TAKING LEAVE OF ABRAHAM

To Don
  – master of humor and melancholy

TAKING LEAVE OF ABRAHAM

AN ESSAY ON RELIGION AND DEMOCRACY

Troels Nørager

Aarhus University Press |

Taking leave of Abraham

© The Author and Aarhus University Press 2008

Cover: Jørgen Sparre

Painting on cover: "Sacrificio di Isacco" by Michelangelo Merisi da Caravaggio (1571-1610)
     with permission from Galleria degli Uffizi, Firenze.

Printed by Narayana Press, Gylling

Printed in Denmark 2008

ISBN 978 87 7934 412 9

Published with the financial support of

Aarhus University Research Foundation

Aarhus University Press

Langelandsgade 177

DK-8200 Aarhus N

www.unipress.dk

INTERNATIONAL DISTRIBUTORS:

Gazelle Book Services Ltd.

White Cross Mills

Hightown, Lancaster, LA1 4XS

United Kingdom

www.gazellebookservices.co.uk

The David Brown Book Company

Box 511

Oakville, CT 06779

USA

www.oxbowbooks.com

CONTENTS

ACKNOWLEDGMENTS

In the process of writing this book I have received a lot of help and support for which I would like to express my sincere gratitude. First of all, I would not have been able to accomplish this work had I not been able to benefit from two very productive weeks (October 2006) in the peaceful surroundings of the "Klitgaarden" retreat in Skagen, sponsored by Aarhus University. Equally important, the Aarhus University Research Foundation accepted my application to spend one month (July 2007) in the serenity of "Møllehuset", Sandbjerg.

Also, I would like to thank my colleagues at the Section of Systematic Theology who, in the context of our monthly research seminar, engaged in constructive discussion on chapters one and three. Further, I am grateful to the students participating in my seminar on 'Religion and Democracy' for having read and commented on the entire manuscript. In particular, however, I wish to express my gratitude to Professor Jan-Olav Henriksen (from the Norwegian School of Theology in Oslo) for having peer-reviewed the manuscript and made several valuable and much appreciated suggestions for improvement.

Finally, my thanks go to Claes Hvidbak and Cecilie Eriksen at the Aarhus University Press and, not least, to the Aarhus University Research Foundation for having generously sponsored the publication of my work.

The book is dedicated to a long-time friend and important source of inspiration, Professor Donald Capps, Princeton Theological Seminary.

INTRODUCTION

Following the terrorist attack of 9/11 a great many books on religion and democracy have been published. The present book, however, claims a degree of originality in that it deliberately *combines* two perspectives which are normally kept separate: that of political philosophy and that of philosophy of religion. But what do the complex relations of religion and democracy have to do with the biblical story of Abraham about to sacrifice Isaac, his son? In fact it is possible to establish a direct link, since the written 'testament' of one of the terrorists, Mohammad Atta, included a reference to Abraham/Ibrahim with the purpose of casting Atta's parents in the idealized role of Abraham who willingly sacrificed his son (cf. Brun et al. 2007, 103).

The present essay, however, is not a book on *sacrifice*, although this vast and complex topic has sparked increased interdisciplinary interest in recent years.[1] Actually, I could imagine someone with at taste for dispute objecting that what we are dealing with here is only a 'near-sacrifice', since in the end Isaac was spared and a ram killed in his place. To any objection along these lines the Biblical text itself is the answer: It makes no secret of the fact that Abraham intended to go through with the killing. Regarding sacrifice (or religion in general), I have no interest in subscribing to a particular definition among the plethora of those available. What is of more concern to me is the gradual *secularization*

---

1 As but one example, the European Society for Philosophy of Religion decided to make 'sacrifice' the general topic of their conference in Oslo, August 28-31, 2008.

of sacrifice which has taken place, plus the fact that the phenomenon of 'sacrifice' may be said to epitomize the religious *per se*.[2]

The *aqedah*, the 'binding of Isaac', is the Jewish term for the story in Genesis 22 of the Hebrew Bible where we read how Abraham was commanded by God to sacrifice his beloved son, Isaac, for whom he had been longing for so many years. Obviously, what we are dealing with here is one of the most influential, and most frequently interpreted, narratives of our Western cultural heritage. No doubt, the many layers of this narrative still form an important part of our cultural and individual unconscious. More importantly, in our current world marred by acts of terror which is at least partly motivated by religious concerns, the story of Abraham and Isaac has gained an acute relevance. For even a superficial reading of Genesis 22 should prompt the reader to think of contemporary acts of terror where individuals see themselves as acting on God's command. In other words, a Biblical story that was always disturbing has become even more disturbing, to the point where we must ask ourselves whether it is time to be 'taking leave of Abraham'.

In the process of writing this book, I have had the opportunity to study what I believe is a representative sample of artistic paintings going back to the 16th and 17th centuries. What struck me (and I believe it would be striking to any contemporary spectator) is how docile, devout and uninteresting most of them are. Isaac is represented as a young (almost adult) man, and he is calmly, confidently, and with an almost angelic expression looking into the sky. Why is this? Well, maybe because the paintings had been commissioned by a church with no interest in arousing our sympathies for the innocent victim. In this long line of artistic glossing over the story, Caravaggio stands out as my personal favorite and hero, because he displays the courage to take the victim's point of view and represent the dread and anguish of Isaac. And indeed, what could be more terrifying than the thought or prospect of being sacrificed and slaughtered by your own father? Thus, having seen the

---

2 In support of this *The Encyclopedia of Religion* (Mircea Eliade, editor in Chief) offers the following general definition of 'sacrifice': "The term *sacrifice*, from the Latin *sacrificium* (*sacer*, 'holy'; *facere*, 'to make') carries the connotation of the religious act in the highest, or fullest sense" (Vol. 12, p. 544).

picture, I decided that it would be fitting to use it for the cover of this book.

What motivated me to write this book is quite easy to tell. During the last years I have had the privilege to teach Kierkegaard's *Fear and Trembling* to university students in their first year of Theology. Two things struck me in that connection: One was the students' general willingness to accept God's command and that Abraham 'just had to do it'; and the other was the fact that they did not more directly relate the thematic of the story to the world in which we live. For, obviously a *tale of terror* like Genesis 22 should have something to do with the *world of terror* in which we live. And thus it dawned upon me that it would be fascinating to use the story of Abraham and Isaac as the overall frame, the test-case as it were, for an analysis of the contemporary debate on the compatibility between religion and democracy and on the role of religion in the public square.

But what, one might ask, is achieved by seeing Genesis 22, Kierkegaard, and the contemporary debate on religion and democracy as interconnected? To this question, of course, the book itself is the answer. Still, what I can say by way of introduction is that part of what kept me going in the process of writing it, is my conviction about two overall points: First, that our current debate on religion and democracy may profit a lot from acknowledging that part of our cultural heritage is a deeply troubling story of a man who has been praised for his willingness to obey God's command to sacrifice his son. The problem here is a radical monotheism demanding blind obedience. And second, that our hermeneutical perspective on Genesis 22 (and the Bible in general) ought to include an awareness of our contemporary problems of defending democracy in the face of the phenomenon of (partly) religiously motivated acts of terror.

I am writing this book as a Christian theologian coming from the field of philosophy of religion. And thus, another way to characterize my book would be to regard it as attempting a conversation between philosophy of religion and political philosophy. For more than a century now, theologians have spent a lot of energy on defending God against a Darwinian account of evolution. I believe it is high time to realize that contemporary political philosophy constitutes an equally (if not even more) important challenge to Christian theology. And, I would argue, not just a challenge to be overcome, but rather an opportunity for critical self-reflection and a chance to clarify the proper role of religion in a democratic society.

This book is not, I should stress, a book on terrorism and its socio-political and religious sources. There are already a great many books on that particular theme. Neither is it a book about those forms and interpretations of Islam that are being used to legitimate much of the terror that we see, for Islam is a subject on which I am not competent to write. At the same time, we would do well to recall here, that the so called *aqedah*, the story of the 'binding of Isaac', is part of the canonical writings of all the three 'Abrahamic' religions: Judaism, Christianity, and Islam. If anything, this book is an implicit call to all people of good will within the three, monotheistic religions to ponder, whether the time has not come for 'taking leave of Abraham' – at least the Abraham who, as it seems, was blindly obedient to a God who demanded human sacrifice.

The book consists of two parts: The first is called *Religion and Morality* in order to denote a cultural context where it is taken for granted that religious authority overrides the norms of morality. Inverting this order, the heading of the second part is *Morality, Democracy, and Religion* which indicates that a constitutive part of what makes us (i.e. we who are living in a Western liberal democracy) 'modern' is that our primary commitment is to morality and the normative foundation of democracy. And then, in turn, our religious commitments should be adapted to find their proper place within that socio-politic context. Fundamentalists, I am of course aware, tend to see things the other way round. My claim to the contrary, however, is more than a matter of taste, for I claim that as a result of *cultural evolution*, and thus in an *irreversible* sense, we have moved from one way of thinking to another.

The internal connection between the two parts of the book may also be stated in the following way: As we shall see, Kierkegaard utilizes Abraham's faith to stage his fierce attack on Hegel's claim that philosophy represents a 'higher' and more advanced viewpoint than that of religion. Today, few people bother too much about philosophy or see a particular form of philosophy as the enemy. Instead, the relevant discussion is whether or not democracy and public reason are 'higher' than religion. The answer, in my opinion, should be yes, if by 'higher' we mean more general, more communal, more obliging. Such a broadly Hegelian response, however, leaves us with the important task of outlining, at the end of this book, what *kind* of religion and faith may be compatible with a genuine commitment to democracy.

Part One contains three chapters: In *Chapter One*, 'A Tale of Terror: The Binding of Isaac', I try to approach this core narrative of the Abrahamic religions by focusing on some influential interpretations, particularly from within the Christian tradition. I end this chapter with a brief reminder on the interpretations put forward by Kant and Hegel, since they may be said to inaugurate the modern 'turning the tables' in the sense of giving priority to morality rather than religion. *Chapter Two*, 'Kierkegaard's *Fear and Trembling*' presents a reading of what I believe is rightly acclaimed as by far the most ingenious and intriguing interpretation of Genesis 22. Part of what makes Kierkegaard interesting in this context, is that he is decidedly modern, fully cognizant of both Kant and Hegel, and yet at the same time struggling to save Abraham as a model of faith. In *Chapter Three*, 'Contemporary Interpretations of *Fear and Trembling*', I look into a selection of contemporary attempts to deal with the complexities of Kierkegaard's reading of Genesis 22. For the most part, these attempts are deeply ambiguous: On the one hand they emphasize that the story is both 'disturbing' and 'troubling', while at the same time going to almost embarrassing lengths in order to save either God, Abraham, or Isaac.

Part Two proceeds by way of four chapters: *Chapter Four*, 'Cultural Evolution and Religion', attempts to establish a coherent argument for seeing religion as embedded in a more general cultural evolution. Since speaking of 'evolution' currently constitutes a grave offense to widespread political correctness within humanities and cultural studies, I hasten to add that my notion of a cultural evolution makes no pretensions whatsoever to universal validity, but is confined to what we usually refer to as the Western world. *Chapter Five*, 'Rawls and Habermas on Liberal Democracy and Religion', addresses the two most prominent representatives of political philosophy, John Rawls and Jürgen Habermas. My purpose, of course, is to outline their familiar, yet distinct, versions of the principles and normative foundation of *deliberative democracy*. And in particular, I focus on the 'constraints' they deem it necessary to impose on those wishing to advance religious reasons in the public sphere. *Chapter Six*, 'Critical Debates on the Role of Religion', presents and evaluates a selection of scholars who have generally been critical towards political liberalism.

Finally, in *Chapter Seven*, 'Integrating Political Philosophy and Philosophy of Religion', I present my own ideas for integrating philosophy of religion and political philosophy. In doing this, I have found valuable inspiration in the Christian philosophy of Russian thinker Nicolas Berdyaev. The important point here, I believe, is that he makes *spirit* and *freedom* the central concepts from which to reflectively construct the relation between God, man, and society. Also, I return to Kierkegaard in order to extract from *Fear and Trembling* what I take to be its contemporary relevance for our continuing efforts to come to terms with how to live as Christians in the world.

Chapter One

A TALE OF TERROR: 'THE BINDING OF ISAAC'

The purpose of this first chapter is to focus on major trends in the history of the reception and interpretation of the *aqedah*, the binding of Isaac. No in-depth study is intended which is why I am content with relying on secondary sources. I take my point of departure in contemporary artistic interpretations; from this I turn to Abraham as the figure connecting the Abrahamic religions (Judaism, Christianity, and Islam). In this connection I raise the question as to the 'price' we have paid for the exclusive monotheism of which Abraham is not only a prime exemplar, but even the renowned 'Father of faith'. The focus of the following section is on New Testament texts reflecting Abraham in general and the sacrifice of Isaac in particular. Having established this, I address the so called 'typological' interpretation which has been the dominant Christian approach to the story. Finally, a big leap in time is taken, since the chapter ends with a section devoted to the two modern interpretations that form the immediate background to Kierkegaard, namely the critical comments on Abraham put forward by Kant and Hegel.

Contemporary Artistic Interpretations: Two Songs and a Movie

Born in 1954, I belong to a generation for whom music has had a profound influence. Obviously, since primordial times when David played his harp to soothe the melancholy of King Saul, music has always played an important role. True, indeed, but what emerged on the scene of popular music in the 1960ies was a powerful combination of music and lyrics that actually carried a *message* – a message going beyond the ever important theme of love and broken hearts. And who knows, perhaps it is more than a coincidence that the two artists who (more than any other musicians) exercised a formative influence on my identity from age 15-16 and onwards, have both written important songs on the story of Abraham and Isaac. I am, of course, speaking here of Bob Dylan and Leonard Cohen who shall serve as our entry into some of the intricacies of the story and the history of its interpretations.

In the frenzied title-song of Dylan's 1965 album *Highway 61 Revisited*, the first verse goes like this:

Oh God said to Abraham, 'Kill me a son'
Abe says, 'Man you must be puttin' me on'
God say, 'No'. Abe say, 'What?'
God say, 'You can do what you want Abe, but
The next time you see me comin' you better run'.
Well, Abe says, 'Where do you want this killin' done?'
God says, 'Out on Highway 61'.[3]

In this somewhat enigmatic text, Dylan, probably with war as the background, uses Abraham to stage an attack on those political leaders who (claiming to have God on their side) send innocent sons into the killing fields of war. In the lyrics just quoted, God acts as if he were a mafia-boss who in a matter of fact way orders a killing by putting out a contract on someone's life. But here it is not *your* son, but just 'a son'. At first, Abraham's reaction is one of baffled resistance, he thinks God is joking and cannot believe that the order to kill is for real. But God is not joking and backs his order with a direct threat. Faced with this, Abraham agrees to perform the killing 'out on Highway 61'.[4]

War is also the interpretive context to Leonard Cohen's beautiful and moving song 'The Story of Isaac' from the album called *Songs from a Room* (1969). The title of the song is aptly chosen, for Cohen explicitly takes

---

3 Lyrics by Bob Dylan. The album was released by Columbia Records on August 30, 1965.
4 For an entry into the many interpretations of Dylan see Michael Gray: *The Bob Dylan Encyclopedia*. New York: Continuum, 2006.

the perspective of Isaac, even to the point of an empathic identification (a dream / nightmare) which forms the contents of the first two verses:

The door it opened slowly,
my father he came in, I was nine years old.
And he stood so tall above me,
His blue eyes they were shining
And his voice was very cold.
He said, 'I've had a vision
And you know I'm strong and holy
I must do what I've been told.'
So he started up the mountain,
I was running, he was walking,
And his axe was made of gold.

Well, the trees they got much smaller,
The lake a lady's mirror,
We stopped to drink some wine.
Then he threw the bottle over.
Broke a minute later
And he put his hand on mine.
Thought I saw an eagle
But it might have been a vulture,
I never could decide.
Then my father built an altar,
He looked once behind his shoulder,
He knew I would not hide.

The emotionally disturbing thing when you read these lines, is that what suddenly happened to the nine-year old boy, might happen to anyone of us: We are utterly alone and defenseless, if it should happen that our father one day changes his personality ('and his voice was very cold') and presents us with a religious motivation for doing something terrible: "I've had a vision / and you know I'm strong and holy, / I must do what I've been told". The perpetrator of child abuse knows that he may count on the victim's complicity ('he knew I would not hide'). The morale of the song is concentrated in the opening lines of verse 3, where the Abrahams of our time are being directly addressed:

You who build these altars now
To sacrifice these children,
You must not do it anymore.
A scheme is not a vision
And you never have been tempted
By a demon or a god.[5]

The children that are being sacrificed nowadays are most likely those who are being sent into war – and perhaps more generally all those who are being abused. But the song urges all those who 'built altars' to stop this practice, since we do no longer buy into its religious legitimation. We know that 'a scheme is not a vision' (or revelation), and none of them 'have been tempted / by a demon or a god'. That was Abraham's situation. We have no way of knowing whether Abraham himself was wondering whether the voice ordering him to kill his son came from a demon or a god. But part of what distinguishes us as 'moderns' is that *we* have to ask ourselves this very question: Was it a demon or a God? As we shall see later in this chapter, this is exactly what a philosopher like Kant has done. But why was this horrific story included in Genesis in the first place? Here we should first of all remember that the practice of child-sacrifice was widely accepted in ancient societies; hence the *sensus communis* among contemporary Old Testament scholars that the primary purpose of the story is etiological, namely to make it clear to Abraham and his descendants that they should no longer engage in child sacrifice.[6]

At this point I find myself wondering whether for a *modern* consciousness it is even possible to imagine and portray the sacrifice of Isaac in a way that is loyal to the Biblical text. A Google search for images of the

---

5 Lyrics by Leonard Cohen. The album *Songs from a Room* was released in January 1969 by Columbia Records.
6 This may well be a correct interpretation (in fact, one cannot help wishing it were); I am no expert on the subject. Still, I wonder why God did not bother to convey this message more explicitly; instead, the text seems clearly to emphasize the theme of Abraham's unquestioning obedience.

sacrifice of Isaac reveals that this motif appears less frequently than in previous centuries.[7] More importantly, perhaps, whereas in pre-modern times the near-sacrifice could be represented directly, the modern approach is either openly critical or, when more positive, an expressionist or more or less abstract version of the typological interpretation.[8] This latter option, however, was not available to film director Joseph Sargent who in 1993 produced *Abraham* with Richard Harris and Barbara Hershey starring as Abraham and Sarah.[9] And thus, in a film which had to remain loyal to the biblical script, I was curious to learn how a contemporary director had chosen to instruct the scene of Abraham's sacrifice of Isaac.

And apparently, this has required a good deal of consideration, for as spectators we are psychologically prepared for this horrific scene by two other scenes of sacrifice, none of them mentioned in the Bible, but at the same time not entirely implausible. In the first, Abraham is telling Ishmael (about 8-10 years of age) how their best sheep can produce a lot of off-spring and thus contribute to Ishmael's future wealth. But then Abraham goes on saying that they ought to sacrifice this sheep as a gift of gratitude to God, for 'nothing is too good for God' and 'nothing on earth should be more important to us than God'. Ishmael is then the one who (instructed by his father) ties the sheep's legs. The sheep is frightened, of course, and Abraham instructs Ishmael to speak softly to the sheep in order to calm it, for it must be calmed down and 'willing'

---

7 Of course there are many exceptions to this overall impression: As examples let me just refer to works by Jewish painter Samuel Bak, American painter Morton Sacks, and German painter Stephanus who, on the background of 9/11 and inspired by Alice Miller and Caravaggio, has portrayed Abraham as a mad butcher, thus at the same time questioning religious fanaticism and taking the perspective of the victim.

8 Chagall may be cited as an example of this. In Denmark, one artist frequently used for decorating the interior of churches, is painter Arne Haugen Sørensen. In 1993 he made an altarpiece (triptychon) to a Middle Age church where the crucifixion is in the center and the sacrifice of Isaac is depicted on the one side. Apart from the typological perspective, however, the artist has tried to portray Abraham in such a way as to facilitate at least some degree of identification: Abraham and Isaac are shown embracing each other; Abraham's left hand is caressing Isaac's head while his right hand is ready to stab the knife into Isaac. Thus, according to the artist, the figure of Abraham may serve to remind us of the basic human ambiguity that we often comfort with one hand while the other is ready to sacrifice.

9 Copyright 2004 PAN Vision AB. www.panvision.com.

before being slaughtered. Finally, although he is not too happy about it, Ishmael is the one who must cut the sheep's throat.

The second preparatory scene is Abraham talking to Isaac sitting with his pet lamb. Here the issue is not the worldly business of material wealth, but teaching Isaac (and the spectators) the lesson that 'we should be willing to sacrifice what we love most to God'. Isaac (about six years old?) is then instructed to pick out his favorite pet lamb, and then father and son go to the altar to sacrifice it. Thus, through these two scenes, the audience is psychologically prepared for the final scene of the movie: the sacrifice of Isaac.

Immediately leading up to this, we meet Abraham in a nightly scene where he reproaches himself for his occasional doubts which he attributes to his having 'abandoned' God. And he promises himself that he will 'not let it happen again'. What follows is God's voice commanding him to sacrifice Isaac. Abraham, of course, is stunned and bewildered: can this really be true? He asks several times, apparently in order to make sure that he has understood the words of God correctly, but as we know from the text of Genesis 22 God offers no further clarifications. At last we see Abraham crying out in frustration: 'WHY'? The scene where they depart for the mountain which God will himself point out to Abraham closely follows the biblical text, including the sparse dialogue between Abraham and Isaac. Abraham and Isaac (at this time seemingly around age 10-12) build the altar together, but after Abraham's placing the wood on the altar, the director has apparently felt the need to employ some artistic freedom: Abraham says 'Stretch out your hands, Isaac', and then he ties Isaac's hands and feet (like we have previously seen with the sacrificial animals). Isaac's compliance borders on the masochistic as he replies, 'Bind me tightly, father!' After this Abraham embraces Isaac for some time, and then lifts him onto the altar where he is placed on his back and lies with eyes closed. Abraham looks into the sky saying, 'God, give me the strength to do what I must'. And then, just before cutting Isaac's throat, the angel intervenes, as we all know. Finally, we see Abraham laughing in utter relief and stretching his arms up to God in gratitude shouting 'My son, my son'.

I began this chapter with two contemporary voices emphasizing the perspective of the victim and questioning the religious legitimation of sacrifice. This, as might be expected, has not been the dominant line of interpretation in history. Before going deeper into this, however, let us take a look at the *aqedah* as a story common to the three Abrahamic religions.

The Aqedah and the Abrahamic Religions

In these days of interreligious dialogue it is widely considered good taste to refer to Abraham as the patriarch and 'Father of Faith', and thus constituting, as it were, a common core to the three monotheistic religions. And in fact, this is historically and textually correct. But what is perhaps even more interesting is the fact that Abraham's sacrifice of Isaac is liturgically enacted once a year in Judaism (Rosh ha Shanah) and Islam (Eid ul-Adha), and – if one adopts a typological interpretation – in the Christian eucharist. In other words, what we find is a strong, albeit different, emphasis on *sacrifice*. Thus, as one commentator has noted "the *Akedah* can be looked upon as standing at the crossroad of these three traditions as one significant sign of their common origin and also of their theological divergence" (Doukhan 1995, 165). The two versions of the story, to be found in the Hebrew Bible and the Quran, may be presented in the following parallel synopsis:

The Bible, Revised Standard Edition

1: After these things God tested Abraham, and said to him, "Abraham!" And he said, "Here am I."

2: He said, "Take your son, your only son Isaac, whom you love, and go to the land of Mori'ah, and offer him there as a burnt offering upon one of the mountains of which I shall tell you."

3: So Abraham rose early in the morning, saddled his ass, and took two of his young men with him, and his son Isaac; and he cut the wood for the burnt offering, and arose and went to the place of which God had told him.

4: On the third day Abraham lifted up his eyes and saw the place afar off.

5: Then Abraham said to his young men, "Stay here with the ass; I and the lad will go yonder and worship, and come again to you."

6: And Abraham took the wood of the burnt offering, and laid it on Isaac his son; and he took in his hand the fire and the knife. So they went both of them together.

7: And Isaac said to his father Abraham, "My father!" And he said, "Here am I, my son." He said, "Behold, the fire and the wood; but where is the lamb for a burnt offering?"

8: Abraham said, "God will provide himself the lamb for a burnt offering, my son." So they went both of them together.

9: When they came to the place of which God had told him, Abraham built an altar there, and laid the wood in order, and bound Isaac his son, and laid him on the altar, upon the wood.

10: Then Abraham put forth his hand, and took the knife to slay his son.

11: But the angel of the LORD called to him from heaven, and said, "Abraham, Abraham!" And he said, "Here am I."

12: He said, "Do not lay your hand on the lad or do anything to him; for now I know that you fear God, seeing you have not withheld your son, your only son, from me."

13: And Abraham lifted up his eyes and looked, and behold, behind him was a ram, caught in a thicket by his horns; and Abraham went and took the ram, and offered it up as a burnt offering instead of his son.

14: So Abraham called the name of that place The LORD will provide; as it is said to this day, "On the mount of the LORD it shall be provided."

15: And the angel of the LORD called to Abraham a second time from heaven,

16: and said, "By myself I have sworn, says the LORD, because you have done this, and have not withheld your son, your only son,

17: I will indeed bless you, and I will multiply your descendants as the stars of heaven and as the sand which is on the seashore. And your descendants shall possess the gate of their enemies,

18: and by your descendants shall all the nations of the earth bless themselves, because you have obeyed my voice."

19: So Abraham returned to his young men, and they arose and went together to Beer-sheba; and Abraham dwelt at Beer-sheba.

Quranic version (Sura 37:99-113) *

Then when (the son)

Reached (the age of)

(Serious) work with him,

He said: "O my son!

I have seen in a dream

That I offer thee in sacrifice:

Now see that is

Thy view!" (The son) said:

"Only father! Do

As thou art Commanded:

Thou will find me

If Allah so will one

Of the Steadfast".

So when they had both

Submitted (to Allah),

And he laid him

Prostrate on his forehead

(For sacrifice),

We called out to him, "O Abraham!

Thou hast already fulfilled

The dream!" – Thus indeed

Do we reward

Those who do right. For this was a clear trial

And we ransomed him

For him among generations

(To come) in later times:

"Peace and salutation to Abraham!"

Thus indeed do we reward

Those who do right

For he was one

Of our believing servants.

And we gave him

The good news

Of Isaac – a prophet, -

One of the Righteous.

We blessed him and Isaac:

But of their progeny

Are (some) that do right,

And (some) that obviously

Do wrong, to themselves.

* This version is quoted from Yunis 1995, 151f.

Let me briefly outline the major differences between these two versions, since the much younger text from the Quran (7th century AD) has changed the 'original' story in more than one respect. First of all, in the Islamic version there is no direct command from God; instead, Abraham has 'seen' the sacrifice of his son in a dream. Therefore, only on the ancient premise that all dreams are God-sent and thus to be considered messages from God, may we regard Abraham to have been actually 'commanded' by God. That this is in fact the case is revealed by Isaac's response to Abraham's declaration of his intention to sacrifice: "Only father! Do as thou art commanded: Thou will find me, if Allah so will, one of the steadfast". Two things are striking in this brief dialogue: One is that Abraham openly reveals the contents of his dream to Isaac. Contrary to this, in the Hebrew version Abraham *conceals* his intention not only to Isaac, but also to Sarah and his servants.[10] The second striking feature of the Islamic version is that Isaac is not just obedient, because he has no alternative; on the contrary, what we find is an Isaac who *encourages* his father to do as commanded! And at the same time he places himself in the position of the one who (almost more than) willingly surrenders his life to a higher, albeit entirely unclear, purpose. This, interestingly, tends to position Isaac, rather than Abraham, in the role of the paradigmatic character to be emulated, although both (in contrast to the Bible) are finally blessed. Submission to the will of Allah is directly stressed, but, more generally, the Bible and the Quran are in agreement on the following points:

- The point of the story (and, apparently, God's / Allah's general idea) is seen as a 'test' or 'trial' of Abraham's faith – with a special emphasis on *obedience*.
- God / Allah is satisfied by the display of obedience; the actual sacrifice is not carried out.
- Obedience is intrinsically linked to God's / Allah's *reward*; it pays off to 'do right', i.e. to follow God's commands.

---

10 As we shall see in the following chapter, Kierkegaard makes an important point of Abraham's silence.

Is There a Price to be Paid for Monotheism?
In 1997 German Egyptologist Jan Assmann published his *Moses the Egyptian: The Memory of Egypt in Western Monotheism*. One year later, the slightly altered German edition came out. Since then, Assmann's ideas, which I shall briefly present here, have generated heated controversy in many quarters, perhaps not least among Old Testament scholars. Some of these critical debates, as well as Assmann's elaborate response, have been included in *Die Mosaische Entscheidung* (Assmann 2003) which has the 'costs of monotheism' in its subtitle. It is this book that I use in the present context, where my purpose is to outline Assmann's basic argument in order to relate it to my chosen paradigmatic test-case: the binding of Isaac. For certainly, Genesis 22 is likely to make us ponder, whether the price we have paid for monotheism might be too high.

In order not to misinterpret the general hypothesis of Assmann, it should be stressed from the outset that his methodological approach is not one of establishing historical facts or truth, but something which he terms 'the history of memory' ('Gedächtnisgeschichte'). Inspired by Freud's *Moses and Monotheism* (1939), Assmann's purpose is to discover a mental revolution in the history of religions and to follow its more or less hidden (because partly unconscious) implications in Western history of ideas. Assmann's impressive learning notwithstanding, it goes almost without saying that this methodological approach has served to make him vulnerable to diverse critical attacks. Nonetheless, the somewhat speculative nature of some of his theses (which he himself does not deny) is, in my view, part and parcel of what makes them new, inspiring and provocative.

More than 3000 years ago, in polytheistic Egypt of the 14th century BC, pharaoh Ekhnaton (1353-1336 BC) enforced a profound revolution in religious life: a strict monotheism. Apparently, for the first time in religious history people were allowed to worship only *one* true God, in this case the god Aton who is generally depicted as the sun. Ekhnaton's religious reform was short-lived and soon to be overturned, however, but its program was subsequently carried through, many scholars argue, by Moses who was probably an Egyptian. Moses (and now we enter more familial Biblical territory) led his followers through the Red Sea and the desert – finally to enter the promised land of 'milk and honey'. As in Freud,[11] a story like this must have its 'primal scene', and Assmann finds this in the story of the golden calf (Exodus 32) which, according to Assmann, is representative of the Egyptian god of Apis. What took place in this decisive scene of cultural memory were the rejection of polytheism and the institution of monotheism. This, in turn, is identical with a basic shift from what Assmann calls 'primary religions' (integral to a particular culture and language) to 'secondary religions' which build on primary religions, but nonetheless, partly due to their origin by divine revelation, sharply demarcate themselves from what is now suddenly considered primitive magic and 'heathen' practices.

The foundation of this more or less constant demarcation is to be found in Assmann's core idea of *the Mosaic distinction*, i.e. the distinction between truth and falsehood in religion: true and false gods, true and false doctrine, and true and false faith. If we follow Assmann, this turn to monotheism is to be considered a major event in the history of religions. He emphasizes, however, that we should not regard it as something that happened once and for all: "The Mosaic distinction is not a historical event that changed the world once and for all; rather, it is a regulative idea which over the centuries has unfolded its world-changing effect in certain 'moves' (German: 'Schüben'). Only in this sense is it possible to speak of a 'monotheistic turn'." (Assmann 2003, 13; my translation).

In Assmann's perspective, the Mosaic distinction between truth and falsehood has done for religion what the distinction of Parmenides and the Greeks has done for science – and both have revolutionized our world; but, more particularly, this distinction has created and shaped the entire mental space of the three Abrahamic religions. Religious truth is originally conceptualized by mentally opposing the worlds of 'Egypt' and 'Israel'. Whereas the former signals polytheism, idolatry (religious 'untruth'), and deification of the world ('cosmo-theism'), the latter signals simply truth, meaning: surrendering to the will of one God and rejecting all others. According to Assmann, there is no way of understanding this turn as a gradual evolution; on the contrary, he speaks of a 'revolution'

---

11 As one would expect, Freud's *Moses and Monotheism* (1939), in which he argues that Moses was in reality an Egyptian Aton-priest, plays an important role in Assmann's attempt to reconstruct the true origins of monotheism.

where monotheism, relying on authoritative revelation positions itself as a *counter-religion* to the idolatry and polytheism of ancient Egypt. Thus, to invoke a metaphor of Assmann, although Egypt is to be considered the 'womb' of the chosen people (Israel), the 'umbilical chord' was decisively cut in order to instigate a point of no return.

Critics have raised a number of important points, for example that the idea of 'the Mosaic distinction' serves as Assmann's version of the 'original sin' of cultural history.[12] One rather obvious objection is the fact that in the Bible it is the religion of the Canaanites, and not the Egyptians, which represents the fundamental sin of idolatry. Faced with this charge, Assmann admits that the role of Egypt in the Exodus-story is *mythological* rather than historical. Another criticism maintains that Assmann over-emphasizes the peaceful nature of polytheism, while at the same time underestimating the importance of monotheism in bringing a *universal* perspective (and the idea of a universal history of mankind) into fruition. Besides, some critics argue, Assmann's portrait of Israelite monotheism misses the important fact that a primary concern of the new Jahve-religion was to be able to live a blessed life in *this* world.

Be that as it may, I shall focus in this context on the more 'political' implications of Assmann's construal of the revolutionary origin of monotheistic religion. Part of this is connected to the fact that Assmann, much like Freud, sees his work as contribution to the mental history of anti-semitism. In this context, Assmann makes no secret of his view that monotheism is basically a *political* idea which primarily has unfolded its violent and hateful potential within Christianity and Islam, rather than in Judaism. What can account for this difference? In Assmann's view, the Jewish people's consciousness of being God's chosen people had the effect of segregating them from the tribes and religions surrounding them – not just back then, but all the way through history. Jews, in other words, were preoccupied with rooting out false religion from their *own* midst, while calmly letting other people serve *their* respective gods. In contrast, "Christianity and Islam have not recognized this distinction, and precisely for this reason they have, time and again in history, become outwardly violent" (Assmann 2003, 31; my translation. Cf. also p. 214).

---

12 For an example of this type of criticism see Koch 1999.

And this is what should prompt the contemporary reader to consider whether the price we have paid for monotheism may not, after all, have been too high.

It should be noted, however, that one critic, Eric Zenger, proposes an alternative reading of the Mosaic distinction. This, according to Zenger (in Assmann 2003, 219ff.), should be interpreted as a distinction of *content*, the point being that Jahveh is the God who led his people out of slavery in Egypt – thus echoing the refrain of several texts in the Hebrew Bible. In other words, the primary 'monotheistic' distinction, claims Zenger, is the one between freedom and slavery, and the 'truth' of Jahveh may therefore be summarized as 'liberation from all forms of un-freedom'. Zenger's interpretation, it seems to me, may well be supported by some Biblical texts that are traditionally considered quite central by theologians, but it nonetheless misses Assmann's attempt to uncover the ideological roots, as it were, of *all* monotheistic religions – or monotheistic religion *per se*.

Another critic, Karl-Josef Kuschel (in Assmann 2003, 273ff.), has been provoked by Assmann's statement that today, as children of modernity, while we must still hold on to the distinction between true and false, we can no longer base these concepts on religious revelation, but instead need to see them as being continually negotiated. Kuschel, opposing this pragmatic idea of negotiation (German: 'aushandeln'), counters that "People may for their convictions – in spite of everything – rely on 'revelations that are fixed once and for all', but they can no longer accept an understanding of revelation without implying the intellectual premises of a modernity which is critical towards religion. Acceptance of unconditional duties presupposes the assumption of something un-conditional. The understanding of the unconditional, however, implies the idea of self-realization (German: 'Selbstbildung') in freedom, and not heteronomous alienation" (285; my translation). As we shall see in chapter two, Kierkegaard may be regarded as one important attempt to combine the idea of something unconditional (Abraham's absolute faith) with the modern idea of self-realization.

Finally, how does Assmann's perspective on the origins of monothe-ism connect to Genesis 22 and the binding of Isaac? It seems to me that this story may be considered paradigmatic and prototypical of monotheism in the sinister sense described by Assmann, because it portrays a God whose commands are beyond questioning, and a human being, Abraham, who is willing to commit a violent, sacrificial act in order to satisfy his 'God'. Thus, in my view, Assmann, despite the fact that his theories may be vulnerable to various criticisms, deserves gratitude for sharpening our awareness of the price we have paid for monotheism.

Genesis 22 *in the New Testament*

Within Christianity the tradition of referring to Abraham as the 'Father of faith' begins with Paul's argument in *Romans*, chapter four, that Abraham is not just the father of those who have been circumcised (the sign of God's covenant with the Jewish people). The premise for this argument is Paul's distinction between 'law' and 'faith': Abraham was righteous in the eyes of God not because he was circumcised, but because of his faith, and therefore the Christians are the true heirs to the promises given to Abraham:

He received circumcision as a sign or seal of the righteousness which he had by faith while he was still uncircumcised. The purpose was to make him the father of all who believe without being circumcised and who thus have righteousness reckoned to them, and likewise the father of the circumcised who are not merely circumcised but also follow the example of the faith which our father Abraham had before he was circumcised. The promise to Abraham and his descendants, that they should inherit the world, did not come through the law but through the righteousness of faith.

If it is the adherents of the law who are to be the heirs, faith is null and the promise is void. For the law brings wrath, but where there is no law there is no transgression. That is why it depends on faith, in order that the promise may rest on grace and be guaranteed to all his descendants – not only to the adherents of the law but also to those who share the faith of Abraham, for he is the father of us all, as it is written, 'I have made you the father of many nations'. (Rom 4:11ff.).[13]

---

13 This and all subsequent New Testament quotations are from *The Bible, Revised Standard Version*.

Paul goes on to relate how Abraham's faith was even strong enough to believe God's promise that Sarah, against all odds, would bear him a child, but, interestingly, he omits any reference to Abraham's subsequent sacrifice of Isaac. And in the following chapter, where Paul reveals that he is no stranger to typological interpretation, the typology is Adam and Christ, not Isaac and Christ. In *Galatians*, we find that Paul has a similar emphasis on the issue of who may claim to be the true sons (and heirs) of Abraham. And again, quoting Gen 15:6, the theological point Paul makes is that righteousness before God comes not by acts of law, but through faith: "Thus Abraham 'believed God, and it was reckoned to him as righteousness.' So you see that it is men of faith who are the sons of Abraham." (Gal 3:6-7).

The first direct mentioning of 'the binding of Isaac' in the New Testament occurs in *James*, interestingly the letter which Luther derogated for its neglect of justification by faith *alone*. Directly opposing this, James insists that "as the body apart from the spirit is dead, so faith apart from works is dead." (Jas 2:26). And as proof that faith without works is null and void, James cites the Abraham who did not only have faith but was also willing to act upon it: "Was not Abraham our father justified by works, when he offered his son Isaac upon the altar? You see that faith was active along with his works, and faith was completed by works, and the scripture was fulfilled which says, 'Abraham believed God, and it was reckoned to him as righteousness'; and he was called the friend of God. You see that a man is justified by works and not by faith alone." (Jas 2:21-23). Interestingly, we may note that Gen 15:6 serves once again as the Scriptural evidence, but now for a markedly different theological purpose. And this purpose is certainly not alien to Kierkegaard where he lets his pseudonym, Johannes de Silentio, insist in *Fear and Trembling* that only the one who draws the knife will get 'Isaac' back again.

There is good reason to let our minds still linger with Kierkegaard when we turn to the final New Testament text referring to the sacrifice of Isaac, for what does it mean to get Isaac back again? This, as we shall see, is an important issue in *Fear and Trembling*, and in pondering this Kierkegaard may well have been inspired by *Hebrews* which in chapter 11 starts with the famous definition of faith ("faith is the assurance of things hoped for, the conviction of things not seen") and then goes on to cite examples of faith from Scripture (Abel, Enoch, Noah). In this connection the whole story of Abraham is briefly recounted, and now with special emphasis on the sacrifice of Isaac:

By faith Abraham, when he was tested, offered up Isaac, and he who had received the promises was ready to offer up his only son, of whom it was said, 'Through Isaac shall your descendants be named.' He considered that God was able to raise men even from the dead; hence, figuratively speaking, he did receive him back. (Heb 11:17-19).

What we find in this dense quotation are two things: One is the important clue that just as God was able to raise Jesus Christ from the dead, so could he have done to Isaac. At any rate, the text in Hebrews claims (obviously against all historical probability) that this was the nature of Abraham's faith. And Kierkegaard, again as we shall see, seems to agree on this point: Isaac, though he never actually died, was already 'dead' to Abraham, and therefore his being spared in the last moment was experienced as a resurrection from the dead. Second (and connected to the first point), by invoking God's power to 'raise men even from the dead' Hebrews establishes a Scriptural basis for the typology between Isaac and Christ which has been so influential through the history of interpretations of 'the binding of Isaac'.[14] Before turning to this, however, I want to introduce the important Biblical theme of sacrificing the first-born and beloved to God.

The Theology of the Beloved Son
A profound and valuable in-depth study of the *aqedah* has been presented by Harvard scholar Jon D. Levenson in *The Death and Resurrection of the Beloved Son* (Levenson 1993). Levenson's approach is philological and historical-critical but it generates almost an entire biblical theology, for he finds the *aqedah* to be inscribed in the larger framework of a theology of

---

14 Another important basis was Romans 8:32 ("He who did not spare his own Son but gave him up for us all, will he not also give us all things with him?") and John 8:56.

the beloved son. The Hebrew term *yahid* (first-born, chosen, and beloved) figures prominently in Genesis where Levenson detects a common theme: the near-death and miraculous restoration of the first-born son. This, in turn, leads Levenson to challenge the dominant view among biblical scholars, namely that the *aqedah* is best understood as a narrative with the etiological function to abolish the tradition of child sacrifice which (although admittedly practiced by the Canaanites and early Israelites) was strongly criticized by the some of the prophets. Levenson, by working out the details of his overall theme, takes a somewhat different view: "Both the rituals and the narrative that articulates this theme suggest that though the *practice* was at some point eradicated, the *religious idea* associated with one particular form of it – the donation of the first-born son – remained potent and productive" (Levenson 1993, ix).

Was child sacrifice a deviation or norm among those who worshipped YHWH? Again, the majority of scholars believe the former, whereas Levenson argues the latter. More specifically, he claims that the divine instruction of Ex 22:28: "You shall give Me the first-born among your sons" should be taken quite literally and as indicative of child sacrifice being the original norm which was later to be gradually transformed. Hence the sub-title of Levenson's book, 'The Transformation of Child Sacrifice in Judaism and Christianity'. In fact, it is Levenson's contention "that only at a particular stage rather late in the history of Israel was child sacrifice branded as counter to the will of YHWH and thus ipso facto idolatrous" (*ibid*, 5). Levenson brings together several pieces of evidence for this claim;[15] prominent among these is the *aqedah*, for as he correctly points out, Gen 22:1-19 "is frighteningly unequivocal about YHWH's ordering a father to offer up his son as a sacrifice" (*ibid*, 12). Equally manifest in the text is that the sacrifice is intended as a test of true devotion. And precisely because Abraham passed the test with flying colors, the angel promises him God's blessings. Hence, Levenson argues, our interpretive efforts should at least fulfill the following condition: "No

---

15 Part of this evidence are archeological findings from the Punic colonies in Carthage which demonstrate that children were sacrificed to Saturn, but also that at some point it was possible to substitute a lamb or kid for a child. Cf. Levenson p. 22 who in this connection makes the important point that the animal did not *replace* child sacrifice but only *substituted* for it.

interpretation of the aqedah can be adequate if it fails to reckon with the point made explicit here: Abraham will have his multitude of descendants only because he was willing to sacrifice the son who is destined to beget them. Any construal of the text that minimizes that willingness misses the point." (*ibid*, 13).

In the Hebrew Bible the theme of the first-born son is part of an overall theology of chosenness: the people of Israel is seen as the first-born son of God, his chosen people. But at the same time the people is his 'property', and since he gives the children he can also legitimately claim them back again. There may be more than one way to 'sacrifice' the first-born son, and stories of fraternal rivalry figure prominently in Genesis with Abel and Cain marking just the beginning. Levenson sees a common thread between the narratives recounting how Abraham expelled first-born Ishmael in favor of his second son, Isaac, how Jacob preferred Joseph over his ten older brothers, and how Isaac favored Esau but was tricked into giving the birthright to Jacob.[16]

Turning again to the aqedah, the fact that in the end the son is spared demonstrates the affinity between this story and that of the first Passover. But this, according to Levenson, has too easily "led to the assumption that the aqedah, too, served as an etiology of the substitution of animal for human sacrifice." (*ibid*, 111). In order to counter this he makes the following argument which serves to highlight important features of Genesis 22: "The cumulative evidence against the ubiquitous idea that the aqedah opposes child sacrifice and substitutes an animal cult is overwhelming: nothing in Gen 22:1-19 suggests that God's command to immolate Isaac was improper, Abraham is commended and rewarded for obeying it, and the text lacks any formal indicators of an etiological motive regarding the nature of sacrificial offerings." (*ibid*, 113f.).

---

16 In particular, Levenson finds important similarities between the two accounts of the expulsion of Hagar and Ishmael (Gen 16:4-16 and 21:9-21) and the aqedah: "They indicate a common structure to the three narratives: in each Abraham is implicated in the near-death of his son, an angel intervenes to reverse the dire situation, and a vision closes the drama. (...) Each of the three stories has its etiological features, but the meaning of none of them *reduces* to its etiological funtion. Each tells the story of the symbolic death and unexpected new life of the beloved son, a story of far more than mere etiological significance." (Levenson 1993, 124).

Levenson also mounts important criticism against the tendency of Protestant-Lutheran interpreters who, inspired by Kierkegaard, regard the *aqedah* as a test of Abraham's *faith*. This kind of interpretation conveniently affirms the Pauline emphasis on faith in contradistinction to works, but at the same time it moves the focus of attention away from the question whether God might really command the slaughter of the beloved son. Thus, opposing both Kierkegaard and biblical scholar Gerhard von Rad, Levenson offers the following elaboration of his own position:

Israel did not always abominate the sacrifice of the first-born son, and some biblical passages are best taken as an endorsement of the practice. Without uncritical harmonization there is no reason to exclude Gen 22:1-19 from the roster of such passages. This being the case, Abraham's willingness to heed the frightful command may or may not demonstrate faith in the promise that is invested in Isaac, but it surely and abundantly demonstrates his putting obedience to God ahead of every possible competitor. And if this is so, then if Abraham had failed to heed, he would have exhibited not so much a lack of faith in the promise as a love for Isaac that surpassed even his fear of God. (...) The aqedah, in short, tests whether Abraham is prepared to surrender his son to the God who gave him. To say, with Kierkegaard and von Rad, that he is prepared so to do because through faith he expects to receive Isaac anew (as indeed happens) is to minimize the frightfulness of what Abraham is commanded to do. (Levenson 1993, 126).[17]

Finally, as regards the New Testament, Levenson reminds us that in the gospel of Mark the very first identification of Jesus is his being the beloved son: "You are my beloved son; with you I am well pleased" (Mk 1:11), an identification which is repeated in the story of the Transfiguration on the Mountain (Mk 9:7). Further, what we see in the New Testament is how the intertextual combination of Genesis 22 and the suffering servant of Isaiah makes it possible to interpret Jesus as the paschal lamb. The fact of the *aqedah* lurking in the background is also present in what consti-

---

17 Cf. also the following quotation demonstrating Levenson's critical distance to Kierkegaard: "To fulfill the frightful command Abraham will have to suppress his paternal affections, placing obedience to God not above ethics, as Kierkegaard would have it, but above his love for Isaac – in some ways a more daunting task." (*ibid*, 128).

tutes the favorite NT text of many contemporary Christians, namely John 3:16, for here, according to Levenson (p. 31) the wording that God 'gave' (Greek: *edoken*) his only son reflects the usual language of child sacrifice. The New Testament transformation of the idea of child sacrifice is completed by Paul. Says Levenson: "As Jesus supplants Isaac in Paul's theology, and the Church, the Jews, so does God supplant Abraham in the role of the father who did not withhold his own son from death itself" (*ibid*, 220). More specifically, in the letter to the Galatians Paul uses the theme of the first-born son (the stories of Ishmael and Isaac) for his own theological purposes. Levenson comments:

At first glance, Paul's elaborate allegorical reading of Genesis 16 and 21 appears so forced as to suggest utter arbitrariness. The apostle to the Gentiles has, it would seem, a theological message to get across, and his choice of the rivalry of Isaac and Ishmael and their respective mothers as his prooftext is without an anchor in the text itself. I submit that the matter is quite the opposite: Paul focuses on Isaac's right of inheritance because, in his mind, the Church is to be identified with Isaac on grounds altogether independent of the particular texts about the expulsion of Hagar and Ishmael. For, as we have seen, Paul believes that Jesus was the promised son of Abraham that Jewish tradition had (and has) always interpreted as Isaac. (*ibid*, 217).

Interpretations in Antiquity

Despite its slim basis in The New Testament, it did not take long for the Church Fathers to develop the so called *typological* interpretation of Abraham sacrificing Isaac. The major elements of this interpretation may be summarized as follows:

Abraham sacrifices his beloved son Isaac = God sacrifices his beloved son Jesus

Isaac offers himself as atonement for the sins of Israel = Jesus offers himself as atonement for the sins of the world

Isaac himself carried the fire-wood for the altar = Jesus himself carried the cross

Isaac was being bound = Jesus was being bound while being interrogated

The ram / lamb = Jesus as the lamb

The ram caught in the bushes = Jesus' crown of thorns

Also, according to some layers of tradition, Isaac was a fully grown up man at the time of the sacrifice, a trait which could well have been inspired from the story of the crucifixion of Jesus. Or, perhaps more likely, it was a necessary corollary of a Jewish tradition which emphasized that Isaac freely agreed to the sacrifice.[18] Finally, I should like to point to a commonality that, at least to my knowledge, has generally been overlooked, namely the fact that both Isaac and Jesus owe their birth to supernatural factors, to divine agency.[19] While Isaac was conceived in Sarah *after* it was humanly possible, Jesus was conceived in Mary *before* it was humanly possible.

In the traditional Jewish interpretation Isaac is, somewhat contrary to the text of Genesis 22, but perhaps inspired by the Christian perspective, seen as the one who willingly offers himself, and this self-offering then atoned for the sins of Israel (Manns 1995, 59).[20] In the more philosophical interpretation of Philo of Alexandria, Isaac's name ('yishaq' meaning in Hebrew 'laughter') symbolizes the joy of wisdom. Thus, Abraham's sacrifice signals his recognition that the essence of God is perfect happiness, wherefore joy belongs to God alone (Damgaard 2007, 9).

One of the earliest examples of a Christian typological interpretation is found in the *Epistle of Barnabas* which contains the following passage: "The Lord [...] was going to offer the vessel of the spirit as a sacrifice of our sins, in order that the type established in Isaac, who was offered

---

18 Thus Josephus (in *Jewish Antiquities* 1.222-236) reports that Isaac was 25 years when the sacrifice took place (cf. Damgaard 2007, 10). And in late 4th century AD, we find in Chrysostomos's homily on Gen 22 a similar emphasis that at the time of the sacrifice Isaac was a young man (ibid, 16).

19 See, however, Levenson (1993, 205f.).

20 Manns (1995, 60) also notes that "The sacrifice of the Passover lamb reminded God of Isaac's perfect self-oblation and invoked his merits". About the role of the *aqedah* in later Jewish tradition see also Levenson (1993), Ch. 14.

upon the altar, might be fulfilled" (quoted from Paczkowski 1995, 105). A similar note is struck by Irenaeus in book 4 of *Adversus Haereses*:

We (with the same faith as Abraham) follow Him carrying the cross, in the same way Isaac took the wood. In fact in Abraham mankind has learned and became accustomed to following the Word of God, voluntarily giving the sacrifice of his son, his only son, his beloved son, so that God might be pleased to make the sacrifice of His only Son, his beloved, for all his descendants, indeed, for our redemption (quoted from Paczkowski 1995, 106).

Typology, however, was just one interpretive strategy in antiquity. Probably even more important was the use of *allegorical* interpretation. To mention just one example, the church father *Origen* argues "that the sacrifice be seen as a struggle between love to God and love to what is carnal and bodily. The fact that Abraham climbs the mountain to sacrifice Isaac is meant to show that Abraham renounces earthly and carnal things in order to ascend to the heavenly things." (Damgaard 2007, 12).

Similarities, however, may also be considered a danger to one's own identity, and thus, also in some of the early fathers one may find attempts to establish a major difference between Isaac and Christ. Most importantly, this consists in the claim that Isaac was not immolated and therefore did not suffer the same way as Jesus. As an example, Paczkowski (1995, 110f.) offers the following quotation from Clement of Alexandria's *Paidagogos*:

He was a sacrificial victim, as was the Lord. Yet, he was not immolated as the Lord was. Isaac did, however, at least carry the wood for a sacrifice, as the Lord carried the cross. And he laughed mystically, prophesying that the Lord would fill us with joy, who are redeemed from corruption by the blood of the Lord. But he did not suffer. Not only did Isaac suddenly yield the first place in suffering to the Word, but there is even a hint of the divinity of the Lord, in Isaac's not being slain.

The notion of Isaac having 'laughed mystically' seems surprising from a contemporary perspective, since his dire circumstances lying bound on the altar seems hardly to have been conducive to laughter. Furthermore, the quotation is interesting for its effort not just to emphasize that Isaac did not suffer, but that he had to 'yield the first place in suffering' to Jesus! This would seem to indicate that between Jewish and Christian commentators there was some kind of competition going on concerning the true nature and value of sacrifice.

This impression is corroborated by Doukhan (1995) who tells us that in fact there was (for centuries) a Jewish-Christian controversy going on which "revolved mainly around the theological meaning of the *Akedah*" (Doukhan 1995, 165). The remarkable thing in this connection is that Doukhan is able to demonstrate that a parallel development took place within Judaism and Christianity: In both traditions the emphasis was first on Abraham and his obedience, but later (in the 2nd century) "as the controversy intensified, the accent shifted gradually from Abraham to Isaac" (*ibid*, 166). Apparently, just as the Christian theologians were concerned to demonstrate that Jesus was the one, true, and universal sacrifice, so on the Jewish side we find polemical attempts to deny that the sacrifice of Isaac should be considered of less value than that of Christ. Doukhan adds the following comment:

The parallel development of the Jewish and Christian traditions concerning the *Akedah* suggests that these two exegetical traditions moved in close relationship to each other. Moreover, just as the Christians responded to the Jews, the Jewish texts give evidence of the Jewish reaction to the Christian apologetic. In order to show that the *Akedah* of Isaac was at least as effective as the sacrifice of Jesus, the ancient rabbis arrogated to the *Akedah* details borrowed from the story of the Passover. Isaac also willingly offered himself as an atonement, crying out and suffering in agony. A passage of *Gen R* (22, 6)[21] goes so far as to describe Isaac as bearing his own cross, just as a condemned man would. (...) [T]he victim Isaac is a type of the suffering Servant and of the Messiah. In his commentary on Gen 22, 11, Ibn Ezra quotes an opinion that Abraham actually did kill Isaac, who was later resurrected from the dead. The basis for this interpretation is the observation that Isaac did not return home with his father. (*ibid*, 167-168).

---

21 *Gen R* is short for *Genesis Rabbah*, an early rabbinic midrash.

Thus, given these surprising examples of Judaism and Christianity borrowing interpretive elements from one another, Doukhan seems entitled to conclude that "the interest in the *Akedah* occurs at the birth of the three Abrahamic religions, serving the purpose of justifying their respective claims to absolute and exclusive truth." (*ibid*, 174).

Later Jewish responses demonstrate the psychological urge to reject or at least reinterpret the story. Thus, Rabbi Yosef Ibn Janach (Spain, 11th century) argued that God only demanded a symbolic sacrifice; and Rabbi Yosef Ibn Caspi (Spain, early 14th century) was of the opinion that Abraham's imagination was to be blamed for leading him to believe that he had been commanded to sacrifice his own son. In Judaism, the *aqedah* was originally tied to the Feast of Passover, but later, probably following the destruction of the temple in 70AD, it became connected instead to the New Year Feast of Rosh ha Shanah. One may well speculate why this happened, and Manns (1995, 60f.) is of the opinion that "The most probable cause of the change was the ending, after 70 AD, of the Passover sacrifice itself. The blowing of the ram's horn which remembered the Binding of Isaac was not affected by the destruction of the Temple."[22] In light of Doukhan's demonstration of examples of polemics and competition from both Jewish and Christian side, it seems more plausible to interpret the change in the liturgical context for the *aqedah* as a way of creating a stronger mark of identity for Judaism.

Also on the Muslim side, the *aqedah* has served as a means of justifying their claim to be the true religion. Thus, the controversy with Judaism has its primary cause in the majority of Muslim commentators claiming that the son who was sacrificed was Ishmael, and not Isaac. And in turn, Ishmael is considered the Father and progenitor of all Muslims. Textually, this is based on the fact that Genesis 22 records that Abraham was told to sacrifice 'his only son', and since Isaac was the second son of Abraham, he could never rightfully be referred to as his 'only' son.

---

22 Doukhan (1995, 168), however, sees this change as reflecting the controversy between Jewish and Christian exegetes over the best and most powerful concept of sacrifice: "The fact also that the *Akedah* is at times related to the Passover and at times to Rosh-Ha-shanah may reflect the liturgical hesitations generated by the controversy."

Later Interpretations: From Religion to Morality

During the Middle Ages the hegemony of religion is still firmly in place. Thus, in Thomas Aquinas, the major theologian of the era, we find an emphasis on the harmonious relation between God, reason, and the requirements of virtue and justice which even Genesis 22 is unable to disturb. Two of Thomas's arguments in relation to Abraham's dilemma go like this:

(...) God cannot command anything contrary to virtue since the meaning of virtue and the uprightness of man's will consist mainly in being in accord with God's will and in responding to his command, even when this runs counter to the usual way in which it works. The precept for Abraham to kill his innocent son was not contrary to justice, since God himself is the author of life and death. (...)

God has sovereign authority over life and death, for it is in accordance with his ordinance that both sinners and the just die. Therefore, anyone who kills an innocent person in obedience to God's command commits no sin, since God whose order he is executing commits no sin; on the contrary he is showing his fear of the lord thereby. (Quoted from Stiltner 1993, 233f.).[23]

With the emergence of early modernity, however, 'the binding of Isaac' begins increasingly to be a source of bewilderment and embarrassment to many theologians. David Pailin (Pailin 1981), who has investigated parts of this interpretive history, illustrates this by English sermons from the 16th and 17th centuries. By this time, the ideas of 'reason' and 'reasonableness' are gaining increasing currency, and in this context many a preacher found it more than difficult to make good sense of Genesis 22. Some rightly debated why an all-knowing God would need to 'test' Abraham's faith, while others took comfort in the fact that since child-sacrifice was common in Abraham's time, it could not have been such a terrible ordeal for him, after all.

One theologian (Chubb) believed, according to Pailin, "that whereas God's command could be justified on the grounds that God never intended it to be executed, Abraham's action in obeying could never be so

---

23 Stiltner refers for these quotations to *Summa Theologica* II-II 104.4 ad 2, and II-II 64.6 ad 1.

justified since he intended to do what could never be morally right" (Pailin 1981, 22). Behind this evaluation lies the more general view "namely, that a man's conduct and, in particular, his entertainment of something as a revelation from God, must be guided by his reason, including his moral sense" (*ibid*). This, as we shall see shortly, anticipates Kant's later criticism of Abraham. A popular solution to the dilemmas of interpretation was to make Abraham's actions more understandable by claiming (based on Heb 11:19ff) that he believed that God would make Isaac alive again. But what, then, is the pious lesson of this Biblical 'tale of terror'? Says Pailin (1981, 27), "By far the most popular 'moral' to be drawn from the story is that Abraham provides us with an eminent example of religious faith, trust, and obedience."

Kant, however, strongly disagreed. First, by cutting the ground beneath the traditional proofs of God's existence and assigning man's relation to God to the domain of *practical* reason alone, Kant established a new agenda for thinking about God in modernity. Focusing on reason and freedom (autonomy), *the moral law* is one that springs out of human reason and one that the modern, autonomous individual freely wishes to abide by. And as his categorical imperative makes clear, the emphasis is on morality as that which is *universally* binding: 'Always act in such a way that the maxim of your action may be elevated to the status of a universal law'. No wonder then that Abraham gets into trouble. As Pailin correctly states, Kant "explicitly rejects Abraham's example as one to be followed. Since he does not accept the voluntarist view of ethics, he holds that God can declare but not determine by his *fiat* what is right and wrong. God's moral uniqueness is that his holy will is 'incapable of any maxim conflicting with the moral law', not that he chooses what the law shall be. Consequently in his understanding faith cannot involve a teleological suspension of the ethical." (*ibid*, 32). As we shall see in the following chapter, Kierkegaard's *Fear and Trembling* argues for the possibility (and legitimacy) of such a 'teleological suspension', namely in the case of Abraham's faith.

As a way of summarizing modernity's tendency of giving priority to morality over religion, I would like to turn to one particular context where Kant directly takes issue with Abraham's situation when he was commanded by God to sacrifice Isaac. Thus, in the relevant passage from his last book *The Conflict of the Faculties* (1798) Kant begins by summarizing his view on our abilities to apprehend 'the Infinite', and then goes on to rebuke Abraham and telling him what he *ought* to have done:

For if God really were to speak to man, the latter could after all never know that it is God who is speaking to him. It is utterly impossible for man to apprehend the Infinite through his senses, to distinguish him from sensible objects and thereby to know him. He can, though, no doubt convince himself in some cases that it cannot be God whose voice he believes he hears; for if what commands him is contrary to the moral law, he must regard the manifestation as an illusion, however majestic and transcending the whole of Nature it may seem to him to be.

For example, consider the story of the sacrifice which Abraham was willing to make at the divine command by slaughtering and burning his only son – what is more, the poor child unwittingly carried the wood for the sacrifice. Even though the voice ran out from the (visible) heavens, Abraham ought to have replied to this supposedly divine voice, "It is quite certain that I ought not to kill my innocent son, but I am not certain and I cannot ever become certain that you, the 'you' who is appearing to me, are God." (Kant quoted from Pailin 1981, 34).

A few years earlier, in *Die Religion innerhalb der Grenzen der blossen Vernunft* (1793), Kant had made a similar point, and once again with Abraham's sacrifice serving as example. Here, in a section entitled 'Vom Leitfaden des Gewissens in Glaubenssachen' ('On Conscience as our Guide in Matters of Faith'), Kant reminds us that the will of God is revealed to us through human beings and then recorded in historic documents (the Bible). Therefore, he continues, "should a revelation seem to someone as coming from God Himself (like the command directed to Abraham to slaughter his own son like a sheep), then it is at least possible that what we have here is a mistake. But in that case, if he dared to do it, he would risk the danger of doing something that would be highly unjust, and precisely in this he acts without conscience" (German: *gewissenslos*).[24]

Whereas Kant's argument reflects the Enlightenment 'either/or between Christian faith and reason' (Westphal 1987, 61), *Hegel* attempts a compromise, if not even to construct a synthesis of the two opposing

---

24 Kant, *Werke*, vol. 6, p. 187 (Akademieausgabe); my translation.

powers. He agrees with Kant that true religion has to do with practical reason and issues from the ethical sphere, but he attacks the formalism of Kantian *Moralität* and claims that it is superseded by a notion of concrete *Sittlichkeit*, where moral life is always part and parcel of society and its basic institutions. Two issues seem particularly important in relation to Abraham and his faithful obedience to God's command. One is Hegel's idea that religion needs to be 'purified' and, as it were, superseded by philosophy. Religion, it is argued, trades in perceptual images (*Vorstellungen*), while the medium of philosophy is 'concepts' (*Begriffe*) having the advantage of clarity of thought. Second, we have the general thrust of Hegel's philosophy of spirit where 'the Idea' gradually permeates history and society on ever more perfect stages in order to reach its pinnacle and perfection in Hegel's own thinking. In this context, 'universality' is not the a priori status of Kant's moral principles, but "the concrete universality of the social order" (Westphal 1987, 76).

Abraham is directly commented upon in the theological writings of the young Hegel. Hence, in "The Spirit of Christianity and Its Fate" (1799), he sets out to chart the history of consciousness, taking as his point of departure the fateful split that occurred in the Fall when man was alienated from God. In this development Judaism obviously plays an important role, and Hegel sees Abraham as epitomizing the spirit of Judaism which he further characterizes as "the spirit of self-maintenance in strict opposition to otherness" (Hegel quoted from Taylor 1977, 309). Hegel has an important point here, and he deserves our respect for having been able to detect, beneath the surface of Abraham's obedient dependence on his God, that this self-same Abraham displays traits of 'self-maintenance' and 'opposition to otherness'.[25] In other words, Abraham represents the exact opposite of the ideal which so captivated the mind of the early Hegel, namely the dialectical model of *love* where "[s]elf-identity and relation-to-other are not exclusive opposites as Abraham had supposed, but in the final analysis, inseparable" (*ibid*, 315). Hegel sees this model of

---

25 Taylor (1977, 310) comments that "From this perspective, it becomes apparent that the Abrahamic 'solution' to the alienation of man from nature replaced one form of slavery with a more profound servitude. The price of the mastery over nature was bondage to a transcendent Lord whose demands upon the individual are infinite."

love (which we may regard as a way of deepening his critique of Kantian morality) represented in Jesus' kingdom of God where the alienation is finally reconciled. Hence, God is no longer pure otherness, but (by virtue of the Incarnation) immanent in the world. And Taylor concludes that Hegel, much like Marcion, "believes Jewish and Christian notions of God and of the God-self relation to be polar opposites" (*ibid*, 316).

At the end of the evolutionary history of Spirit ('Geist'), we find Hegel more or less deifying the state in which he himself lived, i.e. the modern, secular, Protestant state.[26] And this, Westphal concludes, "is to say that true religion affirms the family, the economy, and the state as the decisive presence of God on earth and that true religiosity consists in thoroughgoing socialization. Nothing could be further from the faith of which Abraham is father."(Westphal 1987, 82). Thus, it is no coincidence that in *Fear and Trembling* Kierkegaard stages a fierce battle against the idea that society and its morality is everything. Neither is it a coincidence that for this battle he chooses Abraham of Genesis 22 as his weapon.[27]

My purpose in this chapter has been to demonstrate that 'the binding of Isaac' is a tale of terror which from the earliest times has forced commentators to resort to all kinds of fanciful ideas in order to come to terms with the text. Most prominent in this regard, are the typological and allegorical interpretations of Genesis 22 which, contrary to what is often assumed, are also found on the Jewish side. In the Christian tradition, the *typological* interpretation (seeing Isaac as the forerunner of Christ) may be regarded as primarily responsible for the fact that over the centuries theologians, although at the same time being 'disturbed' by the text, have proved so willing to see the sacrifice of Isaac as a good thing. For when all is said and done, who could be against it, when in the overarching picture of God's plan this sacrifice belonged to salvation history itself?

Another way of putting this point would be to say that in archaic times and up through the Middle Ages there was no morality strong and independent enough to seriously question or destabilize the hegemony of interpretations based on religious and Scriptural authority. This gradually

---

26 I am aware, of course, that some Hegel scholars would dispute this interpretation.
27 The metaphors of 'battle' and 'weapon' are borrowed from Westphal 1987, 62.

begins to change with the Renaissance and Enlightenment, and when we reach modernity, we see philosophers like Kant and Hegel radically questioning the traditional interpretation of Genesis 22. In short, the tables have turned, and 'morality', it would seem, has become more important than 'religion'. This, in turn, forms the challenge and background to Kierkegaard's interpretation in *Fear and Trembling*, the subject of the following chapter.

Chapter Two

KIERKEGAARD'S *FEAR AND TREMBLING*

In 1843, six years before Denmark adopted a democratic constitution, Kierkegaard published *Fear and Trembling* (F&T). As is well known, Kierkegaard was no admirer of the movement towards democracy. He feared that the uneducated masses were in no way suited for power and preferred the monarchy to continue. But what has this got to do with F&T, and why did Kierkegaard bother to write it in the first place?

To this day that question divides and perplexes Kierkegaard scholars. Personally, I make no claim to being a Kierkegaard scholar, and neither do I have any ambitions of solving the many riddles involved in the text. Kierkegaard was a romantic who loved riddles, and this may, at least partly, explain why he chose to publish many of his books under different pseudonyms, in the case of F&T, Johannes de Silentio.[28] As we shall see in the next chapter, this fact is used by some commentators to distance Kierkegaard himself from the eulogizing of Abraham which is undisputedly, I would argue, the basic tenor of F&T. Obviously, an author's use of a pseudonym forces on us a *caveat* not to attribute the 'meanings' and standpoints of the text directly to the author himself. In my case, however, this problem is of little consequence, since I am not going to make any claims either to Kierkegaard's entire work or to him as personally having sworn allegiance to the propositions put forward in F&T. All that matters

---

28 A deeper reason behind the pseudonyms is, as often mentioned in the literature, Kierkegaard's concept of 'indirect communication', i.e. the idea that matters of existential or religious truth can only be communicated in an indirect, Socratic manner. The pseudonyms are helpful in this respect, since they prompt the reader to judge for himself.

to me is the text and the fact that Kierkegaard produced it. Thus, when in this chapter (and later in this book) I refer to 'Kierkegaard', I mean no more or no less than the historic person and genius who once lived in Copenhagen and produced a lot of interesting texts, and among those F&T.

But still, why did he write it? Interestingly, the same commentators who emphasize the pseudonymous character of F&T point to biographical reasons of a highly personal nature. Kierkegaard has himself given occasion for this line of interpretation, not only through several passages of the text, but not least by prefacing the text with a motto taken from German philosopher J.G. Hamann: "What Tarquinius Superbus said in the garden by means of the poppies, the son understood but the messenger did not". The son in this old Roman legend understood that the poppies which Tarquinius (probably to the amazement of the messenger) beheaded with his sword, were a metaphor for the way in which his father admonished him to deal with the leaders of the city he had just conquered. In other words, the motto seems to be an encoded message where a person is ordered by a higher authority to sacrifice (or kill) someone. In this sense, the motto covers also the subject matter of the book, a meditation on Genesis 22 and Abraham's willingness to sacrifice Isaac. In terms of Kierkegaard's biography, however, it is a plausible interpretation to point to two motivating factors. One is Kierkegaard's complex relation to his father whom of course he loved, but who may also be said to have 'sacrificed' his son by a harsh and disciplined upbringing. The other is Kierkegaard's relation to Regine Olsen, the love he himself had chosen to sacrifice not long before writing F&T. That this latter factor weighed on Kierkegaard's mind has been established by entries in his journals, but it is also corroborated by the fact that in F&T (and in other texts as well) Kierkegaard uses examples of young people in love to illustrate the workings of faith. Be that as it may, Kierkegaard could have more than one reason to produce an enigmatic and encoded text where the messenger (Johannes de Silentio) may only understands some of it, whereas the intended reader (Regine?) understands not everything, but what Kierkegaard wanted her to understand in order to explain to her why he decided to terminate their relation and 'kill' their love.

Turning away from biographical and psychological considerations, textual analysis reveals that Kierkegaard had two main targets which furnish us with important clues as to why he found it important to write the book. One of these is the moral and political philosophy of Kant and Hegel, and not least the local, Danish adepts of Hegel's philosophy which at that time was *en vogue* so to speak. Four things enraged Kierkegaard in this dominant philosophy of his time: 1) It put the demands of morality over religion; 2) It presented the 'universal' as being more important than the 'particular' and single individual; 3) It presented the primary task of the individual as that of becoming one with society, of surrendering his private beliefs on the altar of the common good; and 4) it presented religion and faith as a stage to be left behind on the journey to the higher reason of Hegel's absolute spirit. The other target, foreshadowing Kierkegaard's later furious attack on 'Christendom', is his critique of his contemporaries for not taking faith seriously enough. Or to put it stronger: for entertaining completely false and mistaken notions of the true nature of faith. What they lack is *passion* (Danish: *Lidenskab*), and Kierkegaard aims to convince his readers that faith is 'the highest passion'. In the satirical and polemical 'Preface' and 'Epilogue', Kierkegaard effectively uses economic metaphors to display his own time as willing to sell out faith at bargain price. Hence, we may safely assume that in contrast he intends his ghost-writer, Johannes de Silentio, to portray the true value (and highest possible price) of faith.

Now, given these intended targets of Kierkegaard's rare rhetorical and polemical gifts, how could he most effectively strike a blow at both of them? By interpreting the Biblical story of Abraham's sacrifice which had no doubt lingered on his mind since childhood.[29] This story carries the weight of an authoritative tradition (although as we saw in the last chapter, not undisputed), and in the New Testament Abraham is repeatedly referred to as the 'Father of Faith'. So if you want to learn the true nature of faith why not turn to the paradigmatic character himself? Besides, Genesis 22 is perfectly suited for Kierkegaard's polemical purposes,

---

29 On the textual level, I agree with Lippitt (2003, 21) that the man who as a child was so impressed with 'this beautiful tale' is Johannes himself. But since, in a more general sense, we can no doubt agree that the whole point of a pseudonym is that the author (for whatever reasons) is able to hide behind it, I see no problem in assuming that Gen 22 was impressed on young Søren's mind from early childhood.

because it (at least in the interpretation given in F&T) addresses all the four points mentioned above.

However, this may not even be all, for I can think of yet another reason why it is significant that Kierkegaard should choose to deal with the figure of Abraham. The problem with this, however, is that it forces me (but hopefully at this point only) to break my initial promise not to embark on a general interpretation of Kierkegaard's thinking. My personal impression is that the genius and importance, but at the same time the *problem* of (and with) Kierkegaard, is that his overall project could be described as trying to salvage the 'faith of the fathers' (*pace* Pascal) and bring it into modernity. For reasons internally related to the process of secularization (cf. Ch. Four), I doubt that this can be done, but still one cannot help admiring the way Kierkegaard has tried to accomplish this in F&T. Hence, even if and when in the final analysis one chooses to disagree with him, he forces the reader to think and reflect. To put it shortly, I see Kierkegaard as a *radical* Christian thinker, one who likes to go to extremes, and thus I tend to see his late attack on Christendom (which has presented such an embarrassment to contemporary commentators who have generally tried to 'sanitize' Kierkegaard) as a natural, almost logical, consequence of the position worked out in F&T.[30] But once again: we cannot be sure that Kierkegaard himself completely identifies with F&T, and therefore, as stated earlier, I refer to him primarily as the 'producer' of the text.

What I want to do in this chapter, is something rather modest, namely to attempt a reading of F&T focusing on the overall subject of my book, namely the relation between religion, morality, and society in general. I should perhaps add that I do not impose this interpretive perspective on the text of F&T. For, as noted earlier, Kierkegaard himself chose this focus in order to combat Hegel's claim that philosophy be regarded as 'higher' than religion. This debate may seem less relevant today. All one needs to do, however, is to insert 'democracy' instead of philosophy, and suddenly what we have is a text which speaks directly to the major

---

30 I am aware, of course, that my general interpretation of the the major thrust of Kierkegaard's thought calls for further argument. I cannot elaborate on the matter here, but must refer the reader to Nørager 2003 and 2008a.

controversies of our time. Or, to put it differently: The subject matter of the compatibility of religion and democracy, on which I shall concentrate in the second part of this book, is already a core issue for Kierkegaard in *Fear and Trembling*.

Kierkegaard's General Approach to Genesis 22

Kierkegaard adopts a completely independent and original perspective on the *aqedah*. What I particularly like about him is that (much like the cover painting by Caravaggio) he resists so many earlier attempts to gloss over the story and to sanitize it, making it somehow palatable to our taste. On the contrary, no one has untiringly insisted upon and radicalized Abraham's dilemma like Kierkegaard does. And because the way he frames the problem is radical, if not downright impossible, it is only to be expected that the solution be equally radical, complex, and perhaps impossible. This 'solution' or what in F&T is called the 'double movement of faith' will be briefly interpreted in this chapter, and then I shall return to it, and try to make further sense of it, in chapter seven.

As for the *genre* of the work, the title page advertises that we are dealing with 'dialectical lyric'. 'Dialectical' indicates that Kierkegaard's method (and thinking in general) was strongly influenced by Hegel, and 'lyric' reminding us that he is also, as it were, poetically re-enacting and empathically reliving the torments which Abraham had to go through on the 3-day journey to Mount Moriah. Nowhere, and this brings me to the other factor, is this more clearly brought out than in the 'Exordium' where Kierkegaard employs all his imaginative skills in order to put his readers in the right mood for understanding the real drama of the story. He does this by presenting us with four different, but entirely possible versions of what *might* have happened. In each of these imagined versions something goes wrong; either Isaac loses his father or he loses his faith. Faith and love are not always easily reconciled. This, of course, as some commentators have noted, has to do with the fact that none of the four 'sub-Abrahams' (Lippitt 2003, 21ff.) presented is as great as the 'real' Abraham. And thus we, as readers, are prepared for the 'Eulogy on Abraham' which follows. But let us pause a moment here, for Lippitt is surely correct in drawing an important lesson from the difference between the four 'sub-Abrahams' and Abraham 'himself' (i.e. the one favored by

Kierkegaard and his Johannes): "The fact that Johannes clearly considers them all to be inferior to 'the' Abraham shows that mere willingness to obey the will of God no matter how outrageous the ostensible demand cannot be what is being commended. (At the very least, *how* the will is obeyed is clearly a crucial factor)." (*ibid*, 29). No, *mere* willingness is not enough, but at the same time one should not forget F&T's repeated insistence that 'only the one who draws the knife will get Isaac'. My second comment to Lippitt here is that instead of focusing on the sub-Abrahams being 'inferior' to the real one (which of course in light of the following 'Eulogy' is a correct observation), perhaps we should direct our interest to whether or not a given version of the story has a happy ending or not. For, as just noted, common to versions I-IV of the 'Exordium' is that none of them has a happy ending. This contrasts with the Abraham-story (both in Gen 22 and F&T) which, although terrifying, has a happy ending. One must therefore try to discover how the text of F&T accomplishes this. The answer is twofold: First by claiming (without textual basis in Gen 22) that Abraham received Isaac back *happier* than the first time; and, second, by consistently excluding the perspective of Isaac, the victim of the sacrificial violence.

Thus, the initial focus (in version I) on Isaac seems to me noteworthy, since in the remainder of F&T the focus is almost entirely on Abraham. Why this blending out the perspective of the victim? From a psychological perspective, we may speculate that Kierkegaard resisted acknowledging that he himself had been victimized as a child. The all too common 'wisdom' here is that 'the one you love is the one you discipline' and that 'the act of punishment is more hurtful to the perpetrator than to the victim'. Another reason may stem from the somewhat surprising fact that the typological interpretation (Isaac prefiguring Jesus Christ) plays no role whatsoever in F&T. In fact, Christ (or Jesus) is mentioned directly only twice (F&T, p. 28 and 66), and references to the New Testament are (compared to Kierkegaard's other works) relatively few, albeit important.[31]

---

31 I am thinking here of the parable of the rich young man (F&T, p. 28 and 49), the elaboration on Lk 14:26 (F&T, 72ff.), the idea that faith "is convinced that God is concerned about the smallest things" (p. 34), and, perhaps most importantly, Johannes' understanding that "[b]y faith I do not renounce anything; on the contrary, by faith

In this sense, Kierkegaard may be said to connect himself with the earliest layers of the Jewish and Christian occupation with the *aqedah* where the center of attention was Abraham as the obedient Father of Faith.

A crucial question emerges from this fact of F&T being, as it were, an *Abrahamic* book: Is it also a *Christian* book? Or to put it slightly different: We may grant that Kierkegaard's picture of Abraham's admirable faith is one that would gain the sympathetic approval of Jews (and perhaps even more so of Muslims), but does the notion of faith propagated in F&T also qualify as faith in a *Christian* sense? Kierkegaard, as we shall see, tries to convince us of this by portraying a 'knight of faith' who incarnates the New Testament faith which can move mountains and is convinced that for God 'everything is possible'. The answer to our question, then, seems to depend on whether or not we can square Abraham with the knight of faith.

The Portrait of Abraham

Kierkegaard repeatedly refers to Abraham as the 'Father of Faith' and thus as the model for true faith. In this sense he echoes the NT (especially Paul's) understanding of Abraham authorizing the doctrine of justification by faith alone. As indicated above, in his attack on the lame faith characteristic of Copenhagen of the 1840ies, Kierkegaard wants to utilize Abraham as a model and a mirror for critical self-examination on the part of the reader. Abraham is simply the greatest, and no one compares to him.[32]

In agreement with tradition and what one might expect, Abraham is in F&T portrayed as obedient. He willingly subjects to God's command; "He knew it was God the Almighty who was testing him; he knew it was the hardest sacrifice that could be demanded of him; but he knew also that

---

I receive everything exactly in the sense in which it is said [sc. by Jesus in the Gospel, TN] that one who has faith like a mustard seed can move mountains." (F&T, 48f.).

32 In a formulation echoing Paul's theology of the cross in 1 Cor 1:18 (and 3:18ff) Kierkegaard notes that "(...) Abraham was the greatest of all, great by that power whose strength is powerlessness, great by that wisdom whose secret is foolishness, great by that hope whose form is madness, great by the love that is hatred to oneself" (F&T, 16f.). Westphal (1987, 85ff.) sees this 'logic of insanity' as an important element of Kierkegaard's major (pseudonymous) works.

no sacrifice is too severe when God demands it – and he drew the knife" (F&T, 22). The terrible nature of the deed Abraham had to perform is highlighted by Kierkegaard's insistence that Abraham was in a cheerful mood when embarking on the road to Mount Moriah. We can see this in a strange passage where he seemingly directly follows the words of the Bible: "We read in sacred scripture", etc (F&T, 21). In his rendering of the text Kierkegaard implicitly alludes to the dialogue between God and Adam in Gen 3:9; thus he constructs the following inter-text: "And God tempted Abraham and said: Abraham, Abraham, where are you? But Abraham answered: Here am I" (*ibid*). Kierkegaard uses this to critically engage with his reader: "And when your name was called, did you answer, perhaps answer softly, in a whisper? Not so with Abraham. Cheerfully, freely, confidently, loudly he answered: Here am I" (*ibid*). Kierkegaard presses a point here, for obviously we have no textual basis for character-izing Abraham's response as 'cheerful' or 'confident'. But this is not all: "We read on: 'And Abraham arose early in the morning'. He hurried as if to a celebration (...)" (*ibid*). 'As if to a celebration'? My foot! Or perhaps more aptly: Be my guest!

There is another side to the portrait of Abraham, however. This is the Abraham who is in the deepest anguish, in fear and trembling, but who nonetheless manages to display the *courage* that is such a vital part of true faith. And this is the point where Kierkegaard primarily criticizes what he regards as the 'normal' interpretation of Genesis 22. What is typically left out and glossed over is Abraham's anguish and *anxiety*, an anxiety stemming partly from his consciousness of a breach between the ethical and the religious, and partly from the fact that he is in a no man's land, having left behind all the support of his normal society. He is isolated, and stands in a private relation to his 'God' who has allegedly commanded him to perform a terrible deed. Today, we cannot help drawing a parallel to the Palestinian suicide bomber (or Mohammad Atta in the plane on 9/11) who is on route to his target and waiting to enter the pearly gates of Paradise. Obviously, we have no way of knowing whether Kierkegaard, had he been writing F&T today, would have been inclined to demand a less passionate version of faith, but it is certainly a question one cannot help asking.

Given this radicalized and extreme version of Abraham's faith, it is no surprise that Kierkegaard feels the need to answer a question foremost on any reader's mind: How does Abraham (or someone in his position) know that he is 'legitimate' (Danish: 'berettiget') or entitled to do what he is about to do? The text's repeated answer to this is that the legitimation stems from Abraham's anguish, his anxiety, and the fact that he is faced with a *paradox* resisting all attempts at rational penetration. As a continuation of this theme, at the end of 'Problema II' Kierkegaard comments briefly on what he sees as *criteria* by which the individual may ascertain whether or not he is a 'Knight of Faith'. One is that the knight of faith finds himself in absolute isolation; another is that he is always a single individual representing the paradox; a third is that he feels the pain of not being able to make himself understood by others; and, finally, the true knight of faith is always a witness (Danish: 'martyr') – never a teacher (cf. F&T, 79f.). Two comments on these criteria must be made: One is that they are obviously formulated with Abraham on Mount Moriah in mind, albeit nowhere near sufficient to defend his intended sacrifice; another comment is that these criteria do not seem relevant to the mundane knight of faith whom we shall meet later. In other words, already here we have an indication that Kierkegaard's attempt to 'save' Abraham by casting him as an example of a knight of faith performing the 'double movement of faith' will not work.

The portrait of Abraham is highlighted by Johannes imagining how *he* would have reacted, had he been in Abraham's situation. He would have resigned, given up all hope, saying to himself that 'all is lost'. In other words, Johannes could have made the movement of 'infinite resignation' and retained his belief that 'God is love', but this resignation would nonetheless be nothing but 'a substitute for faith' (F&T, 35; the Danish original has 'surrogate'). Another important difference is that Johannes would not be able to *love* Isaac as completely as did Abraham, and Kierkegaard explicitly states that without this presupposition "the whole thing becomes a misdeed" (*ibid*). In other words, Abraham's perfect fatherly love is a crucial feature of what in Kierkegaard's view legitimizes his intention to carry out the sacrifice.

Kierkegaard's interpretation of Abraham walks the tightrope between, on the one hand, praising his courage and willingness to accomplish the deed, and, on the other hand, favoring a solution that only praises Abraham's faith. As to the first, Kierkegaard triumphantly notes that "If faith cannot make it a holy act to be willing to murder his son, then let the same judgment be passed on Abraham as on everyone else" (F&T, 30). Concerning the second aspect, Kierkegaard 'solves', as it were, the problem by being horrified and paralyzed by the prospect of Abraham's *act*, while at the same time admiring his *faith*, and the courage that goes with it. And apparently (although this is not equally clear in all parts of F&T) it is only in the latter respect that Abraham stands out as a model of faith. Thus, Kierkegaard remarks, "As a matter of fact, if one makes faith everything – that is, makes it what it is – then I certainly believe that I dare to speak of it without danger in our day, which is scarcely prodigal in faith. *It is only by faith that one achieves any resemblance to Abraham, not by murder*" (F&T, 31).

But is it legitimate to separate in this manner the motivation and consequences of faith from an idea of 'faith in itself', faith by virtue of the absurd? I doubt it. Despite the general emphasis in theological tradition on distinguishing faith from works, what makes sense philosophically is, rather, to conceive of 'faith' as a cognitive and emotional attitude which engenders a certain practice. In the following two sections we shall see how Kierkegaard, having painted such an extreme portrait of Abraham and his faith, is forced to instantiate a radical break with morality and what we today would see as democratic institutions.

The 'Teleological Suspension' of the Ethical

It is of vital importance to my interpretation that 'the ethical' in F&T is not just equivalent to morality, but has the wider (Hegelian) meaning of 'society', our common life together.[33] Why does Kierkegaard (who is elsewhere not afraid of going to extremes) speak only of 'suspending' the ethical and not abolishing it? Because the whole point (the goal, so to speak) is to *return* to the ethical. Faith, as Kierkegaard repeatedly reminds

---

33 In this regard, it is not particularly helpful that the Hong-translation talks about the ethical as 'the universal' (cf. F&T, 54, and *passim*), since this carries Kantian rather than Hegelian connotations. The Danish original has 'det Almene' which is closer to 'the common life', civil society, or Hegelian 'Sittlichkeit'.

us, is a faith for *this* life. In this sense, Kierkegaard is in F&T presenting an answer to a classic conundrum in Christian tradition: How can and how should the religious person live in society? This is a question Jesus addresses in the New Testament (the story of the rich young man; Jesus saying 'Render unto Caesar', etc,) and which prompted major Christian theologians like Augustine and Luther to make a distinction between two realms or kingdoms, one of them spiritual, the other secular. Kierkegaard clearly belongs in this tradition, but with him the distinction is between the eternal, spiritual and 'inner' on the one hand, and the temporal, material, and 'outer' world on the other. And in our own time this question may take the form in which we will discuss them in part two of this book: Is religion and democracy compatible? And what is the proper role of religion and religious arguments in the public square?

In 'Problema I' Kierkegaard begins with challenging the Hegelian idea that the ethical task of the individual consists in bringing himself into a harmonious relation to society and its norms. Kierkegaard sees in this an annulment of the individual's 'singularity' and counters: "If this is the highest that can be said of man and his existence, then the ethical is of the same nature as a person's eternal salvation, which is his *telos* forevermore and at all times (...)" (F&T, 54). Kierkegaard, it seems to me, has a valid point here. It is important, and not only from an explicitly religious perspective, to insist that each individual is always *more* than his role and value as a citizen. But I think he is in danger of losing this point again, when elsewhere in the text he keeps emphasizing that faith is *higher* than the ethical. Now, of course we may grant that Kierkegaard has been sort of lured into this by Hegel's picture of religion (and faith) as a developmental stage being superseded by the philosophical *apotheosis* of absolute spirit. Nonetheless, it is unfortunate for at least two reasons: One, because it presents the relation between the ethical and the religious as a *competition* (which of the two may claim to be 'higher'?), an antagonistic no-win situation, in reality; and second, because this 'higher' claim is in latent conflict with his important point that faith is a faith for *this* life.

And perhaps at some point Kierkegaard has imagined finding a more constructive, and less antagonistic approach towards the ethical, for in one (but only this one) particular passage of F&T what appears to be nothing less than a major purpose of the book is described in the following way: "We shall see whether this story contains any higher expression for the ethical that can ethically explain his [sc. Abraham's] behavior, can ethically justify his suspending of the ethical obligation to the son, but without moving beyond the teleology of the ethical" (F&T, 57). Note, that here the adjective 'higher' is used in connection with the ethical and in order to announce the search for an explanation of Abraham *within* the confines of the ethical. Not only does this seem to go directly against the main tenor of the book, but quite apart from this Kierkegaard never redeems this promise. At any rate he does not find it in the story of Abraham. Some commentators have tried to find a solution in 'Problema III' where the concept of *sin* emerges in connection with Kierkegaard's complicated interpretation of the story of Agnes and the Merman.[34]

What is involved in the notion of a 'suspension' of the ethical? Clearly, it cannot mean an absolute break with the ethical (although this is often what the text implies). On the contrary, a 'suspension' means that the ethical is put into brackets for a certain amount of time after which it is reinstated again. In this sense, it is a weaker expression than Hegel's *Aufhebung*. This notwithstanding, Kierkegaard is not quite clear on this issue. To see this, look at the following passage:

Abraham's situation is different [sc. from that of the tragic hero]. By his act he *transgressed* the ethical altogether and had a higher *telos* outside it, in relation to which he *suspended* it. For I certainly would like to know how Abraham's act can be related to the universal, whether any point of contact between what Abraham did and the universal can be found other than that Abraham *transgressed* it. (F&T, 59; emphasis added).

Is 'transgression' the same as 'suspension'? Not at all, and Kierkegaard himself attests to this by stressing that there was no point of contact to the ethical.[35] My point here is that Kierkegaard is time and again carried away

---

34 As an example of this strategy, see Søltoft 2000. Other commentators (including Søltoft) rightly point out that the issue is not addressed further until the preface of *The Concept of Anxiety* which directly refers to *Fear and Trembling*.

35 Cf. also the following quotation which speaks of a *contrast* to 'the universal': "But if the ethical is teleologically suspended in this manner, how does the single individual

by his 'will to radicalize', and that this threatens to undermine his two valid points: 1) that the individual should not be reduced to his role and identity within 'the ethical'; 2) that the point of the movements of faith (cf. below) is to be able to *return* to the ethical (and this is why it makes good sense to talk of a 'suspension') and practice a faith for *this* life.

A little later in the text the idea of 'temptation' is applied to the ethical: "As a rule, what tempts a person is something that will hold him back from doing his duty [this is Kant's position, TN], but here the temptation is the ethical itself, which would hold him [sc. Abraham] from doing God's will. But what is duty? Duty is simply the expression for God's will" (F&T, 60). Kierkegaard at this point (and, alas, many others) seems to be playing directly into the hands of a divine command theory, which we shall encounter in the following chapter. But this radicalization has other serious consequences, for once the individual has left the ethical completely, the terrifying possibility of mistake emerges:

But the person who gives up the universal in order to grasp something even higher that is not the universal – what does he do? Is it possible that this can be anything other than a spiritual trial? And if it is possible, but the individual makes a mistake, what salvation is there for him? He suffers all the agony of the tragic hero, he shatters his joy in the world, he renounces everything, and perhaps at the same time he barricades himself from the sublime joy that was so precious to him that he would buy it at any price. The observer cannot understand him at all; neither can his eye rest upon him with confidence. Perhaps the believer's intention cannot be carried out at all, because it is inconceivable. Or if it could be done but the individual has misunderstood the deity – what salvation would there be for him? (F&T, 60f.).

By the end of 'Problema I', however, Kierkegaard seems confident that his analysis of Abraham has yielded the desired answer. In the way he frames it, we see once again how the radicalizing, general thrust of his text makes him stress the *contrast* to the rational, to understanding, and to what can be explained:

---

in whom it is suspended exist? He exists as the single individual in contrast to the universal." (F&T, 61f.).

The story of Abraham contains, then, a teleological suspension of the ethical. As the single individual he became higher than the universal. This is the paradox, which cannot be mediated. How he entered into it is just as inexplicable as how he remains in it. If this is not Abraham's situation, then Abraham is not even a tragic hero but a murderer. It is thoughtless to want to go on calling him the father of faith, to speak of it to men who have an interest only in words. (F&T, 66).

The Absolute Duty towards God

In the opening pages of 'Problema II', Hegel's idea of the ethical is once again the target of Kierkegaard's criticism. He defends, and again this is a valid point, the 'incommensurable' in man which is displayed in faith, but not only here. For Kierkegaard 'the incommensurable' which is so much worth salvaging, has to do with 'interiority', with inner subjectivity. And this, at least from Kierkegaard's perspective, is destroyed by Hegel who demands that the individual should express his interiority in something external. But faith, according to Kierkegaard, only begins where philosophy and reason cannot reach further, and in order to drive home this point he tries to convince his reader that there exists an absolute duty to God. What this entails is that the single individual "determines his relation to the universal by his relation to the absolute, not his relation to the absolute by his relation to the universal" (F&T, 70). If we translate this to the contemporary debate on religion and democracy, we can see that this could be a quite dangerous position. At this point in the text, however, Kierkegaard tries to ease our minds by noting that from "this it does not follow that the ethical should be *invalidated*; rather, the ethical receives a completely different expression, a paradoxical expression, such as, for example, that love to God may bring the knight of faith to give his love to the neighbor – an expression opposite to that which, ethically speaking, is duty." (*ibid*, emphasis added). Is what we have here his answer to the earlier announced search for a 'higher' expression of the ethical? If that is supposed to be the case, it is not a satisfactory answer.

In order to further substantiate his defense of Abraham, Kierkegaard refers to one of the harsh sayings of Jesus, namely Lk 14:26f. ("If any one comes to me and does not hate his own father and mother and wife and children and brothers and sisters, yes, and even his own life, he cannot be my disciple. Whoever does not bear his own cross and come after me, cannot be my disciple"). This inclusion is worth noting, because although (as already mentioned) it is not the only New Testament reference in F&T, it is the only one that Kierkegaard elaborates on and uses for polemical purposes foreshadowing his later attack on Christendom. But of course it cannot and should not be denied that this quotation gives support to his radical version of Christianity.

What are the implications of accepting an absolute duty to God? In relation to Abraham this is brought out in an interesting passage where Kierkegaard struggles to bring together Abraham's faith (his duty to God) and his love for Isaac:

The absolute duty can lead one to do what ethics would forbid, but it can never lead the knight of faith to stop loving. Abraham demonstrates this. In the moment he is about to sacrifice Isaac, the ethical expression for what he is doing is: he hates Isaac. But if he actually hates Isaac, he can rest assured that God does not demand this of him, for Cain and Abraham are not identical. He must love Isaac with his whole soul. Since God claims Isaac, he must, if possible, love him even more, and only then can he *sacrifice* him, for it is indeed this love for Isaac that makes his act a sacrifice by its paradoxical contrast to his love for God. (F&T, 74).

Kierkegaard seems here to buy into the theology of the beloved son which was briefly introduced in the previous chapter. In the meantime, however, the notion (and practice) of sacrifice has undergone a process of secularization (cf. Ch. Four). Hence, today we can only in a metaphorical sense say that love involves an element of (self) sacrifice.

The Solution to Abraham's Dilemma: The 'Double Movement' of Faith

Most commentators agree that the opening part of the 'problemata', the so called 'Preliminary Expectoration' or 'Preamble from the Heart' is of vital importance for understanding the overall message of F&T. A major reason for this is that it is here we find Kierkegaard's famous distinction between 'infinite resignation' and 'faith' which taken together constitute the so called 'double movement of faith'. In what follows, I shall try to give a condensed version of my interpretation of this important part of F&T, but let me begin by presenting two premises of my interpretation:

1) On the basic level of how we approach a given text, I proceed on the hermeneutic assumption that the text 'makes sense' and that it is not internally confused or 'mixed up'. The reader may find it strange that I should emphasize the seemingly obvious, but as a matter of fact (as we shall see in the next chapter) several commentators take refuge in the pseudonymous character of F&T arguing that Johannes de Silentio, being a self-confessed 'outsider' to faith, presents us with a necessarily skewed and inaccurate picture of faith. First, I would object that this is really making too much of the pseudonyms. Granted that just one pseudonym (Johannes de Silentio) and one work (F&T) obviously do not give us the whole picture, in this case of Kierkegaard's view of the nature of faith, I would still maintain that it is simply psychologically implausible that Kierkegaard (assuming that we can agree that he is the *de facto* author of the text) should have written something that he does not himself endorse. Recall, in this connection, that the text is written with such passion and commitment. Second, the text itself explicitly denies that Johannes should not be able to give us an accurate picture of the faith of which Abraham is the paradigm; thus, on page 37 Johannes clearly states that he is able to *describe* the movements of faith (and the text corroborates this). His only 'problem' (if that is to be considered a problem) is that he is unable to 'make' or *carry out* the movements of faith because he lacks the necessary *courage* of faith.

2) I shall argue that much points in the direction that a plausible interpretation of this part of F&T is one that sees the relation between infinite resignation and faith in light of the stage theory, parts of which Kierkegaard had laid out in *Either-Or*. Here the focus was on the relation between the aesthetical and the ethical stage, whereas in F&T Kierkegaard may be said to let Johannes investigate the difference between the ethical and the religious stage. Unfortunately, the text of F&T is ambiguous here: While some passages (fx pp. 37 and 46) indicate that infinite resignation is the last stage before, and at the same time the *conditio sine qua non* for, faith, – other passages (pp. 35f., 36, and notably pp. 40 and 40f.) create the impression that infinite resignation must be performed 'continually' and in 'each and every moment'. This interpretation, somewhat contrary to the stage

theory perspective, seems to be the preferred one in the sense that it has the broadest textual basis. To see this, let me include the following passage from 'Problema III':

> To repeat what was sufficiently [sic! TN] developed earlier, Abraham makes two movements. He makes the infinite movement of resignation and gives up Isaac, which no one can understand because it is a private venture; but next, *at every moment*, he makes the movement of faith. This is his consolation. In other words, he is saying: But it will not happen, or if it does, the Lord will give me a new Isaac, that is, by virtue of the absurd. (F&T, 115; emphasis added).

But, one could ask, are the two interpretations mutually exclusive? Not necessarily. I can see how it could make sense to say from one perspective that reaching the ethical stage and having gained your 'eternal consciousness' is a necessary prerequisite for entering the religious stage. And at the same time, albeit now from the 'internal' perspective of the religious stage, it is plausible to think of faith not as a secure possession once and for all, but, rather as something which must continually be fought for (by way of infinite resignation) and gained (faith by virtue of the absurd).

Let us continue our interpretive efforts by noting three features connecting the 'Preamble from the Heart' with the surrounding sections of F&T. One is the polemic directed against the Hegelians claiming that they have 'moved further' than faith. This theme was brought to the fore already in the 'Preface', and it is repeated in the 'Preamble'. Another is the relation between the ethical and the religious which, as we have seen, is the direct subject of 'Problema I' where Kierkegaard sets out to prove that a teleological 'suspension' of the ethical is possible. At this point it is advisable, I believe, to recall the four sub-Abrahams of the Exordium. Each of these possible variants of the story was flawed; there was no happy ending to either of them, because it proved impossible to reconcile the ethical (Abraham's love of Isaac and his duty as a father) and the religious (Abraham's faith and obedience to God). Now, in the Preamble, Kierkegaard presents his ghost-writer, Johannes, with the task of creating a version of the story which has a happy ending. That this is a 'mission impossible' is clear from the dramatic way in which the problem is formulated: "If faith cannot make it a holy act to be willing to murder his son, then let the same judgment be passed on Abraham as on everyone else" (F&T, 30). Nonetheless, at the end of the Preamble Kierkegaard seems to think that he has argued a water-tight case, for he concludes that faith is the paradox "that makes a murder into a holy and God-pleasing act" (F&T, p. 53). How is this possible? We are now in a position to provide a new answer: by virtue of the double movement of faith and of conceiving faith as a paradox.

What is the double movement of faith, and how may love and faith be reconciled? Let us first take a closer look at the first of the two movements: *infinite resignation*. Johannes, posing here as a faith psychologist with his own private praxis, intends to make it easy for us by presenting us with a 'particular case' of a young lad who fell in love with a princess. This story, supposedly, will cast light over each of the movements' relation to *reality* (the Hong translation has 'actuality') for everything, note, depends on this (F&T, 41). Eventually, the lad must recognize that in reality his love is impossible, because he will not be able to get the princess. This, however, does not mean that he relinquishes his love for the princess. That is just not an option, for this love is nothing less than his identity, the contents of his life. What can he do then? He makes the movement of infinite resignation which contains the following elements:

- He 'resigns' in the sense that he gives up his wish and turns it inward instead. As a consequence, he becomes an individual placed in quiet solitude.
- He concentrates all the passion of his mind and soul and makes the movement of *infinite* resignation. It is 'infinite' in the double sense of a) bringing the lad *away* from finitude and the humdrum of daily reality, and b) turning his love into something *religious*. This again has two aspects: One is that his love for the princess becomes 'eternalized' and therefore secure: nothing can now threaten his private 'princess-religion'. The other aspect is that, similar to the existential choice on the ethical stage, the lad gains not only his 'eternal consciousness' but also a love of God based on the general idea that 'God is love'.[36]

---

36 This basic similarity to the ethical stage is repeated later in the Preamble, p. 46 ("for only in infinite resignation do I become conscious of my eternal validity") and p. 48

In this way, the lad is able to become a 'knight of infinite resignation', something which includes the following benefits: He is reconciled with existence, he is self-contained, and he has found peace of mind and comfort in his pain. This may not sound too bad, but note here that Kierkegaard has instructed Johannes to repeatedly remind us that faith is for *this* life and that everything depends on the relation to reality. Seen from this perspective, the lad is no more than a *tragic hero*[37] which, as we are told, is also the position of Johannes who admits that he can 'get no higher'. At the same time, the lad's religious outlook has not matured sufficiently. Like in the stage theory where Kierkegaard divides the religious stage into religiosity A and B respectively, the point here is that the lad's (and Johannes') conviction that 'God is love' is only faith in a very general sense which does not compare to the absolute, paradoxical faith of *the knight of faith*. What distinguishes him is that compared to the lad "he makes one more movement even more wonderful than all the others, for he says: Nevertheless I have faith that I will get her – that is, by virtue of the absurd, by virtue of the fact that for God all things are possible" (F&T, 46). Thus, faith is the 'paradox of existence'. Faith is the faith that can move mountains. What Kierkegaard leaves unexplained, however, is what exactly (i.e. in reality or 'actuality') it would mean to have the princess in this life and in spite of it being humanly impossible. Consider the following quotation:

And yet it must be wonderful to get the princess, and the knight of faith is the only happy man, the heir to the finite, while the knight of resignation is a stranger and an alien. To get the princess this way, to live happily with her day after day

---

("The act of resignation does not require faith, for what I gain in resignation is my eternal consciousness"). Another feature supporting a stage theoretical perspective is the fact that 'bourgeois philistinism' is mentioned twice, pp. 38 and 51.

37 In F&T the prime example of a tragic hero is the situation of Greek king Agamemnon who was forced to sacrifice his own daughter. Thus, at a first glance, a dilemma quite similar to that of Abraham. The difference, however, is crucial (albeit not for the poor child about to be killed): Whereas Agamemnon remained securely within the ethical sphere (because his breach with a father's duty to his child happened for the sake of a higher ethical purpose, i.e. that of the nation or people), Abraham had to sever himself completely from the ethical, because the rationale behind his intended child-sacrifice was exclusively religious.

(for it is also conceivable that the knight of resignation could get the princess, but his soul had full insight into the impossibility of their future happiness), to live happily every moment this way by virtue of the absurd, every moment to see the sword hanging over the beloved's head, and yet not to find rest in the pain of resignation but to find joy by virtue of the absurd – this is wonderful. The person who does this is great, the only great one; the thought of it stirs my soul, which never was stingy in admiring the great. (F&T, 50).

What unfortunately remains unclear in this passage is the question foremost on any reader's mind, namely, what it would mean to 'get' the princess. Or to state the matter differently: What (in relation to the princess) does the knight of faith 'have' that the knight of infinite resignation is unable to have? I admit that the text apparently *tries* to answer this question, i.e. by stating how the knight of faith is able 'to live happily with her day after day', and even 'to live happily every moment by virtue of the absurd'. But, I venture to ask, what distinguishes this character from a mentally ill person suffering from delusions? Is *this* knight of faith (perhaps Kierkegaard's ideal version of his own 'life' with Regine) not an individual basing his existence on simple self-deception?

Why is it that we (and Johannes) have such a hard time understanding the knight of faith? Not, I would argue, because we are outsiders unable to understand it *cognitively*, but, rather, because *practically* we (at least the great majority) prefer to rest content with the general idea that 'God is love'. This seemed to be the case in Kierkegaard's own time (hence his attack on 'Christendom'), and this seems to be the case today. We are simply not willing to give up our (partly illusory) 'philistine' decision-making and embark on the risky business of Kierkegaard's radical faith (the faith that can move mountains). Again, due to the gradual, but steady, process of secularization many of us are too skeptical to trust that God can solve our problems by interfering directly in our lives.

In this connection it is interesting to focus on the more general and humoristic description which Kierkegaard gives us of the knight of faith. What I am thinking of here, is of course the presentation of the person who looks like a 'tax-collector' (F&T, 39ff.). Outwardly there are no signs whatsoever of the infinite; on the contrary, this man belongs entirely to *this* world. And in this sense he may be seen as embodying and exemplifying Kierkegaard's emphasis on faith being for *this* life. The tax-collector lives a normal, bourgeois life, delights in taking part in everything, and calmly goes about his daily business. In short, he is as normal and average as can be, and yet "this man has made and at every moment is making the movement of inifinity" (F&T, 40); and again: "He is continually making the movement of infinity" (F&T, 40f.). Here is where a stage theory perspective does not give us the whole picture, for what we learn from these quotations is that the movement of infinite resignation is not made once and for all, but must be performed *continually*. Again, I believe a New Testament perspective may provide an answer: The knight of faith is not just a 'new creation' (p. 40), he is also someone whose relation to society, albeit *outwardly* as normal and straightforward as can be, is *inwardly* 'as if not' as we read in *First Corinthians* chapter 7 (verse 29ff.). What I mean by this is that faith needs a certain amount of *distance* from everyday life. This is the first part of the double movement of faith, the other being that which sends us back into the mundane world. Hence, outwardly nothing is visible, but inwardly the knight of faith must balance two kingdoms (the infinite and the finite) by continually performing the double movement of faith. This balancing, as we shall see in the second part of this book (Ch. Six), is equivalent to what philosopher Robert Audi has described as part of an ethics for contemporary citizens, namely that their public reasoning should follow a principle of 'theo-ethical equilibrium'.

Now, how does the above portrait of the mundane knight of faith (and the double movement of faith) fit the case of Abraham? Let us begin by noting what is truly innovative in Kierkegaard's portrait of Abraham. Part of this has to do with what from a more philosophical perspective distinguishes Kierkegaard as a *modern* thinker. Kierkegaard, we may say, endeavours to combine the idea of something *unconditional* (God) with the modern idea of self-realization. Hence he is also a modern thinker in the sense of following the notion of *subjectivity* which had been worked out in German Idealism. Thus, invoking once again the sub-title, 'Dialectical lyric', it is primarily in the 'lyrical' genre that Kierkegaard tries to sell us Abraham's faith as a monstrosity of obedience. In the more 'dialectial' (and philosophical) parts he presents, as demonstrated above, faith as *movements*, invoking (among other things) the images of a dancer or someone learning how to swim. The other part is, in a religious perspective, of paramount importance, namely Kierkegaard's insistence that Abraham's faith is a faith 'for *this* life' (cf. F&T, 20). This, I believe, is where Kierkegaard implicitly superimposes a New Testament perspective on Abraham's faith, but how is that to be understood?

Kierkegaard insists (perhaps inspired by Heb 11) that an important point in Genesis 22 is that Abraham, as it were, received Isaac *a second time*. But this is not enough; Kierkegaard trumps this by saying that Abraham, when getting Isaac back, was even happier than the first time: "He climbed the mountain, and even in the moment when the knife gleamed he had faith – that God would not require Isaac. No doubt he was surprised at the outcome, but through a double-movement he had attained his first condition, and therefore he received Isaac more joyfully than the first time." (F&T, 36).

As we have seen, the first part of the double-movement of faith is the 'infinite resignation' where you realize that you must give up or relinquish your love object. In giving up we distance ourselves (at least to some degree) from society and human fellowship, and Kierkegaard stresses that this is a necessary prerequisite for faith. Why does he do this? It is possible that more than one source of inspiration plays a role. One such source could be his general (and during his later works increasing) emphasis on the hardships of being a Christian who follows in the footsteps of Jesus Christ. Another could be an influence from the mystical tradition which has practiced and taught that in order to encounter God or Christ you must first 'resign' or, as it were, draw back from society and find a place of quiet and seclusion. Whatever the case may be, Kierkegaard says, again in line with the mystics, that anyone can train himself to exercise the infinite resignation. It demands all your strength and concentration, and therefore you can get no further by yourself; the rest (meaning: faith as the second part of the double-movement) must be done by God, or at least he must initiate it. Somewhat surprisingly, the infinite resignation is also termed 'a purely philosophical' movement, the reason probably being that it may be understood and described within a philosophical perspective.[38]

---

38 "The act of resignation does not require faith, for what I gain in resignation is my eternal consciousness. This is a purely philosophical movement that I venture to make

To summarize: First, you must prepare yourself for faith by giving up your most precious love object and thereby distancing yourself from society (becoming the single individual). Then, secondly, you must wait for God to initiate the movement of faith which will in turn give you hope and courage to believe 'by virtue of the absurd' as it is repeatedly stated.[39] But what is so good and important about faith? What's in it for you and me? F&T contains one passage (p. 77) where Kierkegaard explains that since the price of faith is so costly, so equally is the reward: to be able to address God directly – in the 2nd person singular. Nonetheless, Kierkegaard's focus is directed at something else, which may well have a biographical background in his relation to Regine. What truly fascinates him is the possibility of giving something up and getting it back again in a new and even better form! – a theme which is elaborated further in *Repetition*. Another aspect to this is the relation to the temporal world. The infinite resignation is clearly a movement *away* from 'this world'; but as we have already heard, 'faith' is a faith for *this* world, and consequently the movement of faith must be seen as sending us back into society and human fellowship again.

Before concluding, let us look at some of the passages where Kierkegaard underscores just how much faith can do. In relation to Abraham, the 'father of faith', he comments that "it is great to give up one's desire, but it is greater to hold fast to it after having given it up; it is great to lay hold

---

when it is demanded and can discipline myself to make, because every time some finitude will take power over me, I starve myself into submission until I make the movement, for my eternal consciousness is my love for God, and for me that is the highest of all. The act of resignation does not require faith, but to get the least little bit more than my eternal consciousness requires faith, for this is the paradox." (F&T, 48). We may infer from this that Kierkegaard makes a sharp distinction between 'love of God' and (real) 'faith'.

39 That the movement of faith must be *initiated* by God reflects, of course, a Lutheran emphasis on faith as a gift from God. Seen in this light, the following passage is somewhat perplexing: "The knight of faith realizes this [the impossibility, TN] just as clearly; consequently, he can be saved only by the absurd, and this he grasps [note here that the Danish verb 'griber' is active and does not (like 'grasps') carry the meaning of 'understands'] by faith. Consequently, he acknowledges the impossibility, and in the very same moment he believes the absurd" (F&T, 47). A formulation like this may, I suppose, be inspired from Kierkegaard's characterization of the ethical choice (in *Either-Or*) where the individual chooses himself – and in the same moment chooses his 'eternal consciousness' and gains the idea of God as love.

of the eternal, but it is greater to hold fast to the temporal after having given it up" (F&T, 18). Later he emphasizes that "the movement of faith must continually be made by virtue of the absurd, but yet in such a way, please note, *that one does not lose the finite but gains it whole and intact* (F&T, 37; emphasis added). Echoing this, Kierkegaard can also characterize the movement of faith in the following way: "The next [movement] amazes me, my brain reels, for, after having made the movement of resignation, then by virtue of the absurd to get *everything*, to get one's desire *totally* and *completely* – that is over and beyond human powers, that is a marvel" (F&T, 47f.; emphasis added). The explanation or solution offered to us, where Kierkegaard struggles to combine the philosophical ('modern') and religious (partly 'archaic' / 'Abrahamic', partly Christian) aspects of his brilliant interpretation, consists, as we have seen, in the double-movement of faith.

What, then, may be the answer to the question raised earlier in this chapter as to whether *Fear and Trembling* can be considered as conveying a *Christian* message? Although I generally favor clear answers, in this case I believe the answer should be both 'no' and 'yes'. *No*, because Abraham's God-relation can hardly be considered Christian (for one thing this would be patently anachronistic), and *yes* because the double movement of faith which Kierkegaard imposes on Abraham may be interpreted as mirroring the duality of Christ's death and resurrection. Be that as it may, I would still maintain that it is more than difficult to square Abraham with the mundane knight of faith.

In conclusion, we may thus have ample reason to ask whether the argument of *Fear and Trembling* adds up in the end, and whether it makes sense when seen from a contemporary perspective. Personally, I would argue that Kierkegaard in the end becomes a victim of what is at the same time his strength: his impressive rhetorical skills and his tendency to go to extremes in portraying Abraham as the model of true faith. Moreover, from a systematic perspective it is possible to detect in the text an unresolved tension between two strands in Kierkegaard's interpretation of Genesis 22: One is the radicalized Abraham who is placed in an unmediated opposition to the ethical and who determines his relation to the universal by way of the absolute. Although one cannot help admiring Kierkegaard's masterful eulogy of this figure, I would nonetheless claim that to embark on this interpretive road leads nowhere, – or to be more precise: It leads to religious absolutism which may in turn lead to religiously sanctioned acts of terror. The other strand is Kierkegaard's idea of the double movement of faith as well as his (albeit unsuccessful) search for a higher form of the ethical. If these ideas could be combined with his justified insistence that there is something incommensurable in the individual, something that cannot and should not be subsumed under 'the ethical', we might in the end have something useful. To this more constructive task I shall return in Chapter Seven. For the moment, however, I turn in the next chapter to a selection of contemporary efforts to make sense of *Fear and Trembling*.

Chapter Three

CONTEMPORARY INTERPRETATIONS OF *FEAR AND TREMBLING*

As we have seen in Chapter One, the *aqedah* was always a disturbing story, and up through history major theologians have struggled to make at least some good sense of it. One would have rather strong reasons, I believe, to assume that in our own time this had changed dramatically. However, as we shall see in this chapter, surprisingly many theologians and philosophers of religion still engage in torturous attempts to defend both God and Abraham.

Some of these religionists adhere to the so called 'Divine Command Theory' in ethics which may trace its antecedents all the way back to one of Plato's dialogues, the *Euthyphro* where Socrates at one point poses a central question to Euthyphro, namely "whether the pious or holy is beloved by the gods because it is holy, or holy because it is beloved of the gods?" (quoted from Wainwright 2005, 73). Wainwright correctly notes that whereas the former alternative (the Socratic position) has been the dominant line of Christian philosophical theology, "[s]ome important Christian thinkers have embraced the second alternative, however – what is good or right is good or right only because God wills or commands it" (*ibid*). And this point of view is the defining feature of divine command theory which has seen a remarkable resurgence in recent years, particularly (almost exclusively) among analytic philosophers.[40] As an example

---

40 Wainwright (2005, 84) offers an interesting comment to this development: "Few modern philosophers have taken divine command theories seriously. They have either not discussed them (…) or attacked them as an assault on moral autonomy. The recent resuscitation of divine command ethics thus took many by surprise. Yet, in retrospect, its re-emergence could have been anticipated. For the past quarter of

of this position I have included in this chapter C. Stephen Evans who has written extensively on Kierkegaard.

But of course, other commentators have more complex reasons for trying to come to terms with Genesis 22. A common feature, however, is that they 'reframe' the story in ways that sometimes borders on the embarrassing. In this regard, they inevitably fall short of Kierkegaard. I have also chosen to include a psychological interpretation (Donald Capps) of Genesis 22 and *Fear and Trembling*. This is no coincidence, but reflects my conviction that philosophy and psychology are often complementary perspectives, perhaps not least in religious matters. When all is said and done, however, all I can do in this chapter is to discuss a representative selection of contemporary commentaries on Kierkegaard's *Fear and Trembling*. In the first section, I deal with attempts to defend God and Abraham. In the second, I present a quite different psychological and theological interpretation that insists on taking the perspective of Isaac and his mother, Sarah. Finally, I include a few interpretations by contemporary philosophers.

Saving Abraham, God – and Kierkegaard

C. Stephen Evans (Evans 2004 & 2006) is an example of a divine command theorist having dealt explicitly with *Fear and Trembling*.[41] Evans makes no effort to conceal the challenges and problems arising from Kierkegaard's meditation on Genesis 22. Thus, regarding Abraham's willingness to sacrifice Isaac he admits: "This is certainly a case whose implications are troubling for advocates of a divine command ethic"

---

century, analytic philosophers of religion have turned their attention from standard topics like the proofs for the existence of God, the coherence of the divine attributes, and the problem of evil to traditional theological doctrines such as the trinity or the atonement." In his own treatment Wainwright has chosen to concentrate on two contemporary proponents of a divine command theory, Robert Adams and Philip '.

41 "A divine command theory is committed to the claim that whatever God commands humans to do is morally obligatory for them" (Evans 2004, 304). A few pages earlier, however, Evans has assured us "that moral obligations are grounded in the commands of a *good* and *loving* God" (*ibid*, 299; my emphasis). And this, of course, is what makes the immoral story of Gen 22 such a formidable challenge.

(Evans 2004, 73f.).[42] Given this, how could one still save Abraham and his God? For only if that is possible, may a divine command theory present itself as a plausible account of the nature of moral obligations. And in this connection it is equally important for Evans to save Kierkegaard himself, since his works in general (not least *Works of Love*) are seen by Evans as supporting a divine command view of ethics.[43]

If Kierkegaard needs 'saving' then (which I personally doubt), how could this be done? One possible move, and a rather obvious one, would be to point to the pseudonymous nature of F&T. As noted in the previous chapter, this could be done in relation to the *motto* of the book, and, accordingly, to Evans (2004, 63) it seems "quite plausible that Johannes de Silentio is himself the messenger of the book, and that he communicates something that he himself does not really understand." Later in the same book, however, Evans has realized that this is not enough to save Kierkegaard – or for that matter, a divine command theory: "One might try to save Kierkegaard here [...] by noting the pseudonymous character of *Fear and Trembling* [...]. All of this is perfectly correct, but unfortunately does not get Kierkegaard, or a divine command theory of moral obligation, off the hook. Insofar as Abraham is praised as a model of faith, then his unquestioning obedience to God is implicitly recognized in the book as a praiseworthy ideal to emulate" (*ibid*, 305). I fully agree but wonder whether 'implicitly' should not be replaced by 'explicitly'.

Evans tries to broaden the perspective to other parts of Kierkegaard's *oeuvre*, and argues that the notion of faith as the absurd (or more correctly: faith *by virtue* of the absurd) appears only in the pseudonymous works.[44] Evans comments that this is "one more clue that the perspective

---

42 In a similar vein Wainwright (2005, 181), having paraphrased Gen 22, continues: "This is troubling, and not just if we assume that the account is historical. Even if it is not, it remains true that the God in whom Jews, Christians, and Muslims believe is represented in the story as commanding something that seems clearly immoral."

43 For a discussion on "the extent to which *Fear and Trembling* commends a divine command morality" see also Stiltner 1993, 227ff.

44 Evans quite correctly notes that: "What is 'absurd', and what de Silentio claims not to understand, is not Abraham's willingness to sacrifice Isaac, but rather Abraham's *faith*. This faith does *not* show itself in Abraham's willingness to draw the knife, but in Abraham's ability to receive Isaac back with joy" (Evans 2004, 71). I would only slightly modify it by adding that faith does not *only* or primarily show itself in

of Johannes de Silentio is the self-confessed perspective of an outsider who lacks faith. It is clearly distinct from the perspective of Kierkegaard himself, though this of course should not be taken to imply that Kierkegaard must be thought to disagree with everything de Silentio affirms" (Evans 2004, 66).

On the same note, in his latest book, having quoted passages from other works by Kierkegaard indicating a more harmonious relation between faith and the ethical, Evans (2006, 213) continues: "Since the passages I have appealed to are all later than *Fear and Trembling*, it is possible Kierkegaard changed his mind on this subject after writing about the Abraham case. Alternatively, one might appeal to pseudonymity here: perhaps the view that ethics and religious faith conflict is an opinion of Johannes de Silentio which Kierkegaard did not share." In light of this, it is somewhat confusing, when Evans only a few lines later takes the idea of a strong disagreement between Johannes and Kierkegaard back again, because, as he puts it, "I do not think that Johannes himself holds that the two [the ethical and the religious] are in fundamental opposition" (*ibid*, 213).

If the argument from the pseudonymous character of F&T does not work, or at least is nowhere near sufficient to get Kierkegaard and divine command theory 'off the hook', a more promising avenue might be trying to *reframe* the book by answering the question 'what is F&T *really* about?'. Evans tries out more than one answer to this pertinent question, and the answers seem to go in slightly different directions. First of all, it is important for him to stress that F&T is not about ethics but "primarily about the nature of the self and its identity" (Evans 2004, 62). Or, as he later puts it, "[t]he possibility that Abraham represents is that there is another path to selfhood than cultural conformity" (*ibid*, 80). This is an important point which could find support in at least two interconnected features of F&T where Kierkegaard vehemently opposes the dominant Hegelian view of his time: One is his insistence that faith cannot and should not be absorbed into *Sittlichkeit*, and the other is that faith requires each person to become (like Abraham) a single individual

---

Abraham's willingness to sacrifice his beloved son; nonetheless, obedience is still an important part of what makes Abraham, the 'father of faith', a normative model.

before God.[45] On this note, Evans (2006, 210) comments: "The main point of *Fear and Trembling*, on my reading, is not that faith is opposed to morality, but that genuine religious faith cannot be *reduced* to a life of moral striving, or completely understood using only the categories of a rationalistic morality."

This point of view is then in turn argued by way of the following three theses which taken together may be said to summarize Evans' reframing of F&T:

(1) The book is primarily about faith, and the role faith should play in the formation of the self's identity [...] (2) The conception of the ethical the book embodies is not identical with the view of the ethical Kierkegaard develops under his own name [...]. (3) *Fear and Trembling* is a pseudonymous work, and its pseudonymous author, Johannes de Silentio, is most emphatically distinct from Kierkegaard. (Evans 2004, 62f.).

The urge or the need felt to reinterpret what is the 'real' meaning of F&T is also evident, when Evans points to what he sees as "the true theme of *Fear and Trembling*, which is not, I think, whether God might require a person to kill his or her child, but how an individual becomes a self in the truest and deepest sense of the word, how a person achieves 'salvation'." (Evans 2006, 217). Evans argues this point from 'Problema III' where Kierkegaard mentions some incommensurable characters (Gloucester, the Merman, etc.) that from the outset (like Kierkegaard himself) are like the 'anguished', i.e. outside 'the general' (Danish: 'det Almene'). Thus, argues Johannes, "if ethics is the final word, then their lives are hopeless" (*ibid*, 218). From this, Evans goes on to claim that in light of original sin this is in reality the situation of *all* of us. Johannes, he continues, has seen this in relation to these marginal characters, "but he then spoils this insight

---

45 Thus, Evans thinks there is hope "[o]nce we see that the main point of the work is to call into question the identification of faith with ethics [...]" (*ibid*, 83). And in the same vein (in Evans 2006, 214) he claims that "The tension between religious faith and the ethical in *Fear and Trembling* is between faith and a form of the ethical life that claims to swallow up faith". This may all be correct, but the problem, I would argue, is that today this is precisely *no longer* a relevant issue! Who would today identify faith with ethics, other than perhaps proponents of a divine command theory?

by seeing these individuals only as exceptional characters" (*ibid*, 219).

Sin, on this reading, is the crucial category which (alas) is only briefly, almost in passing, mentioned in F&T, and, according to Evans, "[f]rom this it follows that it is a mistake to take *Fear and Trembling* as giving us a positive account of faith" (*ibid*, 220). This, I believe, is a daring conclusion! What Evans means by this, however, is that Johannes de Silentio has a reasonably good grasp of what faith is *not*, but being an 'outsider' he is, almost by nature, cut off from sorting out what faith positively *is*. On the contrary, I regard Johannes' self-confessed position of being outside faith as a strategic and rhetorical move on Kierkegaard's part designed to better enable Johannes to fight Kierkegaard's battle against the Hegelian philosophers of his time.

Divine Commands and Pluralist Democracy

In connection with his adherence to a divine command theory of moral obligations, Evans (2004, 305f.) sets out to defend the following three claims:

(1) It is indeed the case that a person ought to perform any action God commanded, and this implies that *if* God commanded someone to take the life of a child, that action would be right. (2) It is not possible for God to command an act that is unloving; if a being whom we thought to be God made such a command, that being would no longer warrant being thought of as divine, and its commands would not be moral obligations. (3) In our current epistemological situation, a person could not rationally believe that God has commanded an act of child sacrifice unless God supernaturally took control of the person's beliefs.

As for the first claim, what we find here is first of all a standard version of a divine command view; applied to Genesis 22, however, serious problems emerge. I believe Evans wants us to see this claim in close connection with the first part of the second claim, namely that 'it is not possible for God to command an act that is unloving'. But how do we know that, and how can we be sure about it? After all, Genesis 22 does not exactly point in this direction. But of course you could say that God was just joking, or that what we humans perceive to be an unloving act looks differently in God's eyes. So when Evans frames the conditional clause as '*if* God commanded someone to take the life of a child', it is because he does not regard it as a possibility to be taken seriously. In other words, we have moved quite a distance from the uncomfortable territory of *Fear and Trembling*.

The second claim amounts to an interesting admission on Evans' part where one is immediately reminded of Kant's main objection to Abraham's obedience in Genesis 22. And in fact, in the same context as the above quotation, Evans states: "I believe [...] that something like Kant's view is correct for someone in a contemporary cultural context, though it was not right for Abraham" (*ibid*). Surely, this is an important admission on Evans' part, not least because it raises the issue of *change* which is potentially devastating for a divine command theory. We find ourselves in a different 'cultural context' from that of Abraham, and I would emphatically agree that it makes little sense to condemn Abraham for not having had Kantian doubts as to whether he had actually heard the voice of 'a demon or a god' – to put it in the words of Leonard Cohen. But what about God, has he changed, too? I doubt that Evans would agree to this, and nonetheless it seems to be implied in his '*if*' in the above quotation: God might have commanded it *then*, but there is no realistic chance that he would do it *today*. The implicit prospect we are dealing with here, is the idea of a *cultural and mental evolution* (cf. the following chapter) which covers religion and gradually brings about changes in the relationship between man and God.

And, reasonably enough, Evans finds that Abraham was somehow justified in complying with God's command: "Does my argument imply that Abraham should not have believed that God had asked him to sacrifice his son? Not at all. I take it that Abraham is not in the same epistemic situation as contemporary Christians and Jews" (Evans 2004, 310). The third claim made by Evans, the idea that God might supernaturally take control over a person's beliefs, appears to me so exotic that I shall refrain from commenting on it.

What is particularly noteworthy in the context of this book, however, is that Evans (at least according to my research) is the only contemporary commentator who has explicitly addressed the issue of whether or not F&T (and a divine command theory) may be regarded as compatible with a liberal and pluralistic democracy. In this respect, he is aware that the two seems to be in tension, to say the least. He further admits "the fact that religious sectarianism seems to many to be what generates many of our moral problems, rather than constituting a possible solution. The contemporary world is wracked with violence, and much of the violence is at least partially grounded in religious divisions." (Evans 2004, 319).

But let me ponder, for a moment, Evans's point that there is a fundamental difference between 'the epistemic situation' of Abraham and that of ours. To this troubling issue Evans offers the following clarification: "To be more precise, I want to claim that no such person could reasonably believe that God has today issued such a command. This is not the same thing as a claim that God could never have issued such a command" (*ibid*, 306). Again, Evans is not unaware of the problems which his admissions along the way pose for divine command theory, for later in the same context he feels the need to pull the emergency brake: "One might think that I have thereby deserted a divine command theory of obligation [...] However, this is not necessarily the case" (*ibid*, 307). And he elaborates on this in the following way: "I think we can certainly understand that God could give some commands that are in some way limited: applicable only to a particular time, people, or even individuals. Such commands could indeed be revoked" (*ibid*, 309). What I can understand is that God changes over time, – and in actual fact he changes quite a lot from The Old Testament to The New Testament. So surely, our 'current epistemological situation' must also influence our understanding of God and his relation to ethics and society?[46]

Returning to F&T, what, according to Evans, are the contemporary relevance of this work? What he points to in this regard seems similar to what in the last chapter I emphasized as the 'valid point' that Kierkegaard is making, namely that religion is not *reducible* to morality, and that the individual is always *more* than his role as a citizen in society. Evans (2004, 327) formulates it in the following way: "We cannot rule out the possibility that God may require us to take a stand that will bring down the wrath of the establishment on us. When any human society forgets this, then it is in effect in rebellion against God's authority and it seeks to deify itself. When Christians identify their faith with the *Sittlichkeit* of

---

46 Besides, Evans himself discovers that his interpretation creates a problem regarding God's omnipotence.

a particular society they have betrayed their faith and become complicit in such a rebellion." Personally, I would not formulate the point in this way (what I have in mind is the possibility of a religiously motivated 'civil disobedience'), and I cannot help getting the impression that – despite his claims to the contrary – Evans is actually prepared even today to accept the basic premises of Genesis 22.

Earlier on in the same book he has raised an important question: "However, exactly where does the contemporary relevance of the story lie?" (Evans 2004, 312). Again his answers, it seems to me, go in different directions. The first one is rather uncontroversial, I believe: "Why should we care about whether such a possibility of radical challenge to existing values is kept open? Well, we might worry about the dangers that stem from deifying existing social and cultural norms [...] I think that the possibility of this kind of cultural critique is indeed important to keep alive" (*ibid*, 79). His second answer is that we should be aware that we could come in a situation parallel to that of Abraham, i.e. where our faith brings us into 'a conflict with prevailing moral standards'. Here I am more doubtful, but of course it all depends on what is implied in the idea of 'a conflict with prevailing moral standards'. At any rate, my point here would be that Evans' interpretation of F&T in and by itself implies the necessity of a more thoroughgoing reflection on the relation between democracy and religion. The second part of this book is devoted to this task.

Saving Isaac

In his important and moving book, *The Child's Song: The Religious Abuse of Children* (Capps 1995), Princeton theologian Donald Capps has devoted a chapter to the story of Abraham and Isaac, including Kierkegaard's interpretation in *Fear and Trembling*. Under the heading 'Abraham and Isaac: The Sacrificial Impulse' (pp. 78-95), Capps utilizes insights from depth psychology to paint a markedly different portrait of the characters involved in the drama of Genesis 22. During the more than ten years since its publication, however, it has lost none of its relevance and timeliness. In fact, as I am writing these passages, the BBC has just released its documentary of the habitual and widespread sexual abuse of children by Catholic priests and bishops.

Capps takes his point of departure in Alice Miller who has studied many of the paintings depicting Abraham about to sacrifice his son. In this connection Miller asks:

Why did all of these artists accept the story as valid? The only answer I can think of is that the situation involves a fundamental fact of our existence, with which many of us became familiar during the first years of life and which is so painful that knowledge of it can survive only in the depths of the unconscious. Our awareness of the child's victimization is so deeply rooted in us that we scarcely seem to have reacted at all to the monstrousness of the story of Abraham and Isaac (Miller quoted from Capps 1995, 82).

This prompts Capps to raise a related question: "Why does Isaac allow himself to be his father's victim?" (*ibid*, 83). Of course this question may seem anachronistic, for we know that paternal authority was so much stronger in those archaic times, but still? And the question gains increasing relevance if we assume (with some layers of tradition, cf. Ch. One) that at the time of the horrible incident Isaac had already entered into adulthood. From a psychological perspective Capps surmises that Isaac had 'identified with his aggressor', for it is (at least in our times) a well established fact "that the child adopts the parent's perspective as his own, and the fact that he is filled with fear only reinforces this basic fact" (*ibid*, 84). Capps then, partly inspired by Miller, turns his attention to the idea of *sacrifice* itself:

The idea of sacrifice – that payment is demanded – is so deeply rooted in the human psyche, and in the structure of human society, that we rarely question its validity. Abraham does not challenge the notion that a sacrifice is required, nor does Isaac. Nor do most readers of the story question the storyteller's assurance that Abraham was commanded by God to do this thing, and that it was also by divine agency that Isaac was spared. Why do most readers of the text accept this claim and why do they not entertain the alternative theory that Abraham [...] was out of his mind? Why we do not dispute the storyteller's assurance that God commanded Abraham to act as he did, thus questioning the whole premise of the story, tells us something about how deeply rooted is the sacrificial view of human life, both personal and societal, and how deeply rooted is the belief that this view has a religious legitimation. (Capps 1995, 84).

In turning to *Fear and Trembling*, Capps deliberately settles for a selective reading focusing on the 'Exordium' which has been the cause of some confusion and bafflement in Kierkegaard scholarship. What Capps finds significant is that here Kierkegaard actually "imagines the different scenarios that might have substituted for the one presented in the biblical text itself" (*ibid*, 85). What is also important about these four scenarios is that in two of them the perspective of Isaac figures prominently, and besides, Sarah is mentioned, albeit only briefly, in all four.[47] Nonetheless, Capps is aware that in Kierkegaard's book the Abrahams of the four scenarios fall short of the real Abraham, the one who in the immediately following section of F&T receives a passionate eulogy.[48] Capps talks, and I believe quite correctly, about Kierkegaard's 'idealization of Abraham', a feature of the text which is mostly ignored or quickly dismissed by commentators. Capps' approach, therefore, deserves to be quoted at length:

The question we have to ask is, Why does Kierkegaard himself, once having envisioned the alternative scenarios, which take account of the moral and religious ambiguities of the sacrificial idea, proceed to extol Abraham for his own utter disregard of these moral and religious ambiguities? If readers of the biblical story have difficulty comprehending Abraham, is this because Abraham is a man of such great faith that he allows nothing – even his beloved son – to come between

---

47 In the last section of his analysis, Capps offers a psychoanalytic interpretation of the enigmatic 'weaning metaphor' following each of the four scenarios of the 'Exordium'. I would assume that Kierkegaard may have been inspired here by Gen 21:8 which tells us that Abraham threw a grand party on the day that Isaac had been weaned. A psychological approach seems not only highly adequate to the imagery of weaning; it also helps shift the focus from Abraham to Sarah, and Capps argues that "[t]he critical event in this story is not, as the storyteller claims, what happens between Abraham and Isaac, but what is happening between Sarah and her son". And a little later he continues: "The question this scenario raises, a profoundly religious question, is whether she will have even stronger sustenance at hand so that his spirit does not perish, so that he is fortified to go out again, believing in himself when he can no longer believe in his father and his father's God." (Capps 1995, 93).

48 "What impresses Kierkegaard about Abraham's decision to go through with the sacrifice of Isaac is that by doing so he was a man of absolute faith." (Capps 1995, 88).

himself and his God, or is it because he is so certain of himself, so sure that he is acting in response to the command of God, that we necessarily wonder – precisely because he *is* so certain of himself – whether he is not deluding himself? Why should he not consider the alternative scenarios that Kierkegaard has put forward? Why are they not even worth his consideration? And why is Kierkegaard so willing to reject these scenarios in favor of the one in which Abraham proceeds with the sacrifice as though it were a celebration? Why should Abraham not ask God to forgive him for even considering the sacrifice of his son? Why should Abraham not exhibit such despair that Isaac cannot but conclude that the God his father is trying to serve is unworthy of him? (Capps 1995, 89f.).

Of course, asking such passionate and highly relevant questions may by some be considered both anachronistic and somewhat futile. Besides, I do not think that Capps is entirely fair to the text of F&T when he says that Kierkegaard paints a portrait of an Abraham who is certain of himself, or rather, this is not the whole truth. For later in the book, i.e. in the 'Problemata', it is repeatedly emphasized that what characterized Abraham on the road to Mount Moriah was distress, anxiety and the feeling of being in a terrible dilemma or paradox. In fact, as we have seen, this 'dark side' of the matter is considered by Kierkegaard to be his legitimation. So, not only does Abraham cause fear and trembling in the readers, he himself is also, according to Kierkegaard, in fear and trembling. Nonetheless, he possesses the courage of faith and is willing to do as commanded by God.

Now, Abraham is one thing, and we obviously have little hope of being able to know what went on in his mind. With Kierkegaard however, things look somewhat different, and I believe Capps is right not only in characterizing his relation to Abraham as that of an *idealization*, but also to ask why this is the case, and why "he is unable or unwilling to face the initially disturbing but ultimately liberating truth that human sacrifice, whatever form it may take, has absolutely no religious legitimation" (*ibid*, 90). Capps surmises that, much like Isaac, Kierkegaard identified with the aggressor, but a more profound reason seems to have been "his intense desire to be a son to a man like Abraham" (*ibid*). On a first glance this may appear far-fetched, but Capps is able to detect in the 'Eulogy' phrases and expressions that are "spoken like a son for whom Father Abraham is a powerful ideal, a father figure" (*ibid*, 91). Furthermore, drawing on entries from Kierkegaard's *Journals* on his troubled and ambivalent relation to his father, Capps makes a rather convincing case that "one can easily imagine that Kierkegaard envied Isaac, who had a father who could be idealized because he was a man of absolute faith" (*ibid*, 91f.). Besides, Capps' interpretation may, I believe, find additional support in what at first glance appears as an enigmatic phrase from the opening of the 'Preamble from the Heart'. Here, Kierkegaard utilizes the New Testament saying that 'Only the one who works gets bread' to make the point that this finds its real truth in the spiritual world – as opposed to the temporal world. And then he adds the following passage: "Here it does not help to have Abraham as father [cf. Matthew 3:9] or to have seventeen ancestors. The one who will not work fits what is written about the virgins of Israel: he gives birth to wind – but the one who will work *gives birth to his own father*." (F&T, 27; emphasis added).

Thus, by accomplishing the arduous work of producing *Fear and Trembling*, Kierkegaard may have envisioned the possibility of creating his own imaginative, wished-for, and spiritual father: Abraham, the 'Father of Faith'.

Saving the Internal Coherence of the Bible
In the context of dealing with the problem of evil, systematic theologian Ingolf U. Dalferth has recently made some interesting suggestions regarding the interpretation of Genesis 22 and the *aqedah*.[49] From the basic hermeneutical point that we always understand something in terms of something else, he goes on to make an important distinction between God as an *explanatory category* and God as a *category of orientation*. In the former case, more or less futile debates on theodicy arise, whereas in the latter we get a much more realistic picture of what makes people turn to God when faced with evil.

In a section of the paper entitled 'Disambiguating the Notion of God', Dalferth then goes on to distinguish two ways in which monotheistic religions may solve their continuing "need for clarifying and purifying

---

49 Ingolf U. Dalferth: "Problems of Evil. Theodicy, Theology, and Hermeneutics" (unpublished MS, presented at Aarhus University, October 2006).

their understanding of God" (Dalferth 2006, 16). One is the way of *theological reflection*, while the other is through *practical solutions*, i.e. "by acting and living in ways that in a sense force God to clarify and decide the issue Himself". What this means is that "God Himself is made to give an answer that decides the issue on whether or not he is trustworthy in times of need. The idea is to create a situation in which there are only two options: Either God turns out to be trustworthy and reliable after all, or we can simply forget about God" (*ibid*, 16f.). Dalferth calls this practical way the *experimentum crucis* approach. Immediately following is a passage which deserves to be quoted in full:

The most important examples of this *experimentum crucis* approach in the biblical tradition are the *Aqeda*-story in Genesis 22 and the gospel story of Jesus' death on the cross. In the first, Abraham, whom God had promised to make the father of a great people, is ordered by God to sacrifice his only son and thus destroy the very token of God's promise. This turns God into someone utterly ambiguous and self-contradictory, someone whose will is not only inscrutable and enigmatic but totally incomprehensible. A God like this is indistinguishable from no God at all and of no help in orienting the life of his people. You cannot trust such a God. You cannot count on Him. You do not know to whom you should turn in time of need. This is why Abraham, who is presented in the biblical stories as one who loves to argue with God, says not a word but simply acts and would have killed Isaac if God had not intervened at the very last minute. By acting out the *aporia*, Abraham forces God to either identify with his promise or prove to be no God after all. The outcome of the story is that there is no way around God's promise: God is forever the God whose promise can be trusted. God may be difficult to discern in the ambiguous ups and downs of human life, but his people can be sure that God will stick to his promises: Either God is a God whose word can be trusted or there is no God at all. (Dalferth 2006, 17).

What is one to make of this intriguing interpretation of Genesis 22? To begin with, I think Dalferth deserves credit for his clear insight that the God who commanded Abraham to kill his own son is 'indistinguishable from no God at all'. In light of this sinister realization, however, one is almost puzzled to find that Dalferth's version of Genesis 22 has an almost happier (and certainly more devout!) ending than the original:

'The outcome of the story is that there is no way around God's promise: God is forever the God whose promise can be trusted', etc. But apart from this, it seems to me that there are a number of inherent problems in Dalferth's interpretation.

One is that the *sacrificial* element of the story has evaporated, and consequently Isaac plays no role whatsoever. There are no victims in Dalferth's version of the *aqedah*, only two winners, Abraham and God. In this casting of the drama there is no role for Isaac, or rather: He just serves as the instrument necessary to Abraham's test of God's reliability. But surely, seen from Isaac's (not to mention Sarah's) perspective, a religious poker game with such high stakes ought to be forbidden by law? Second, Dalferth's perspective entails that the burden is shifted from God to man; God only *appears* evil and not to be trusted. This 'shifting the burden' is clearly expressed in Dalferth's daring idea that the point of Genesis 22 is that Abraham allegedly 'forces God to either identify with his promise or prove to be no God at all'.[50] To this idea I would first remark that it seems incompatible with the text of Genesis 22 which in verse 1 explicitly states that it was *God* who put Abraham on a test – and not the other way around. That we are dealing with a test of Abraham's 'fear of God' is also clear from verses 12 and 16. And speaking of fear: Is it really a likely and credible scenario that Abraham should have dared to 'force' God into showing his true colors? Quite apart from this, Dalferth's approach seems to create two theologically unwelcome problems: One is that God is not independent and sovereign in relation to man, and the other is that the idea of 'forcing God' might be seen as opening the door to the Feuerbachian point of 'man makes God' and not the other way around.[51]

Having come this far, it is time to let Dalferth himself reveal why he has chosen the name *experimentum crucis* for the idea of creating (who creates: the story-teller or Abraham?) a situation "that in a sense force[s] God to clarify and decide the issue Himself" (Dalferth 2006, 16). This becomes clear in the following passage focusing on Jesus' death on the cross:

---

50 One is reminded here of Carl Jung's *Answer to Hiob* where Hiob by arguing with God forces Him to change.

51 I am aware, however, that the idea of 'forcing God' might gain a firmer biblical footing if seen in connection with the psalms (laments) and the Book of Hiob.

What the *Aqeda* story does for the Jewish tradition, the gospel story of Jesus' death does for the Christian one. According to the oldest gospel stories, Jesus died with a cry of "My God, my God why hast thou forsaken me?" Jesus is depicted in the gospels as having placed all his hope in the imminent reign of God's benevolent love. He too [sc. like Abraham] did not argue it out with his skeptical fellow-countrymen or with God but lived it out, and he did not [sc. contrary to Abraham] put someone else's life at stake in testing the reliability of God's love but solely his own. In his case the outcome was that Jesus apparently died convinced that his trust in God was misplaced. It was only when his followers became convinced of his resurrection that they began to see his death as evidence that God's love is trustworthy after all. That which for Jesus was a disaster became for them the definitive proof of God's love. So there are important dissimilarities between the tale of Abraham and the story of Jesus, but in their different ways they make a similar point: in order to disambiguate one's understanding of God one has to live and act in a decisive way, and one does this by taking God at His word. If God does not prove Himself to be trustworthy and a God of hope, then humans are better off without Him. In the light of these stories, what has become unthinkable and indeed self-contradictory in the Jewish and Christian tradition is that God may change his mind and turn out to be not a God of promise or a God of love after all – not because God couldn't in principle do otherwise but because he in fact has chosen to do *this* and not something else. (*ibid*, 17).

I must admit that the last sentence is not quite clear to me, but I *think* it is intended to indicate that there is an element of *contingency* inherent in the notion of God. But let me return to some final thoughts on Dalferth's *experimentum crucis* approach to Genesis 22. First of all, the name itself signals that we are dealing with a New Testament idea which is then claimed to have relevance for interpreting the Bible as such. This may well be problematic, but at the same time one should grant that Dalferth's move is an elegant theological solution: Without simply adopting the traditional, typological interpretation, he is still able to establish an important thematic coherence between The New Testament and The Old Testament. The price to be paid, however, may be seen in the problems briefly outlined above.

Major Issues in Contemporary Interpretations

In light of the many perplexing issues in the text of F&T (cf. Chapter Two), one would more or less expect to find a wide array of contemporary interpretations. The disagreement among scholars, however, is so pronounced that Lippitt (2003, 135ff.) has provided his chapter surveying some of these interpretations with the headline 'What is *Fear and Trembling* really about?' A major dividing line is among those who argue that the text is primarily about *ethics* and those who see the text as conveying a message about the nature of true *faith*.[52] This disagreement, in turn, is connected to another dividing line, namely whether you tend to read F&T 'straight', or whether you prefer to embark on an allegorical reading. Recalling the embarrassment which prompted many early interpreters of the *aqedah* to take refuge in a typological interpretation (cf. Chapter One), it should come as no surprise that the majority of contemporary commentators have preferred an allegorical reading centering on a particular view of ethics as constituting the 'hidden' message of Kierkegaard's famous text. In what follows, I shall briefly survey some variations of the ethical reading and then give my reasons for disagreeing with it.

Jerome Gellman (Gellman 1994) may be as good a place as any to start. Right from the beginning the understanding of 'the ethical' in F&T is the focus of his interpretive efforts. The 'standard interpretation', according to Gellman, is wrong in assuming that Abraham's dilemma consists in a moral rule ('thou shall not kill') conflicting with a specific divine command ('thou shall kill your beloved son'). Instead, counters Gellman, "The issue is whether we are individuals in relation to God. The story is not about Abraham's daring to kill his son, but about Abraham's having the courage to define himself as an individual, other than as a father, *willing* to 'sacrifice' his son to this self-determination" (Gellman 1994, 7).[53] If this is the morale of the story, it means that the voice of God is not a command to perform a specific, gruesome act, but, rather,

---

52 A sort of combination, of course, could be a divine command theory of ethics as supported by Evans, as we have seen earlier in this chapter.

53 Immediately following this quotation Gellman advances a general interpretation of F&T with which I am in agreement: "If this is correct, then *Fear and Trembling* is best seen as a polemic against the Hegelian idea that a person is *defined* within her social/ethical contexts." (*ibid*).

a call to self-definition before God. Gellman, it must be said, makes no secret of the fact that this is clearly an allegorical interpretation turning Kierkegaard's rendering of Genesis 22 into "a *parable* for the choice between two kinds of self-definition" (*ibid*, 5). Further, Gellman claims that the sacrifice of Isaac is "a metaphor for Abraham's ability to transcend his familial role into individual subjectivity. (...) Indeed, by being *prepared* for the 'sacrifice', that is, by defining himself as an individual rather than a father, Abraham 'gets Isaac back'" (*ibid*, 13).

Gellman's approach may seem attractive in more than one respect, but it should not be overlooked that the text of F&T speaks against an interpretation along these lines. First, one reason that Johannes is both admiring and appalled by Abraham has to do with the fact that he is not just 'prepared for' the sacrifice (as Gellman says), but actually prepared to *carry out* the sacrifice. Second, Johannes explicitly emphasizes Abraham's role (and ethical duty) as a father and his fatherly love of Isaac. Nonetheless, Gellman maintains that his allegorical reading captures at least two important elements of Genesis 22:

Conceiving the *akedah* story as an allegory, in the way proposed, against the standard interpretation, supports what are two prominent elements of the Biblical story for Kierkegaard. One is that Abraham was asked to kill his son, and not, say, himself or a stranger, and the second, that in the end Abraham was not required to kill Isaac. If the ethical aspect of the story were the moral prohibition of the act of murder, as it would be on the standard interpretation, there would be no special significance in Abraham's having been asked to kill specifically his son; and if God's command were really commanding murder, and the real issue were the superiority of God's word over the ethical, then there would be no reason why the act should not have been carried out. Why should Abraham's hand have been stayed? (Gellman 1994, 16).

Once again, I think Gellman has got it wrong, or to be more precise: He may well be able to make an interesting point, but he must pay the price of having the text against him. Recall, here, that Johannes more than once warns us not to take the easy way out by comforting ourselves that after all the whole thing was nothing but a trial or test. And, in the same vein, in Problema I he directly attacks and ridicules those who rest content with looking at the 'outcome' of the story. In fact, *this* is the 'standard interpretation' which Kierkegaard is so eager to attack, because it overlooks the anguish and paradoxical nature of Abraham's situation.

But, the reader may well ask, is there nothing at all symbolic or allegorical in the text of F&T? My response to this question would be 'No', but with two qualifications. The first has to do with the text itself, for I can think of only one instance (apart from the weaning metaphor utilized in the 'Exordium') where the text itself opens for an allegorical reading. This is in Problema II where we find the following passage: "Only the single individual can ever give himself a more explicit explanation of what is to be understood by Isaac" (F&T, 71). Clearly, at this particular point 'Isaac' is intended as a symbol of what each of us loves the most and therefore will have the hardest time giving up. The second relates to the motto of F&T (Tarquin's poppies): this may well point in the direction of F&T being 'allegorical' in the sense of having a double biographical relation to Kierkegaard's life, namely his aborted relation to Regine, and his partly troubled relation to his father.[54] Granted that much can be said in support of a (partly) biographical reading of F&T, I would still agree with Lippitt (2003, 139) that this gets us nowhere in terms of discerning in the text a message relevant to our times and our problems. In order to accomplish this, what is needed is obviously some sort of constructive re-interpretation, but, as a minimal requirement, it must be able to find support in the text itself. This, alas, is not the case in Gellman, whose allegorical reading leads him to the following conclusion: "The 'trial of Abraham' for Kierkegaard, to conclude, takes place entirely within Abraham's soul, not atop a mountain. For Abraham to pass the trial means for him to take up a specific self-defining attitude toward himself and his role within the family. It means to be bound only by possibility, and not by the existing structures within which he finds himself." (Gellman 1994, 19).

A former debate between Ronald Green and Gene Outka may also

---

54 Green (1988, 125), to take one example, argues that "[t]he whole theme of *Fear and Trembling* concerns the relationship between a father and a son, indeed, a father whose conduct physically imperils his son's life, just as the elder Kierkegaard's conduct had spiritually imperilled Soren's."

be illustrative of some of the issues at stake in interpreting F&T. Green, opposing the many 'ethical' interpretations and claiming that "[f]ew books have been as badly misunderstood as this one" (Green 1993, 191), states the problem in the following manner:

The interpretive problem I am signaling can be stated succinctly: although *Fear and Trembling* has largely been read as a book dealing with ethics, its central problem lies elsewhere, in the realm of soteriology. Not *human* conduct (the question of which norms should govern our behavior) but *divine* conduct (whether God can suspend justice in the name of forgiveness) is the book's central preoccupation. In this respect, *Fear and Trembling* is best thought of as a modern discussion of the classical Pauline-Lutheran theme of justification by faith. What makes *Fear and Trembling* so complex and what has misled generations of readers is that Kierkegaard uses a *surface* discussion of ethical questions to present his more soteriological concerns. (*ibid*, 192).

Here, evidently, something important is being argued, for the metaphor of 'surface' invoked by Green implies that he has been able to discover, as it were, the hidden 'depths' of F&T.[55] To be fair, Green does not deny "that there are ethical concerns in *Fear and Trembling*" but he holds these to be "radically secondary to its deeper soteriological purpose" (*ibid*, 193). Further, he acknowledges that the text may be read as supporting a divine command theory of ethics; to this view, however, he offers the following relevant criticism:

Unfortunately, this interpretation fits less well into *Fear and Trembling* itself, for the fact is that *Fear and Trembling* offers little or no development of the moral content of Abraham's faith. We hear no praise of God's righteousness, and we are never told that Abraham's obedience must be understood within the framework of an ethical trust in God. Instead, the emphasis is on the fearful nature of God's command, the horror of Abraham's conduct, and his defiance of any

---

55 Invoking once again the surface-metaphor in the conclusion of his article, Green writes that "Kierkegaard meant *Fear and Trembling* to be an encoded massage to all those capable of seeing beyond its surface treatment of Abraham's singular trial to a more universal message concerning our common failure before the stringency of God's moral demands and our shared need for God's grace." (Green 1993, 204).

conceivable ethical norms. Like all efforts to make ethical and religious sense of the book's admiration of Abraham, this approach achieves its purpose by softening the contours of *Fear and Trembling's* emphasis on Abraham's violation of ethical norms. (Green 1993, 197).[56]

How then, does Green substantiate his Christian reading focusing on soteriology? Here, alas, he makes two moves – none of them particularly convincing: First, being positioned as a sinner before God, Abraham is allegedly used in F&T as "a 'figure' or 'type' to establish a Christian ontology in which the order of merit – of ethics, 'the law', or 'works righteousness' – is subordinated to the realm of grace" (*ibid*, 199).[57] Hence, the point of the 'teleological suspension', according to Green, is not to justify Abraham's action, but to show that "God acts to suspend his justified wrath" (*ibid*). Second, Green (here in line with some other commentators) makes a lot of the fact that the issue of *sin* emerges (although only very briefly) in Problema III. According to Green, the condition of sin applies not only to the merman but even more so to Abraham; to his good fortune, however, God suspended the ethical judgment and saved him by His grace. The near absurdity of this claim is revealed in the following anachronistic statement: "It is precisely because he knew himself to be justified by grace alone, that Abraham is deservedly the 'father of faith'" (*ibid*, 204). But, we must surely ask: How can Green know what goes on in Abraham's mind? And even if he could, how could Abraham know that he was justified by grace alone? Had he been reading Paul – not to mention Luther?

In his sobering response to Green, Gene Outka notes not only the slim textual basis for Green's emphasis on Abraham as figure or 'type' of the universal condition of sin; he also correctly sees that "the trouble comes

---

56 Later Green adds the following pertinent remark: "A more serious problem is that if *Fear and Trembling* defends a divine command ethic, it is a forbidding and frightening ethic. The God of *Fear and Trembling* and his loyal devotee, Abraham, are more shockingly 'beyond good and evil' than most commentators have been willing to admit" (*ibid*, 198).

57 Thus, in direct contrast to my claim that F&T displays no interest in a typological interpretation, Green is of the opinion that "Kierkegaard's project in *Fear and Trembling* stands self-consciously in a long tradition of similar uses of Abraham for soteriological purposes" (*ibid*, 199).

from Green's attempt to assimilate *Fear and Trembling* too unqualifiedly into the classical Pauline-Lutheran doctrine of justification through faith alone, including assumptions about sin associated with it" (Outka 1993, 212f.).[58] In contrast, I find it much easier to agree with the conclusion reached by Outka: "Abraham learns what obedience to God can require; he exemplifies a life dominated by the first great love commandment. What is religiously decisive in *Fear and Trembling* is simply this: we must *cleave to God as the subject of unique veneration.*" (*ibid*, 215).

Returning to Lippitt's (Lippitt 2003, 135ff.) survey of contemporary interpretations, one rather obvious approach would be to read F&T as a 'call to Christian commitment' (*ibid*, 140). This would find support not only in the mercantile imagery of the 'Preface' and the 'Epilogue' where Kierkegaard has Johannes scorning his contemporaries for selling faith at bargain price. Moreover, it fits with the continued demand for 'passion' (Danish: *Lidenskab*) and the emphasis on faith as the 'highest passion'. To this it should also be added that we find in the text more than one passage foreshadowing Kierkegaard's later attack on 'Christendom'. The most relevant, in my opinion, is found in Problema II where Kierkegaard utilizes the harsh words of Lk 14:26 in a severe (and highly satirical) attack on those who try to evade and reinterpret the real message of this particular saying of Jesus. These words, Kierkegaard continues, "are terrible, but I dare say that they can be understood without the necessary consequence that the one who has understood them has the courage to do what he has understood. One ought to be sufficiently honest, however, to admit what it says, to admit that it is great even though one himself lacks the courage to do it" (F&T, 73). In particular, it is the demand for 'being honest' (Danish: *redelig*) which Kierkegaard is later to repeat when in 1854-55 he fought to make the dignitaries of the Danish state church admit that they were not Christians in the New Testament sense of Christianity. Lippitt (2003, 140) concludes that "Johannes' aim, on this view, is to draw attention to the true value – and potential cost – of faith."

---

58 What is more, one could argue that there is a markedly *non*-Lutheran strand in F&T, namely in its emphasis on the need to *work*, and work hard, for one's salvation. As we recall, in F&T it is necessary to prepare oneself (by way of infinite resignation) for receiving faith.

In my view, this 'theological shock treatment' (to use Lippitt's expression) is certainly a major message of F&T which no interpretation should overlook and which serves as a reminder that the text is concerned with faith rather than ethics. Nonetheless, the text's highly rhetorical (at times even hyperbolic) eulogy of faith does not in itself explain what is presented as the solution to Abraham's tragic dilemma, namely the 'suspension' of the ethical and the double movement of faith. In the literature on F&T two major answers to this can be found; one finds a new idea of ethics to be the intended message, whilst the other argues for a Christian reading.

As for the first approach, it has been the focus of the interpretive efforts of (among others) Edward F. Mooney who in a number of publications has argued that F&T is 'really' about replacing a universal, 'objective' picture of ethics (as in Hegel) with a deeper, 'subjective' picture (cf. Lippitt 2003, 147). Mooney's interpretation may be captured in the idea that Abraham's trial on Mount Moriah is really a 'call to selfhood' in the sense of giving up one's habitual claim to possess the things and persons we love, and instead coming to regard them in a more receptive mode, as gifts from God. In these two aspects, it is not difficult to discern the two movements of 'infinite resignation' and 'faith'. On this reading, then, what appears to be a 'suspension' of the ethical is really a *transformation* instead: What Abraham (and others whose souls have been tempered by an ordeal) acquires is a new character by virtue of which he comes to realize that "Isaac is 'his' only as a gift from God" (*ibid*, 152).

Lippitt, being largely sympathetic to Mooney's interpretation, argues that instead of seeing Abraham's situation as utterly unique, we should interpret it as a reminder that life is full of *tragic dilemmas* meaning: situations where ethics is 'suspended', in the sense that it is unable to guide us. Therefore, according to Lippitt, the distance between Abraham (the knight of faith) and Agamemnon (the 'tragic hero') is much narrower than Johannes de Silentio tries to convince us. Further, seizing upon the text saying that Abraham is great by 'a purely *personal* virtue', Lippitt struggles to combine his account of the nature of tragic dilemmas with a solution based on the tradition of virtue ethics. Besides, to the inspiration from Mooney Lippitt wants to add an idea which he takes from Ronald L. Hall, for whom "the faithful reception of the world from the hands of the

Eternal *presupposes an ongoing possibility of doing otherwise* – an ever-present temptation not to receive it" (quoted from Lippitt 2003, 63). In other words, the movement of infinite resignation must me made *continually*, because the temptation to refuse the life of faith must constantly be 'annulled'.

Concerning the second (Christian) interpretation, Lippitt's point of departure is an attempt to answer the question 'What does Abraham believe at the point of drawing the knife?' (Lippitt 2003, 66ff.). He is not content with "a common traditional interpretation which has Abraham believing two incompatible things: first, that he will have to sacrifice Isaac (and so Isaac will die), and second that somehow he will not have to sacrifice Isaac (and so Isaac will not die)" (*ibid*, 67). To avoid this reading, Lippitt finds it "[f]ar better to embrace as the knight of faith an Abraham who believes and trusts in the possibility of divine grace" (*ibid*, 74) and thus he reaches the conclusion that,

All of the above provide reasons to think that, at the point of drawing the knife, Abraham believes, against overwhelming evidence, that somehow Isaac will be spared. But a vital part of his faith is the need continually to annul the temptation to give in to 'infinite resignation'; to take heed of the evidence, lose hope and trust in God, and resign himself to the loss of Isaac. That Abraham does *not* do this is a vital part of what makes him, for Johannes, the paradigm exemplar of faith. (*ibid*, 75f.).

Echoing this, in his conclusion to the chapter on contemporary interpretations of F&T Lippitt (2003, 171f.) makes two points: One is that "there is much to be said for the Christian reading" where he leans toward Stephen Mulhall who has reinvigorated an "allegorical or analogical reading of Abraham's ordeal as a prefiguration of Christ's atonement" (*ibid*, 169). The other is that "much of Mooney's interpretation is well worth serious consideration" (*ibid*, 172). In the following conclusion I shall briefly outline my reasons for disagreeing on both counts.

My Personal Conclusion

Although it must be admitted that an *ethical* reading of F&T is able to deliver an interesting and contemporary message, I fail to see how it can find sufficient textual basis. While it is comprehensible that Kierkegaard chose Genesis 22 to argue his case against Hegel that faith is a *paradox* which cannot be mediated, I find it implausible that we should be able to find in this 'tale of terror' the idea of a 'deeper' or more 'subjective' ethics. And, as we have already seen, Johannes' own search for a 'higher expression' of the ethical remains unsuccessful. Thus, it is no surprise that those who favor an ethical reading have found it necessary to incorporate ideas from other works by Kierkegaard (*Concept of Anxiety*, *Sickness unto Death*, etc.). At the same time, it is revealing, I believe, that the attempts to detect an 'ethical' message must all resort to an allegorical or symbolic reading of F&T. And, although one would have strong reasons to deem it a hopelessly naïve approach, the interpretations claiming to find in F&T a 'hidden' Christian message do not even shy away from utilizing a typological understanding of Abraham.

As far as a *Christian* reading is concerned, I must first of all disagree with Lippitt's complaint above that a 'traditional' reading is at fault for having Abraham believing two incompatible things at the point of drawing the knife. In fact, I think that the textual evidence is massive at this point: Abraham's perfect love for Isaac is undiminished; yet he realizes that he will have to sacrifice Isaac, and he is willing to go through with it. This is Abraham's infinite resignation. At the same time, however, Abraham has faith (by virtue of the absurd) that somehow 'it will not happen' or that in some form 'he will get Isaac back again'. This is his faith (the second aspect of the double movement) which will eventually enable him to return to (and embrace) the finite again. That this, admittedly, amounts to believing two incompatible things at the same time is not a relevant objection to a text that untiringly insists that faith is a *paradox*. Also, I believe that many of us could come up with examples from our personal life, when our situation might have been accurately described as 'believing two incompatible things at the same time'.

A more important aspect of the 'Christian' reading is, as we have noted, the typological interpretation and the attempt to 'smuggle in', as it were, the notion of Divine grace. None of these moves have, I would claim, any foothold in the text of F&T. This is also the case even in Problema I (F&T, 65f.) when the figures of Virgin Mary and Christ are introduced. First of all, the point here is *not* to facilitate a typological reading (which seems to have had no appeal whatsoever to Kierkegaard). Instead, what 'unites' them with Abraham is, according to Johannes, the fact that they experienced what we as readers tend to forget or to delete from the story, namely "the anxiety, the distress, the paradox" (F&T, 66). What the text neglects to tell us here, is that Mary and Christ *differ* from Abraham in one respect that ought to be more relevant to F&T, namely that none of them suspended the ethical. Or to be more accurate: When Christ suspended the ethical (i.e. the law of Sabbath) he did it not to obey a commanding God, but for the sake of humanity.

So, should we opt for a straight or an allegorical reading of F&T? As indicated earlier, my answer is 'straight', not least because this is what the text demands, and rather explicitly, in fact.[59] Thus, in commenting on Lk 14:26 Kierkegaard remarks that, "It is easy to see that if this passage is to have any meaning it must be understood literally" (F&T, 73). And, as we already know, Johannes time and again attacks the all too 'normal' reading which fails to take the anguish and distress of Genesis 22 seriously.[60] A straight reading should also be preferred because it keeps us on 'the straight and narrow' in the sense of adhering to what the text itself highlights as the major theme, namely faith – and not ethics.[61] To put it differently, the overwhelming textual evidence points in the direction that F&T is first and foremost about *faith* and its relation to the ethical, i.e.

---

59 Another example of a 'straight' reading is Levinas who takes issue with the 'violence' he perceives in Kierkegaard's breaking away from the ethical stage. Closely related to this is his "idea that the real point of the Akedah story may be quite different from what Johannes supposes" (Lippitt 2003, 137). Thus, for Levinas, "the highest point of the whole drama may be the moment when Abraham paused and listened to the voice that would lead him back to the ethical order by commanding him not to commit a human sacrifice" (Levinas quoted from Lippitt, *ibid.*).

60 In fact, albeit somewhat surprising in light of his sympathy for allegorical interpretations, Lippitt himself acknowledges that the text forces us in the opposite direction: "It is important to note that Johannes' treatment of this passage [Lk 14:26, TN] parallels his treatment of the Abraham story, insofar as he insists that it not be watered down, that it be *taken literally*". (Lippitt 2003, p. 104).

61 As already mentioned, at one particular point in Problema I, Kierkegaard sends Johannes on a 'mission impossible', namely to investigate "whether this story contains any higher expression for the ethical that can ethically explain his behavior, can ethically justify his suspending the ethical obligation to the son, but without moving beyond the teleology of the ethical" (F&T, 57). Within the text of F&T, however, this search remains unsuccessful.

in the sense of Hegel: to society and its institutions – or in my contemporary version: the relation between religion and democracy.[62] If this is the *problem* that the text poses (and tries to elucidate by way of the story of Abraham and Isaac), the *answer* it provides is the idea of the double movement of faith. The posing of the problem as well as the answer may both contain many perplexing, at times even enigmatic, details, but any interpretation which does not remain faithful to this overall theme, has, in my view, effectively *left* the text of F&T and thereby our only court of appeal.

Provided that the goal of our interpretive effort is not just a re-telling or paraphrase of F&T but a productive re-reading relevant to the problems of our time, I see no alternative to *taking leave of Abraham*. From him we can learn nothing. If anything, he is an early warning of the contemporary dangers of absolute faith and listening to the alleged voice of a 'strong' and commanding God. But does this dismissal of Abraham not precisely amount to being disloyal to the text? I have two reasons for being convinced that this is not the case.

The first relates to a reflection on the possible *motives* behind Kierkegaard's choice of Genesis 22. These motives, I would claim, are partly biographical, partly determined by his intention to find a model of faith which would be 'incommensurate' and impossible for Hegel's philosophy of spirit to 'mediate'. In short (and as noted in the last chapter), Abraham is Kierkegaard's major weapon against Hegel. The biographical motives would presumably have been deeply relevant to Kierkegaard himself, as the attack on Hegel was relevant to the intellectual climate of Copenhagen in the 1840ies. But none of these two motives are relevant *to us*, and this leads me to my second reason for taking leave of Abraham without necessarily being disloyal to the text.

To our good fortune, Abraham is not F&T's only example of a 'knight of faith'. In fact, in marked tension to Abraham stands another example, a very ordinary man who looks like a 'tax-collector' and is even outwardly indistinguishable from a bourgeois philistine. From him, I would argue,

---

62 This, as we have seen, is supported by the 'Preface' and the 'Epilogue' which agree in framing the book as aiming to convince its readers of the nature and value of true faith.

we may be able to learn a thing or two about individual faith and its relation to society and its institutions. To this, therefore, we shall have good reasons to return in Chapter Seven.

Chapter Four

CULTURAL EVOLUTION AND THE SECULARIZATION OF RELIGION

Already in Chapter One I dealt briefly with Kant's and Hegel's way of reacting to Abraham's situation in Genesis 22. A major characteristic of their response was to give preference to the concerns of morality and *Sittlichkeit* rather than religion. And in the last chapter, we noted how Evans pointed to a 'different epistemic situation' as both an indirect excuse for Abraham, and an explanation for our difficulties in understanding his blind obedience to religious authority. My overall aim in this chapter is to elaborate on this and at the same time to make the case for a stronger reading of what separates us from Abraham, and thus to argue that differences of 'epistemic conditions' are part and parcel of a broader cultural evolution which, of course, encompasses and affects also religion.

More specifically, I want first of all to emphasize the point in recognizing a general, historical trend of *secularization* – and at the same time to explicate wherein this trend consists. Second, I want to encourage my readers to regard a modern Christian consciousness not as heresy or apostasy, but, rather, as the result of a gradual 'purification' of Christian doctrine and belief. And, finally, I am going to ask whether it is possible to see a certain overall *pattern* in the process of secularization, and in this connection to raise the question as to whether this pattern is so clear and has exerted such a pervasive influence on our culture and mentality that we may take the next step of conceiving of this process in terms of a cultural *evolution* consisting of certain stages or phases. Now, I am aware of course that just to mention the word 'evolution' raises a plethora of difficult issues and that the concept of evolution is an abomination to the majority of contemporary scholars within the humanities. I hasten, therefore, to add a number of *caveats*. One is that I leave it entirely open whether evolution in the cultural domain may constitute a universal process; in the present context, however, I emphasize that it is a *cultural* process, in this case a discernible process which has taken place in what we generally refer to as the Western world. Another important modification is that I do not conceive of evolution as pre-planned of pre-figured, as in the famous paradigm of an embryo. On the contrary: 'cultural' means in this connection that the process was driven forward by many complex factors, and also that there were occasional and temporary backslides. The important point to grasp here is that it is only 'after the fact' or in hindsight that we are able to rationally reconstruct certain stages or phases.

In other words, my primary purpose for buying into the controversial concept of a cultural evolution is to argue for a 'strong' reading of secularization. Strong in the sense of *irreversibility*, i.e. recognizing a certain overall direction and that there is 'no going back'. The added value of arguing this way is, of course, that it gives access to a *norm* or normative perspective from which to assess the many faces of the contemporary religious scene. And *contemporary* religion is what I am interested in, since I believe that it matters quite a lot whether a particular religious group (be it Christian, Buddhist or Muslim) is more or less authoritarian, or violent, or compatible with modernity and the civic virtues of democracy. Thus, contrary to the 'evolutionistic' historians of religion in the early 20th century, I can easily resist the temptation to establish a hierarchy of the historic manifestations of religion and label each of them as being more or less 'primitive'. This is not to say that I do not believe that a case can be made for regarding societies and their cultural products (including religion) as being more or less 'developed'; in fact, it would be kind of odd if this was *not* the case. Only this is not my project in this chapter. My aim is more modest.

I begin by outlining some of the common wisdom put forward regarding secularization by major sociologists of religion. Next, I devote a section to presenting and briefly discussing the impressive history of Western secularization recently published by Charles Taylor (Taylor 2007). Immediately following, and intended as a bridge to the discussion of cultural evolution and religion, I insert a short section on the anti-evolutionism which is characteristic of the influential contemporary ideology of 'multiculturalism'.

The Return of Religion and the Death of Secularization?

The so called 'return' of religion (did it ever disappear?) is manifest in a great many ways. One of them is easy to discern and almost quantifiable, namely the fact that in recent years the number of treatments of (and references to) religion in newspapers and the media at large has markedly increased. This is an uncontroversial fact. Controversies begin, however, as soon as we move from superficial description to critical evaluation and try to answer the pertinent question: *Why* has religion seemingly gained new momentum, and what are the implications for the relation between religion, culture, and public life?

Before trying to answer, let me offer just a short list of examples of the kind of stories which are reported in the media:

- Catholic priests in US churches guilty of sexual abuse of children. The responsible bishop did little or nothing to prevent it.
- The issue of homosexuality threatens to cause a split within the Anglican Church.
- Charismatic or Pentecostal Christianity is rapidly growing in China, Africa and Latin America.
- Catholics and Protestants embark on a journey of peace in Northern Ireland.
- Sharia Law enforced: A young woman accused of adultery has been stoned in Pakistan.
- Muslim suicide-bombers revered as martyrs who will go directly to Paradise.
- Danish Mohammad-cartoons create massive demonstrations in the Middle-East.
- Parents go to court in order to make sure that their children are not exposed to Darwinism.
- Evangelical leaders lobby to ensure that the Christian Right can influence the election of the next U.S. President.

It goes without saying that the list could be continued page after page. The point I am getting at, however, is whether examples like the above warrant headlines such as 'the return of religion' or 'the revival of religion'. Many have interpreted the facts in this way. In fact, more than one sociologist of religion has repented his past erratic ways and instead pronounced the 'death' or 'end' of secularization (cf. Berger 1999). Peter L. Berger is an interesting example in this context, since three or four decades back he was (as he himself honestly admits) one of the leading proponents of a gradual and steady process of secularization. But now things have changed: We no longer, according to Berger, live in a secularized world. On the contrary, the world is as religious now as it has always been, and nothing seems to indicate that this is going to change. Religion is here to stay. We must therefore conclude, argues Berger, that the earlier theories of secularization have been empirically falsified. The basic idea which, as it were, has now been proven wrong, is that modernization by necessity leads to a *decline* in religion – in society at large as well as in individual consciousness. Berger, however, does not deny that modernity has involved some secularizing effects, but it has also (and this is what now seems to be the more important feature) produced "powerful movements of counter-secularization" (Berger 1999, 3). Language and choice of words are always revealing, though; it seems to me that when someone talks of 'counter-secularization' he is basically accepting an underlying or previous secularization.

Noteworthy on the global scene is that within almost all religions it is the *conservative* versions that are on the rise and gaining followers. Taken together this, according to Berger (1999, 6) amounts to "a massive falsification of the idea that modernization and secularization are cognate phenomena." At the very least, he adds, this development shows that *counter*-secularization is an equally important feature. And it is at this point that Berger admits at least *some* truth to the old theories of secularization, i.e. in the sense that fundamentalism must be understood as a reaction *against* a widely secular culture. But why do we see all these signs of religious revival? Berger advances the three-step hypothesis that 1) modernity undermines almost all taken-for-granted truths; 2) many people find it difficult or even impossible to live with this kind of insecurity; and hence 3) they turn to those types of religion which trade in security and clear-cut answers. While the basic tenor of Berger's account is that secularization theories have generally been mistaken, he does admit two exceptions to this overall picture. One is the existence of an international and elitist sub-culture of intellectuals marked by a more or less pronounced secular attitude and world-view. In relation to this position, the resurgence of religion may to some extent be explained as a protest against secular elites. This, as Berger notes, is characteristic of the ongoing cultural battle in the USA. The other exception is Europe where traditional theories of secularization seem to hold.

But *is* Europe really the exception that proves the rule? This is the question animating sociologist Grace Davie's contribution to the same volume (Davie 1999). A lot of empirical data (Davie in particular refers to the European Values System Study) seem generally to confirm a high level of secularization in Europe, although there are of course important differences from one country to another. At the very least one would do well to distinguish between the following four types of religious commitment: a) the Catholic countries; b) the Protestant countries; c) a mixed type like Germany, and d) a 'laicistic region' with countries like France, Belgium or the Netherlands (cf. Davie 1999, 71). From an overall perspective, however, the dominant picture is that "Western Europeans are *un-churched* populations" and that the general situation may be characterized as "believing without belonging" (*ibid*, 68). At this point Davie presents three different sociological interpretations of the data pertinent to the European situation. One is Steve Bruce whose basic intention is to hold on to a secularization thesis. In his perspective the Protestant Reformation, in particular, played a decisive role in advancing the key factors of individualism and rationality. Another perspective comes from José Casanova who argues that the concept of secularization should not be abandoned but needs, rather, to be clarified and refined, since it covers at least three elements: a) secularization in the sense of increasing differentiation between secular spheres and religious influence; b) secularization as decline in religious faith, and c) secularization as religion's being marginalized to the private sphere. According to Casanova, the core of the hypothesis of secularization is the first element, i.e. increasing differentiation (cf. Davie 1999, 77f.). Finally, French sociologist Danièle Hervieu-Léger advances the interesting, broadly Durkheimian perspective that religion should first and foremost be conceptualized in terms of collective memory. Hence, if one wishes to understand the role of religion in the modern world, one's attention should be focussed on two questions in particular: 'What is the nature of the *tradition* forming the basis of a given religious community?', and how can we analyze "the *chain* that makes the individual believer a member of a community" (*ibid*, 80). According to Hervieu-Léger, a major problem (and at the same time an important element in 'secularization') is that modern societies may be characterized as 'amnesiac societies'. At the same time, however, the process of modernization tends to open up 'utopian spaces' which, apparently, only religion is able to fill.

What is one to believe amidst this apparent empirical and theoretical confusion? Is religion growing or declining? If by 'religion' we mean organized religion, the empirical facts prompts us to answer: 'Both'. Thus in the case of Christianity, the number of active followers are growing due to an Evangelist-Pentecostal revival in some parts of the world (China, Africa, and Latin America), while it is (still) decreasing in many European countries, where the general attitude towards the church has been aptly characterized, as we saw above, by the phrase 'believing without belonging' (Grace Davie). Once again, the empirical facts may be uncontroversial, but evaluating their significance is not.

Returning to my initial list of examples of 'religion' in the media, what is characteristic of it? Let me offer the following suggestions:

- 'Religion' (particularly in connection with scandalous aspects of sexuality) is 'good news' in the sense that it sells a lot of newspapers.
- Religion is used (perhaps not least in the Muslim world) for political and/or nationalistic purposes.
- Fundamentalist, traditionalist and conservative religion causes many court cases, because believers claim that their religious liberties are being infringed upon.

Personally, I would tend to summarize this by saying that contemporary religion makes a good deal of 'noise'. We are, as it seems, increasingly reminded that religion may be used for many different purposes, some of them nobler than others. In religion and religious life, as William James once remarked, 'seraph and snake abide side by side'. This seems to be as true now as it was hundred years ago.

We may regard it as a fact that the general hypothesis of secularization has come under heavy attack in recent years. In this connection it is worth noting that one of the severe blows has come from what is commonly referred to as 'postmodernism'. The way this story is most often told, the collapse of Communism signalled the loss of faith in grand narratives of the gradual progress of humanity. Thus, the 'end of history' (Francis Fukuyama) could also mean the end of theories of secularization, since these theories were often connected to the idea of the gradual progress of reason and enlightenment. Moreover, in the epistemology of the humanities, postmodernism manifested itself as an emphasis on the constructed and contextual nature of human knowledge and culture, including religion. This trend, somewhat ironically, has been taken to heart and celebrated by protagonists of conservative or fundamentalist religiosity. And it is easy to understand why: When we all have certain presuppositions, and nothing is more inherently reasonable than something else, 'anything goes' and a conservative religious world-vies suddenly looks less odd and suspicious than before.

But is secularization really nothing but a hoax? This, in my opinion, would be a premature verdict. To illustrate why, let us turn to what is likely to be for quite some time regarded an influential and highly important account of Western secularization.

The Historical Process of Secularization

Charles Taylor's Templeton Prize-winning book *A Secular Age* is undoubtedly one of the most important contributions to the contested topic of secularization for many years. A major point of Taylor's general approach to the subject is to conceive of 'secularization' and 'secularity' as covering (at least) three semantic layers (he refers to them as secularity 1, 2, and 3). The first one is understanding secularity in terms of *public places* being increasingly 'emptied of God'.[63] The second one is regarding secularity

---

63 Taylor elaborates on this in a way reminiscent of Habermas' account of the historical differentiation between independent validity spheres. Says Taylor, "as we function within various spheres of activity – economic, political, cultural, educational, profes-

as "the falling off of religious belief and practice, in people turning away from God, and no longer going to Church" (Taylor 2007, 2). In other words the 'decline' in religion noted earlier. While these two perspectives on secularization are not only widespread and the ones favored by sociologists of religion, Taylor, however, makes a point of highlighting secularity in a third and different meaning, i.e. as a profound change in the *conditions of belief*. Thus, for Taylor the fact that we live in 'a secular age' has to do with religion turning into "one option among others, and frequently not the easiest to embrace" (*ibid*, 3). Obviously, then (and Taylor is aware of this), this third sense of secularity is not unrelated to the other two. But I believe he is right in seeing the changed conditions of belief as the more interesting subject matter for a philosophical as well as a theological perspective. Hence, in this *opus magnum* of more than 800 pages Taylor impressively charts and philosophically reflects on the cultural and mental history which has led to our current situation of religion and faith being just 'one option among others'. He describes his particular focus in the following way:

[T]he change I want to define and trace is one which takes us from a society in which it was virtually impossible not to believe in God, to one in which faith, even for the staunchest believer, is one human possibility among others. I may find it inconceivable that I would abandon my faith, but there are others, including possibly some very close to me, whose way of living I cannot in all honesty dismiss as depraved, or blind, or unworthy, who have no faith (at least not in God, or the transcendent). Belief in God is no longer axiomatic. There are alternatives. And this will also likely mean that at least in certain milieux, it may be hard to sustain one's faith. There will be people who feel bound to give it up, even though they mourn its loss. This has been a recognizable experience in our societies, at least since the mid-nineteenth century. There will be many others to

---

sional, recreational – the norms and principles we follow, the deliberations we engage in, generally don't refer us to God or to any religious beliefs; the considerations we act on are internal to the 'rationality' of each sphere – maximum gain within the economy, the greatest benefit to the greatest number in the political area, and so on. This is in striking contrast to earlier periods, when Christian faith laid down authoritative prescriptions (…)." (Taylor 2007, 2).

whom faith never even seems an eligible possibility. There are certainly millions today of whom this is true. (Taylor 2007, 3).

But still, why does Taylor want to move beyond the massively influential perspective of secularity 2 (the decline in religious belief and practice)? A major reason is that he is not convinced by the dominant explanation behind this version of secularity, namely that *science* and scientific progress has made religion obsolete. And, in turn, behind this opposition lies Taylor's important point that 'belief' and 'unbelief' are not to be considered (as has so often been the case) rival *theories*, but instead should be seen as "different kinds of lived experience" (*ibid*, 5). The relevance of this move becomes fairly obvious, once we think of contemporary critique of religion along the lines of Richard Dawkins or Daniel Dennett. But what does it entail to think of religion in terms of 'lived experience'? It means conceiving of each human being as searching for fulfillment, for a sense of fullness and investing in different 'places of fulfillment'. In this perspective, then, to be religious means to experience fullness as coming from a power *beyond* the individual. At the same time, belief and unbelief are constantly related to a changing 'background' or 'framework', and this, in particular, is what Taylor aims to trace and portray:

It is this shift in background, in the whole context in which we experience and search for fullness, that I am calling the coming of a secular age, in my third sense. How did we move from a condition where, in Christendom, people lived naïvely within a theistic construal, to one in which we all shunt between two stances, in which everyone's construal shows up as such; and in which moreover, unbelief has become for many the major default option? This is the transformation that I want to describe, and perhaps also (very partially) explain in the following chapters. (Taylor 2007, 14).

As concerns the concept of religion, Taylor (wisely it seems) avoids entering the ever-controversial terrain of *defining* religion. Instead, he rests content with "a reading of 'religion' in terms of the distinction transcendent/immanent" (*ibid*, 15). To see why we need to look at another quotation:

The great invention of the West was that of an immanent order in Nature, whose working could be systematically understood and explained on its own terms, leaving open the question whether this whole order had a deeper significance, and whether, if it did, we should infer a transcendent Creator beyond it. This notion of 'immanent' involved denying – or at least isolating and problematizing – any form of interpenetration between the things of Nature, on one hand, and 'the supernatural' on the other, be this understood in terms of the one transcendent God, or of Gods or spirits, or magic forces, or whatever. (*ibid*, 15f.).

In other words, broadly defining religion in terms of the transcendent/ immanent distinction is appropriate to the task at hand, since the gradual working out of this distinction is itself a core element of Western secularization. Hence, the important question to ask, according to Taylor, is "whether people recognize something beyond or transcendent to their lives" (*ibid*, 16). Some do, and some don't. Nonetheless believers and unbelievers have something very important in common, since both groups are trying to come to terms with basic existential questions like 'What is human flourishing?' or 'What constitutes a fulfilled life?' Around 1500 this kind of questions could only be perceived and answered in a religious mode, whereas five centuries later the default mode for answering may well be from an attitude of unbelief. Perhaps we can now see why the core element in Taylor's secularity 3 is the gradual development of a 'self-sufficing' or 'exclusive' *humanism*. Says Taylor, "I would like to claim that the coming of modern secularity in my sense has been coterminous with the rise of a society in which for the first time in history a purely self-sufficient humanism came to be a widely available option. I mean by this a humanism accepting no final goals beyond human flourishing, nor any allegiance to anything else beyond this flourishing. Of no previous society was this true." (*ibid*, 18).[64]

---

64 Or, as Taylor (2007, 19f.) succinctly puts the difference in relation to earlier times: "a secular age is one in which the eclipse of all goals beyond human flourishing becomes conceivable; or better, it falls within the range of an imaginable life for masses of people. This is the crucial link between secularity and a self-sufficing humanism."

An important step along this way was Providential Deism; Taylor calls it a 'halfway-house' on the road to contemporary secularity. In Providential Deism God still has a plan for the world, but he has drawn back ('retired') in order for humans to carry out and realize his benevolence. But still, what is Deism's internal connection to the rise of 'exclusive humanism'? The point is that humanism gained increasing plausibility due to a number of *anthropocentric shifts* implied in Providential Deism:

These involved, first, that the central moral concern becomes the imposition of a disciplined order on personal and social life, ensuring high standards of self-control and good behaviour in the individual, and peace, order and prosperity in society. Even many of the devout came to place great importance on this ordering project. The highest goals of human beings seem, even in the sphere of religion, to aim at purely human goods. When, on top of this, there begins to be serious progress towards these goals, the idea can gain currency that these ends are within the scope of unaided human powers. (Taylor 2007, 260f.).

Taylor sets his own view in opposition to what he calls 'subtraction stories' of secularization, according to which modernity and secularity "is to be understood in terms of underlying features of human nature which were there all along, but had been impeded by what is now set aside. Against this kind of story, I will steadily be arguing that Western modernity, including its secularity, is the fruit of new inventions, newly constructed self-understandings and related practices, and can't be explained in terms of perennial features of human life." (*ibid*, 22). As already indicated, a first stage on the road leading to our secular age is getting used to the distinction between immanent and transcendent, and distinguishing in one's own experience 'natural' from 'supernatural' causes and influences. What is at first sight remarkable, however, is that this 'disenchantment' (in the sense of Max Weber) went hand in hand with an intensification of religious faith. But the point here is that this intensification was in itself a modern trait, in that it reflected an increasing individualization of faith, of faith becoming a matter of personal commitment. The Protestant Reformation obviously played an important role in this regard.

Concerning the overall process of Western secularization, Taylor, basically, advances three claims: 1) Reform and reformation involves a 'push towards disenchantment' (*ibid*, 266) in the sense that the two spheres (natural and supernatural) tend to collapse into each other. Nonetheless it seems fair to wonder how this breaking free from a more or less closed religious world-view could happen in the first place. Taylor offers the following answer: "How does the break-out occur? Because the very attempt to express what the Christian life means in terms of a code of action in the saeculum opens the possibility of devising a code whose main aim is to encompass the basic goods of life in the saeculum: life, prosperity, peace, mutual benefit. In other words, it makes possible what I called the anthropocentric shift." (*ibid*).

Taylor's second claim is that 2) 'it could not have been otherwise'. Part of what he means by this is the historic irony that it was religion itself which gave rise to exclusive humanism. And as he asks, "How could the immense force of religion in human life in that age be countered, except by using a modality of the most powerful ethical ideas, which religion itself had helped to entrench?" (*ibid*, 267). It may be illustrative to think of Luther here, for how could he hope to advance his case and gain a hearing, were it not for the fact that he argued from what everybody (and even the Catholic Church) had to accept as the highest authority, namely Holy Scripture? Finally, Taylor's third claim is 3) "that all contemporary unbelief is still marked by that origin" (*ibid*, 268), i.e. by stemming from an originally religious framework. He speaks in this context of 'the sedimentation of the past in the present' and means by this expression "that our understanding of ourselves as secular is defined by the (often terribly vague) historical sense that we have come to be that way through the overcoming and rising out of earlier modes of belief." (*ibid*). Thus, even in our contemporary 'culture of authenticity' "God is still a reference point for even the most untroubled unbelievers, because he helps define the temptation you have to overcome and set aside to rise to the heights of rationality on which they dwell." (*ibid*).

We may begin, perhaps, to perceive here that Taylor's impressive account, so rich in historical, philosophical and theological details, is not that of an objective or detached observer. While gathering all the material necessary for understanding how we have landed in a secular age where religion is optional, and often not even the default option, at the same time he does not conceal that his way of telling the story is influenced by his own perspective as a believer. Thus, at one place he admits being moved by the life of Francis of Assisi, and hence he is not willing to accept secularization as encompassing 'the disappearance of independent religious aspiration' (*ibid*, 436). Moreover, he makes it quite clear that in relation to the major theories of secularization (what he calls 'subtraction theories') it is his general purpose to "set out an alternative take on the last centuries, which offer a different picture of secularization" (*ibid*). What is the difference then? Well, according to Taylor, his different picture of secularization tells us that the decline in religion is not linear and, therefore, that the "vector of this whole development does not point to a kind of heat death of faith" (*ibid*, 437). On this background, then, Taylor's more personal evaluation of Western secularization is marked by a certain optimism and hope:

Thus my own view of 'secularization', which I freely confess has been shaped by my own perspective as a believer (but that I would nevertheless hope to be able to defend with arguments), is that there has certainly been a 'decline' of religion. Religious belief now exists in a field of choices which include various forms of demurral and rejection; Christian faith exists in a field where there is also a wide range of other spiritual options. But the interesting story is not simply one of decline, but also of a new placement of the sacred or spiritual in relation to individual and social life. This new placement is now the occasion for recompositions of spiritual life in new forms, and for new ways of existing both in and out of relation to God. (Taylor 2007, 437).

In other words, we may conclude that the story of secularization is one of decline and religion becoming (just) an 'option', but at the same time this has opened up new possibilities for 'recompositions' of spiritual life. This is an important and, I believe, generally valid conclusion.

Multiculturalism as Anti-Evolutionism

In many ways similar to the spirit of postmodernism, one prominent approach to globalization and the ensuing plurality of cultures, religions, and forms of life, is 'multiculturalism'. As a contemporary ideology wide-spread among Western intellectuals, multiculturalism signals the idea 1) that all cultures are of equal worth and value deserving not only

Lockean tolerance but 'respect', and 2) that many different cultures living together in the same society is in itself a good thing. When all cultures are equal and none may be regarded as 'higher' (more developed) than anyone else, it is not surprising that proponents of multiculturalism have as their favourite hate-objects 'evolutionism' and 'ethnocentrism'. Untiring, and partly fuelled by the spirit of political correctness, multiculturalist researchers have taken pleasure in revealing the grave sins of evolutionist researchers in the late 19th and early 20th centuries. Nowhere has this been more dominant than in the study of religion ('Religionswissenschaft') where 'culture' has gained the status of a new 'Leitbegriff'. And once religion is culture, it has become elevated to a plane beyond criticism: You may still criticize products of literature or art, but in the realm of religion there is, apparently, no kitsch and nothing to criticize: only interesting and valuable products to be respected for what they are.

Of course, as one would expect, anti-evolutionism also carries the day in cultural and anthropological studies. One need only open a standard text-book on cultural anthropology to learn what students are taught to think about their predecessors who studied 'other' cultures and their religious ideas. Thus, in the chapter on 'Religion' we find the following appraisal:

In the nineteenth and early twentieth centuries, many anthropologists were concerned with trying to find the origin, and trace the development, of religion. For the most part, they wanted to demonstrate that religion had evolved from primitive superstition to enlightened Christianity. E. B. Tylor, one of the founders of anthropology, saw religion as beginning with ANIMISM, the notion that all objects (living and nonliving) are imbued with spirit, and evolving through polytheism to monotheism. Tylor and many of his contemporaries believed the evolution of religion was part of the more general human progression toward logic and rationality. *This view of religion has long been discredited; no religion is any more or less logical than any other and none is more evolved than another.* (Nanda & Warms 2007, p. 375; emphasis added).

The last part of this quotation should give us pause to reflect. It is said that 'Tylor and many of his contemporaries believed the evolution of religion was part of the more general human progression toward logic and rationality'. And then, immediately following, the authors calm their readers by emphasizing that 'this view of religion has long been discredited'. In other words: we may relax, we don't need to take it seriously. But why, looking back over, say, the last thousand years, should it not be possible to discern a 'progression toward logic and rationality'? I tend to find that a rather plausible claim. And in fact, the authors do not directly oppose this idea. What they apparently wish to attack is the view that *religion* has been part of this progression. But why, given that religion is a product of culture and society, should this development leave religion unaffected? The answer is blowing in the wind and one begins to understand why the authors use the verb 'discredited' to distance themselves from any evolutionary perspective on religion. Thereby they reveal that what ought to be a proper subject of scientific curiosity is turned into a matter of taste: By the rules of political correctness it is simply bad taste to entertain the notion that one form of religion (and the culture in which it is embedded) may be more evolved than another. Be that as it may, the 'correct' and tasteful view that the authors are so keen to pass on to the students who read their text-book runs contrary not only to common sense but also to the nature of scientific inquiry.

Common sense first: Whenever we visit a foreign country, just as ordinary tourists, we cannot help making judgments about their way of life (including the role and function of religion) and comparing it to what we know from our own background. Doing this is quite simply an integral part of the process of understanding. This evaluation and comparison may be quite superficial and full of prejudices, but new experiences may lead us to revise our prejudices, and then we have the hermeneutical circle as described by Gadamer. My point here is just to say that this is the way we understand something in humanities as well as in theology. Hence it would be strange and counter-intuitive if scientific inquiry did not cultivate the same interest in comparison and different levels of development. Put differently: those who state from the outset that 'evolutionary' perspectives can have no proper place in research on religion and culture ought to offer good reasons to the rest of us (and these days we are surely in the minority) why this should be the case. We all know that in the past the evolutionary perspective was applied in a heavy-handed and 'ethnocentric' fashion, but is this really sufficient reason to forever banning it from the halls of science?

The 'Early' Habermas on the Evolution of Religion

In the 1970ies and early 80ies Jürgen Habermas did some interesting work from an evolutionary perspective. The background to this was partly his awareness that for a contemporary Marxist it was necessary to 're-construct' a historical materialism which had been empirically falsified, and partly his attempt to better understand the development of the in-dividual's capacities for interaction. This latter interest, of course, served as part of what was later to become his general theory of communica-tive action. Methodologically, Habermas was inspired by Jean Piaget's structural-developmental perspective and Lawrence Kohlberg's theory of moral development. In both cases 'development' is conceptualized as an irreversible sequence of stages.[65] Care had to be taken, however, when these theoretical insights were to be applied to the evolution of cultures and societies. Could it really be the case that *ontogeny* and *phylo-geny* mirrored each other? This certainly looked very much like the old, evolutionist mistake.

Habermas seems to have been aware of this danger, for he is cau-tious in two respects: One, because he makes a distinction between the *logic* and the *dynamics* of development, respectively. The 'logic' covers what we might call 'the big picture' or the overall trend of development, whereas the 'dynamics' refers more to the actually realised development which will always be the result of several constraining factors. Second, Habermas seems to acknowledge that it is problematic to assume that the ontogenetic stages are also reflected in the phylogenetic development of cultures. Says Habermas,

The ontogenetic models are certainly better analyzed and have received more confirmation than their social-evolutionary counterparts. That homological

---

65 Piaget's theory, focusing on the child's cognitive development, is generally considered uncontroversial. Kohlberg's theory, although still convincing, is more problematic because it privileges a broadly Kantian morality (universalist perspective) as the highest level of moral thinking. And even more problematic is James Fowler's theory (*Stages of Faith*, 1981) of 'faith development'.

structures of consciousness may be found in the history of the human species is not surprising, however, when one reflects on the fact that the linguistic intersubjectivity of understanding marks the phylogenetic innovation which only made possible the level of socio-cultural learning. At this level, the reproduction of society and the socialization of the members of society are two aspects of the same process; they are dependent on the same structures (Habermas 1976, 13; my translation).

A few pages later (16f.), Habermas explicitly mentions some reasons why one should be very careful not to be too quick to draw parallels between the development of the individual ('Ich-Entwicklung') and the evolution of world-images ('Weltbilder'). Not only is there the danger of confusing structure and contents; one should also be aware that the pattern of ontogenetic development does not simply mirror the structures of human history. In spite of these reservations, however, Habermas finds it possible to point to 'certain homologies', particularly with respect to the *cognitive* aspects of development. This, in turn, leads him to present the following four stages of social evolution:[66]

I. Archaic societies
The social structure of archaic societies is determined by kinship relations (family and tribe). The image of the world is structured by myths, mythological thinking and an anthropomorphic conception of nature. The prevalence of myths makes it possible to absorb and interpret all kinds of contingencies (cf. Habermas 1976, 97f.).

II. Early High-Cultures
New factors in the social structure at this level of social evolution are cities or nascent states with a ruling king. Here we find polytheistic gods acting very human-like, and we also find the beginning of a de-sacralization of the natural environment, which Habermas interprets as 'indication of the

---

66 It is more than a coincidence that Habermas presents these ideas in an implicit dialogue with Hegel; thus, the text entitled 'Können komplexe Gesellschaften eine vernünftige Identität ausbilden?' formed the basis for his acceptance speech when in 1974 he was honoured with the Hegel-award in Stuttgart.

opening of a field of possible surprises' (*ibid*, 98). In man's relation to the gods, new forms of interaction emerge: prayer, sacrifice, and adoration.

III. Developed High-Cultures

Here we find a further development of the state and class-societies marked by extreme inequality. At this stage we encounter the great world religions (we are here in what Karl Jaspers famously termed 'the axial age') to which Habermas accords a special significance: "A general or universalistic validity claim ('Geltungsanspruch') is first represented by the great world religions, among which Christianity is perhaps the most completely rationalized. The one, transcendent, all-knowing, perfectly just and gracious God of Christianity made possible the formation of a personal identity independent of all specific roles and norms. This 'I' is able to conceive himself as a completely individuated being. The concept of an immortal soul before God paves the way for the idea of freedom, according to which 'the individual has an infinite value' ([Hegel] Enzyklopädie, par. 482)" (*ibid*, 99; my translation).

IV. Modernity

The problem of modernity, for Hegel as well as for Habermas, is the advent of a thoroughgoing *split* between the personal identity of the individual, framed by universalistic structures, and the collective identity tied to the 'nation' or the 'state'. Religion is no longer able to mediate between these two types of identity, for 'God' is more or less reduced to a structure of communication which in turn is indicative of a broader development "where not much more is left from the universal religions than the core content of a universalistic morality" (*ibid*, 101; my translation). In other words, religion is forced to give up its former status as world-picture ('Weltbild'). We shall see, shortly, how this diagnosis informs some of Habermas' later thoughts on religion.

The ideas briefly paraphrased above are more than 30 years old, and in the meantime they have become unfashionable. There are exceptions, however. Thus, in the domain of art history, my colleague at Aarhus University, professor of art history Jakob Wamberg, has recently, and inspired by Hegel and Habermas, presented an elaborate theoretical argument as well as empirical evidence for the hypothesis of evolutionary stages in the history of Western paintings. His claim, more specifically relates to the gradual development of depth and perspective in the way in which landscape is presented in paintings right from the earliest depictions in caves like Lascaux, France (cf. Wamberg 2006). Furthermore, Wamberg is able to relate this evolutionary (i.e. irreversible sequence of stages) development to corresponding developments in social and personal understanding. The history of Western landscape painting reaches its maturation and climax with the advent of modernity (here: 19th century) where the depth of perspective (corresponding to individual self-reflection) is most fully developed.

Wamberg's research is an inspiring and courageous attempt to apply an evolutionary perspective to the history of art. But of course it has its inherent problems, too. One such problem is the apparent fact that the evolutionary stages *end* with modernity. Obviously, as is well known, in post-modernity (which is here the 20th century) we have all sorts of –isms in art, beginning with the cubism of Braque and Picasso; in fact, we even have what looks like a return to a naturalistic and 'primitive' way of painting. Does this, then, invalidate Wamberg's general hypothesis? I think not. To see why, think of Piaget's stages of cognitive development which end once the individual has reached puberty ('formal operational thinking'). In adult life, of course, the individual continues to develop in so many ways, but from a strictly cognitive perspective she continues on the level that was reached already in puberty. In a similar fashion, we might assume that in the domain of landscape painting there is nothing more to learn about depth of perspective after painters like Caspar David Friedrich in the 19th century. And then in another sense (no longer linear development) there is a lot more to learn and discover: you can deconstruct it (Picasso) or play with it in so many other ways, some of them including what on the surface looks like a return to a 'childhood' long gone.

There may be an interesting lesson for our subject of religion involved here. Thus, Habermas' four-stage model of social and religious evolution similarly implied that in Western Europe religion (i.e. Christianity) became fully developed in modernity. What this means is that it had exhausted its learning potential and in this sense reached 'maturation'. In a sense, then, *evolution* may have stopped, but *development* and transformation goes on. The problem is how to read or interpret this continuing development. One possible approach is the broadly Hegelian adopted by the early Habermas: the core of religion is reduced to a universalistic morality anchored in the very structures of communication.

Only a few years later than *Zur Rekonstruktion*, Habermas published his *opus magnum*, *The Theory of Communicative Action* (Habermas 1981). Here, rather than relying on Hegel and evolutionary thinking, Habermas utilizes Max Weber's concepts of 'rationalization' and 'disenchantment'. In order to understand where we have come from, Habermas draws upon Durkheim's analysis of the function of the sacred in primitive society: the sacred, in sharp distinction to the profane, is what normatively binds people together. What gradually changes this, however, is the new 'motor' which Habermas now sees at work in history, namely communicative action. Thus, in *Theory* Habermas advances the hypothesis of a gradual 'Versprachlichung des Sakralen' (the sacred being turned into language). Thanks to the validity claims inherent in communication, the 'banning' function of the sacred is gradually replaced by the 'binding' functions of communicative action. One of the problems, obviously, facing this kind of theory is the fact that religion today seems to be very much alive and well. And this fact, we may assume, serves to explain why Habermas has since left his 'early' approach to religion. Now, as we shall see in the following chapter, instead of evolution and 'Versprachlichung' he speaks more cautiously of historical 'learning processes', and concedes that religion (i.e. Christian tradition) harbours valuable semantic resources for which philosophy is unable to offer a secular equivalent. And in turn, as we shall also see, this is part of what prompts him to accord religion an important role in the public sphere.

In the context of the present chapter, however, let us return to the issue of what we can learn from Wamberg's approach to the history of art. My point here would be that after modernity religion in the West may well have 'matured', but it nonetheless continues its development in ways similar to art. In other words, it develops in so many surprising and unexpected ways that reflect the multiplicity of life-worlds in contemporary society. Religion has become a choice of life-style and a mark of identity.[67] But just as post-modern 'naturalistic' paintings are something quite different from the naturalism of previous centuries, so we should be wary of the wide-spread talk of a 'return of religion'. Nothing returns as what it once was. And no amount of conservative, Bible-believing Christianity can hide the fact that the form and function of religion has irreversibly changed.

Meme-Theory and Religion

A promising, but still relatively undeveloped approach to religion and culture in general, is the theory of *memes* constantly competing for space in the human mind. Meme-theory goes back to neo-Darwinist Richard Dawkins (presently leader of an atheist crusade against religion) who in the early 8oies was one of the first to take the step from 'genes' (biology) to 'memes' (culture). To invoke the title of a book by J. M. Balkin (Balkin 1998), memes may be considered our 'cultural software'. Says Balkin,

I argue that there is a significant Darwinian mechanism at work in cultural evolution. However, it does not operate through the natural selection of human beings or groups of human beings. What is replicated and selected in cultural evolution is not human beings but cultural information and cultural know-how in human beings. What is replicated and selected in cultural evolution is cultural software (Balkin 1998, 42).

But what *is* a 'meme'? According to Balkin, memes are "primarily skills and abilities, but they also include beliefs about the world (. . .). Memes encompass all the forms of cultural know-how that can be passed to others through the various forms of imitation and communication." (*ibid*, 43). What memes have in common with genes is that both are 'units of inheritance'. Balkin is aware, however, that "if we rely too heavily on biological analogies, we will inevitably be misled, because biological evolution is only one possible form of evolutionary development" (*ibid*,

---

67 Interestingly, this general picture is also corroborated by seeing religion in the light of Habermas's 'validity claims' corresponding to the objective, the social, and the subjective worlds respectively. In terms of validity, religion, as a consequence of secularization and the differentiation of independent value spheres, belongs to the subjective world, and its 'validity' is that of 'truthfulness' and 'authenticity'.

48). Moreover, one important difference that cannot be overlooked is the fact that in contrast to genes memes are not living organisms. And yet, Balkin argues, they exercise an important influence, albeit without being intentionally acting. How then do they affect us? By acting like a *virus* (another metaphor from biology); memes are more or less contagious, and the memes that survive are those with the best ability to replicate and spread.

It is very difficult, however, to make predictions about memic, cultural evolution. The reason for this is that individuals are creative and that their minds make combinations and adjustments when confronted with new memes. So, instead of linear development in one direction, Balkin wants us to see culture as *bricolage* and he concludes, "In sum, one of the most important distinctions between genetic and cultural evolution is that while biological lineages increasingly diverge, cultural lineages often recombine" (*ibid*, 53).

From a memetic perspective cultural evolution "is not possible until there are sufficiently powerful information-processing devices capable of storing information and reliably transmitting it to or replicating it in other information-processing devices" (*ibid*, 55). Going back in history, Balkin points to the importance of language, writing, and even later the invention of printing-presses. There is nothing new in this, and scholars (fx Walter Ong) have long since pointed to the profound effects of the shift from an 'oral culture' to a culture based on writing. In fact, once we reflect on the stunning development within the technology of communication, it becomes clear, in my opinion, that what primarily makes meme-theory worth considering is that it seems perfectly suited to describe the cultural effects of the seemingly unlimited proliferation of 'memes' made possible by the spread of personal computers and the constant extension of the internet. Put differently, cultural developments in our globalized information society often occur in a surprising, sometimes seemingly *stochastic* fashion, and meme-theory may help us to understand why.

There are, however, constraints or 'blockages' to the spread of memes. First, notes Balkin, "the human mind is a natural bottleneck for memetic evolution, because memes usually must reside in a human mind before they can be transmitted to others. The scarcity of human minds is an important element of the natural selection of memes" (*ibid*). Second, each individual develops a repertoire of *filtering mechanisms*. In fact, according to Balkin we may think of it much like an 'arms race' going on: new technologies for the spread of memes must be met with new filters. A filter, then, is a cognitive mechanism, but not necessarily in the form of a propositional belief. Says Balkin, "Many cognitive mechanisms, including prejudices, narrative structures, metaphoric models, and metonymic associations, act like filters. They let in ideas that conform to particular patterns of thought while rejecting those that do not. (...) Hence these meme filters are part of the mechanism of natural selection that occur within each individual human mind." (*ibid*, 58).

But is 'natural selection' really what we are dealing with here?[68] And who is in the driver's seat, the memes or the individual human being? 'Both' seems to be the answer favoured by Balkin as is clear from the following quotation:

The account of cultural evolution that I have been developing suggests that not only do people have ideas, but ideas have people. Memes "use" people for the purpose of their own propagation. We should not understand such anthropomorphic language literally: memes no more than genes have wants, desires, purposes, or interests. Rather, this is merely a shorthand way of describing how natural selection works on units of cultural transmission.

This approach removes the need to explain human cultural development and proliferation solely in terms of its survival advantages for human beings. To the contrary, we may assume that much cultural development is largely irrelevant to human survival in the short term, although it may have many profound and unexpected long-term effects. Memes do not necessarily reproduce and propagate because this process confers an evolutionary advantage on human beings

---

68 Without adopting the concept of natural selection, Stephen L. Carter exemplifies how an evolutionary perspective may even be used for apologetic purposes. Thus, in his *The Culture of Disbelief* which attacks the secular thrust of liberal democracy, we find the following surprising statement: "There is an economy about religious belief – an economy and a tendency toward evolution. Over the centuries, the religious traditions, like traditions of other kinds, tend to abandon what is useless and preserve what is useful. (...) This evolution matters because it suggests that a religion that has survived must include some kernel of moral truth that resonates with broader human understandings, whether or not most people share the epistemic premises of the religion itself." (Carter 1993, 231).

(although this may in fact occur). Rather, they survive, reproduce, and propagate because it advantages them (Balkin 1998, 61).[69]

But still, does it make good sense to speak of 'natural selection' in the realm of culture? At any rate, Balkin's attempt to calm us by noting that his anthropomorphic language should not be taken literally cannot hide that meme-theory (in the versions presented so far) relies heavily, and perhaps too heavily, on the paradigm of natural selection. Another problematic feature of meme-theory is its implicit deterministic conception of the human person. It must be admitted, though, that at one point Balkin offers an original point of view when he suggests that, "Indeed, we might define a person as an entity that is continually at a loss what to do" (*ibid*, 62).

More to the point, Terry Rambo makes no secret of the consequences of an evolutionary perspective: "Above all, however, understanding cultural evolution necessitates abandoning many of our most deeply held beliefs about the nature of humanity and our place in the universe." (Rambo 1991, 93). Moreover, although finding meme-theory promising, he puts his finger on what is probably the primary weakness of meme-theory, namely the fact that the very definition of a 'meme' remains unclear. Says Rambo, "The lack of any convincing specification of the nature of these information units is a major obstacle to development of this approach to cultural evolution. (...) How will we know a 'meme' or a 'culturgen' if we discover one?" (*ibid*, 69). Or, as he later concludes: "The meme and its equivalents are still at best metaphorical suggestions" (*ibid*, 90).

Conclusion

It is time to take stock and put some of the ideas presented in this chapter into a concluding perspective. In the context of this book we needed to take a look at cultural evolution and religion for at least two reasons. One is the need to account for the 'different epistemic situation' that separates us from Abraham and makes his relation to God look archaic and obsolete.

---

69 Later in his book Balkin proposes that "we can understand human culture as a compromise and conflict between the interests of persons, their genes, and their memes" (Balkin 1998, 71).

The other is the disturbing fact that in contemporary arguments about religion the tendency is that 'anything goes'. To put it differently, what is discernible, in my opinion, is an intellectual irresponsibleness in matters of religion and the question of how it relates to culture and politics. No doubt, this state of affairs is partly caused by the wide-spread conception that secularization is 'dead' and that religion has 'returned'.

My claim is that this is a superficial conception. This claim, I should add, covers only the cultural evolution which has taken place in the Western world dominated by Christianity. Here, what we find may be summarized in the following points:

- From archaic times and until modernity secularization has exerted its influence in the form of a gradual *dis-enchantment* (Max Weber's 'Entzauberung') of God, nature, and self.[70] This process may be characterized as a cultural evolution in the sense of a development passing through a sequence of stages. The number and nature of these stages or phases are of course matters open to debate. Although in society as well as on the individual level occasional and temporary relapses to a former stage may occur, the overall process of cultural evolution (of which religion is part and parcel) is *irreversible*. Abraham's relation to his God will not 'return'; neither is it a live option for our times.
- Those theories of secularization that predicted the 'end' of religion have been proven empirically wrong by the resurgence of religion during the last decades. Rather, therefore, after modernity we should speak of a *transformation* in the way in which religion is used. In fact, as 'symbolic capital' (Pierre Bourdieu) religion has demonstrated a remarkable flexibility in being used for many different needs: nationalistic, personal, economic or political.
- 'Religion' has become more a mark of identity, a choice of lifestyle.
- Religion (in the form of 'fundamentalism') can be interpreted as a protest reflecting a dis-like of modernization. Or, in the terminology of meme-theory, as a filtering mechanism aiming to limit the influ-

70 A more elaborate account of the consequences of this may be found in Gauchet (1997).

ence of pluralism and of what is perceived as dangerous, 'secularizing' effects.

To conclude, then, the point is not so much 'evolution' in any universal sense but, rather, recognizing a 'developmental logic' (Habermas), a socio-cultural development of an *irreversible* nature. In other words, there is no turning back as regards 'the big picture'.[71] In the beginning of this chapter I said that understanding secularization in terms of a cultural evolution gives us access to a *norm* by which to assess the plethora of contemporary forms of religion. Now the time has come to indicate what is implied in this. Recall that I established a certain parallel between the evolution within art history (landscape painting) and the evolution implied in the conditions of what it means to have a religious consciousness. The basic similarity is related to the fact that within both areas the contemporary situation is characterized by an open field of significant 'recompositions' – to borrow the expression used by Taylor. But whereas a 'recomposition' may be a real possibility in a postmodern culture, a simple return to (or repetition of) the past is not. In aesthetics as well as in religion we may in this connection speak of *kitsch*. Despite these important similarities between art and religion, however, we should not overlook an equally important difference. For although (guided by Habermas) we may establish that art and religion share the validity claims of 'truthfulness' and 'authenticity', religion differs from aesthetics in that its source of meaning and authority has a *transcendent* origin.

Thus, a major consequence of cultural evolution is not the end of religion, but a *pluralism* of world-views. Jeffrey Stout has given an, albeit somewhat weak, expression of this: "The mark of secularization, as I use the term, is rather the fact that participants in a given discursive practice are not in a position to take for granted that their interlocutors are making the same religious assumptions they are. This is the sense in which public discourse in modern democracies tend to be secularized" (Stout

---

71 What we do see, however, are occasional re-lapses into archaic patterns of reaction and ways of using religion (as in the ethnic cleansing in former Jugoslavia). We humans may be technologically and culturally advanced, but we are still capable of both good and evil.

2003, 97). Whether this also entails the *priority* of the secular over the religious is a highly controversial matter, as we shall see in the following two chapters.

Chapter Five

RAWLS AND HABERMAS ON LIBERAL DEMOCRACY AND RELIGION

What is the nature of a modern, constitutional democracy, and how does religion fit into it? This question will be the focus of the present chapter. To deal with this topic, I have chosen to consult what is generally recognized as the two major representatives of contemporary political philosophy, namely John Rawls and Jürgen Habermas. They both belong within the same family of political philosophy which is concerned to defend the normative principles of a 'deliberative democracy'. In the way they perform this task, they differ and part ways in certain central regards, but at the same time they may also be said to complement each other in interesting ways. At any event, what is decisive for my purposes is that they both give special concern to the role of religion in the sphere of public reason.

In the first section, I shall outline the approach to liberal democracy and religion that Rawls adopts in his seminal book, *Political Liberalism* (1993), and in what is an even more interesting text for my purposes, i.e. the somewhat later version of his position put forward in the article entitled 'The Idea of Public Reason Revisited' from 1997. As one might expect, Rawls' political liberalism has been paraphrased before, frequently in fact, and thus I make no claim whatsoever to originality. Readers who are already familiar with Rawls may therefore wish to skip some sections of this chapter. To me, however, it is important to present what I intend and hope to be a correct and loyal picture of the central ideas of political liberalism. It is important, I think, because only a quick survey of the debate on Rawls reveals several recurring examples of distortions (or at least misrepresentations) of his basic standpoints. And yet, as we shall have the opportunity to see, Rawls himself may not be entirely beyond possible blame here, since over time he has not only substantially modified his basic position, but also left the reader with an ambiguous description of the central ideal of an 'overlapping consensus'.

In the second section, I turn (as in the previous chapter) to Habermas who in his latest writings has dealt extensively with the role of religion in the public sphere. In connection with commenting on the American debate (Rawls and others), Habermas has developed what he considers a less restrictive and more sympathetic framework for the political participation of religious citizens. Finally, in the last section of this chapter, I briefly ponder whether Rawls' or Habermas' perspective is better suited to deal with the current dilemmas surrounding the role of religion. This chapter is thus intended to constitute the necessary background to the critical debates which will be treated in the following chapter.

Rawls: Political Liberalism and Religion

In *A Theory of Justice* (henceforth: *Theory*) from 1971 Rawls had, on a broadly Kantian and contractarian basis, been able to reconstruct the basic principles (liberty, equality) of a society which all of its members would consider fair and just. Rawls accomplishes this by hypothesizing an *original position*, a situation where a group of people is debating what kind of society they could possibly agree to wish to live in together. For this thought experiment to work, it is a requirement that the people deliberating this have no knowledge as to their own position in the future society. This condition of 'no knowledge' regarding one's future role in society is what Rawls in *Theory* famously labelled *the veil of ignorance*. In other words, the participants must, as it were, be forced to reflect on the principles of justice forming the basis of this society according to the *principle of reciprocity*, i.e. granting all other members the same rights as one would oneself wish for, or feel the need for. What emerged from this experiment was that rational individuals, given this situation and these constraints, would choose to form a society whose basic principles of justice look very much like the well-ordered society of a liberal democracy.

What then is the major difference between *Theory* and *Political Liberalism* (henceforth: PL), and what prompted Rawls to develop the idea of a political liberalism? While the former may be considered a *philosophical* enterprise and has the status of a comprehensive doctrine, it eventually became important to Rawls to transform the fundamental idea of justice as fairness into a *political* conception of justice.[72] The primary reason lies in what he perceives to be the basic problem calling political liberalism to its task: "How is it possible that there may exist over time a stable and just society of free and equal citizens profoundly divided by reasonable though incompatible religious, philosophical, and moral doctrines?" (Rawls 2005, xviii).[73] Or, as he later phrases it, "the question should be more sharply put this way: How is it possible for those affirming a religious doctrine that is based on religious authority, for example, the Church or the Bible, also to hold a reasonable political conception that supports a just democratic regime?" (*ibid*, xxxvii).[74] Hence, already in this formulation we may perceive the acute relevance of Rawls to the 'Abrahamic' dilemma of religious authority vs. common (political) morality which I rehearsed in the first part of this book. In this connection it should be emphasized that Rawls repeatedly reminds us that this 'division' between a political conception on the one hand and a plurality of comprehensive doctrines on the other, which constitutes the basic challenge to PL, is in no way to be considered a defect or a societal disease to be cured. On the

---

72 Looking back, Rawls (1997, 489) describes the difference as follows: "justice as fairness is presented there [sc. in *Theory*] as a comprehensive liberal doctrine (although the term 'comprehensive doctrine' is not used in the book) in which all the members of its well-ordered society affirm that same doctrine. This kind of well-ordered society contradicts the fact of reasonable pluralism and hence *Political Liberalism* regards that society as impossible."

73 Cf. also the way in which Rawls (1997, 485) begins his concluding remarks to 'The Idea of Public Reason Revisited': "Throughout, I have been concerned with a *torturing* question in the contemporary world, namely: Can democracy and comprehensive doctrines, religious or nonreligious, be compatible? And if so, how?" (emphasis by me).

74 This formulation reveals two things: One is that although comprehensive doctrines may be of a religious, philosophical or moral nature, what first and foremost creates problems in relation to public reason is *religion*, precisely because (and in so far as) it is 'based on religious authority'. The other important thing to note is that Rawls distinguishes between a *doctrine* (religious, philosophical or moral) and a *conception* (political): "I shall use the term 'doctrine' for comprehensive views of all kinds and the term 'conception' for a political conception and its component parts, such as the conception of the person as citizen." (Rawls 1997, 441).

contrary, the fact of a pluralism of comprehensive, and often mutually exclusive, doctrines is the *normal*, natural and to be expected outcome of reasonable citizens living in a free society. Thus, Rawls says of reasonable comprehensive doctrines that "they are in part the work of free practical reason within the framework of free institutions", and therefore "the fact of reasonable pluralism is not an unfortunate condition of human life" (Rawls 2005, 37).[75] What is crucial, however, and what we may be justified in regarding as the overall aim of political liberalism, is to succeed in transforming the fact of pluralism into a situation characterized by *stability* 'for the right reasons'.

And now we can provide the answer as to why Rawls saw the need to transform the basic elements of *Theory* into the political conception of PL: For if PL were itself a philosophical doctrine, we would have a situation where 'democracy' was *one* doctrine and 'religion' *another*. And confronted with such a scenario, anyone can probably see that it would be futile to imagine or hope for the possibility of an overlapping consensus.[76] Therefore, it is necessary for Rawls to clarify what PL *is not*. For only on this background may we appreciate what it positively *is*.

First, in relation to historical precedents, he emphasizes that PL is not a form of Enlightenment liberalism which more often than not regarded itself as being in a hostile relation to religion and churches. Contrary to this, claims Rawls, PL is not 'secularist' – no matter how often this complaint appears on the side of religious critics. Also, PL is not a comprehensive liberalism in terms of a political ideology. In fact, and this is the important point to make for Rawls, PL is not a comprehensive doctrine at all (philosophical or otherwise), but something much more modest, namely a political conception trying hard to be impartial to the

---

75 In this connection it is important to note that Rawls makes a distinction between *pluralism* and *reasonable pluralism*: "The crucial fact is not the fact of pluralism as such, but of reasonable pluralism. [...] The fact of reasonable pluralism is not an unfortunate condition of human life, as we might say of pluralism as such, allowing for doctrines that are not only irrational but mad and aggressive." (Rawls 2005, 144; cf. also p. 63f.).

76 "For rather than confronting religious and nonliberal doctrines with a comprehensive liberal philosophical doctrine, the thought is to formulate a liberal political conception that those nonliberal doctrines might be able to endorse." (Rawls 2005, xlv).

comprehensive doctrines.[77] Still, he acknowledges that PL has a *normative* content: "political rights and duties are moral rights and duties, for they are part of a political conception that is a normative (moral) conception with its own intrinsic ideal, though not itself a comprehensive doctrine." (*ibid*, xlii). Another way that Rawls expresses this is to insist on characterizing PL as a 'freestanding view':

Political liberalism tries, then, to present an account of these values as those of a special domain – the political – and hence as a freestanding view. It is left to citizens individually – as part of liberty of conscience – to settle how they think the values of the political domain are related to other values in their comprehensive doctrine. For we always assume that citizens have two views, a comprehensive and a political view; and that their overall view can be divided into two parts, suitably related. [...] History tells of a plurality of not unreasonable comprehensive doctrines. This makes an overlapping consensus possible, thus reducing the conflict between political and other values. (Rawls 2005, 140).

In other words, the overall aim of PL is to secure stability and social unity (cohesion) in the face of 'the fact of pluralism'. And as we shall see below, it is of paramount importance to Rawls that citizens choose to contribute to the stability of society for the *right* reasons.

In what follows, I shall try to sketch the major elements of PL, some of which we have already encountered above. Thus, this section will form the background for understanding Rawls' views on the role of religion in the public sphere.

The Reasonable Citizen and Civic Virtues

What kind of anthropology is implied in the political conception of Rawls? First of all, it sees the person as a free and equal citizen, but of course this calls for further elaboration. In a section of PL entitled 'The

---

77 It should be noted, however, that Rawls sometimes uses the expression 'political philosophy' which is likely to create some confusion. Cf. for instance the following passage: "Political liberalism sees its form of political philosophy as having its own subject matter: how is a just and free society possible under conditions of deep doctrinal conflict with no prospect of resolution?" (Rawls 2005, xxviii).

Political Conception of the Person', Rawls mentions three ways in which citizens are conceived to be 'free':

1) "they conceive of themselves and of one another as having the moral power to have a conception of the good" (Rawls 2005, 30);
2) "they regard themselves as self-authenticating sources of valid claims" (*ibid*, 32); and, finally,
3) "they are viewed as capable of taking responsibility for their ends and this affects how their various claims are assessed" (*ibid*, 33). What is important in this connection, is that Rawls deliberately eschews questions of philosophical anthropology (since this would lead him into a comprehensive doctrine), and, instead, delimits himself to addressing individuals as *citizens*.

The above criteria, however, are not sufficient. PL needs also to attribute to citizens the following features: "their readiness to propose and to abide by fair terms of cooperation, their recognizing the burdens of judgment and affirming only reasonable comprehensive doctrines, and their wanting to be full citizens" (*ibid*, 86). This, according to Rawls, is equivalent to saying that they have 'a reasonable moral psychology' which in turn lies behind what he refers to as 'the great civic virtues'. Among these virtues he mentions "the virtues of tolerance and being ready to meet others halfway, and the virtue of reasonableness and the sense of fairness. When these virtues are widespread in society and sustain its political conception of justice, they constitute a very great public good, part of society's political capital." (*ibid*, 157). But, one might still ask, when is a citizen a *reasonable* citizen? Rawls offers the following answer:

Citizens are reasonable when, viewing one another as free and equal in a system of social cooperation over generations, they are prepared to offer one another fair terms of social cooperation (defined by principles and ideals) and they agree to act on those terms, *even at the cost of their own interests* in particular situations, provided that others also accept those terms. (Rawls 2005, xlii; emphasis added).

Another way to elaborate on this is to say that citizens are reasonable, when in public life they think and act according to the *criterion of reciproc-*

ity which states that "our exercise of political power is proper only when we sincerely believe that the reasons we offer for our political action may reasonably be accepted by other citizens as a justification of those actions." (*ibid*, xliv). From another context we can get additional insight into the ideal that Rawls has in mind regarding reasonable citizens, and what is noteworthy about this example is that here the necessary gap between ideal and reality should be at its minimum: What I am hinting at is that Rawls has an interesting section called 'The Supreme Court as Exemplar of Public Reason' (cf. Rawls 2005, 231ff.). In this connection he makes the following point:

> To say that the court is the exemplar of public reason also means that it is the task of the justices to try to develop and express in their reasoned opinions the best interpretation of the constitution they can, using their knowledge of what the constitution and constitutional precedents require. [...] The justices cannot, of course, invoke their own personal morality, nor the ideals and virtues of morality generally. Those they must view as irrelevant. Equally, they cannot invoke their or other people's religious or philosophical views. (*ibid*, 236).

A similar idea emerges in another context where Rawls (1997, 444f.) asks the following question: "How, though, is the ideal of public reason realized by citizens who are not government officials? [...] To answer this question, we say that ideally citizens are to think of themselves *as if they were legislators* and ask themselves what statutes, supported by what reasons satisfying the criterion of reciprocity, they would think it most reasonable to enact."[78]

Reasonable Comprehensive Doctrines
In defining reasonable comprehensive doctrines, Rawls points to three main features:

> [It] is an exercise of theoretical reason: it covers the major religious, philosophical, and moral aspects of human life in a more or less consistent and coherent man-

---

78 See also Rawls (1997, 478): "Recall that public reason sees the office of citizen with its duty of civility as analogous to that of a judge with its duty of deciding cases."

ner. It organizes and characterizes recognized values so that they are compatible with one another and express an intelligible view of the world. [...] a reasonable comprehensive doctrine is also an exercise of practical reason. [...] Finally, a third feature is that while a reasonable comprehensive view is not necessarily fixed and unchanging, it normally belongs to, or draws upon, a tradition of thought and doctrine. Although stable over time, and not subject to sudden and unexplained changes, it tends to evolve slowly in the light of what, from its point of view, it sees as good and sufficient reasons. (Rawls 2005, 59).[79]

Rawls has, wisely it seems, restricted the political conception (NB: *not* philosophy) of PL to the bare minimum of the constitutional essentials and the basic principles of justice. By this move he hopes to attain two things: First, to be able to stay out of trouble, i.e. not having to get entangled with any of the comprehensive doctrines. In fact, we might say that this is Rawls' version of the constitutional *neutrality principle* in relation to religion, which again combines with the liberty of conscience guaranteeing citizens the right to form their own world view or comprehensive doctrine. In other words, the Rawls of PL wants to 'leave philosophy as it is' in order to remain *impartial*. Second, he hopes that the different comprehensive doctrines will freely endorse the political conception – precisely because its content is neutral with respect to each of the reasonable comprehensive doctrines.[80] Nonetheless, Rawls recognizes that there may be cases where, as he puts it, "we may eventually have to assert at least certain aspects of our own comprehensive religious or philosophical doctrine (by no means necessarily fully comprehensive). This will happen whenever someone insists, for example, that certain questions are so fundamental that to insure their being rightly settled justifies civil strife. The religious salvation

---

79 It seems clear that the ideal of an overlapping consensus (cf. next section) gets into trouble if a comprehensive doctrine sees itself as covering *everything* relating to society and politics. Consequently, Rawls must hope that the following situation prevails in practice: "[...] I have supposed that the comprehensive doctrines of most people are not fully comprehensive, and this allows scope for the development of an independent allegiance to the political conception that helps to bring about a consensus." (Rawls 2005, 168).

80 Significantly, Rawls states that "by avoiding comprehensive doctrines we try to bypass religion and philosophy's profoundest controversies so as to have some hope of uncovering a basis of a stable overlapping consensus." (Rawls 2005, 152).

of those holding a particular religion, or indeed the salvation of a whole people, may be said to depend on it. At this point we may have no alternative but to deny this, or to imply its denial and hence to maintain the kind of thing we had hoped to avoid." (Rawls 2005, 152).

I believe that we now know more or less what a *reasonable* comprehensive doctrine is. It is both internally and externally open to reasons and reasoning, and in this sense it is (at least to a certain degree) marked by what Habermas would call a fallibilistic consciousness. Moreover, it is willing to abide by the criterion of reciprocity. But when do we have the situation of being confronted with a doctrine that is *un*reasonable? To elucidate this, Rawls offers the following imaginary example which appears as a modern parallel to the Catholic church of the Middle Ages:

If it is said that outside the church there is no salvation, and therefore a constitutional regime cannot be accepted unless it is unavoidable, we must make some reply. (...) we say that such a doctrine is unreasonable: it proposes to use the public's political power – a power in which citizens have an equal share – to enforce a view bearing on constitutional essentials about which citizens as reasonable persons are bound to differ uncompromisingly. [...] Here it is important to stress that this reply does not say, for example, that the doctrine *extra ecclesiam nulla salus* is not true. Rather, it says that those who want to use the public's political power to enforce it are being unreasonable. (Rawls 2005, 138).

In 'The Idea of Public Reason Revisited' Rawls makes some remarks which supplement the above description. Thus, having (once again) outlined the ingredients of a constitutional democratic society he emphasizes that "all reasonable doctrines affirm such a society with its corresponding political institutions: equal basic rights and liberties for all citizens, including liberty of conscience and the freedom of religion." And then he adds: "On the other hand, comprehensive doctrines that cannot support such a democratic society are not reasonable. Their principles and ideals do not satisfy the criterion of reciprocity, and in various ways they fail to establish the equal basic liberties. As examples, consider the many fundamentalist religious doctrines, the doctrine of the divine right of monarchs and the various forms of aristocracy, and, not to be overlooked, the many instances of autocracy and dictatorship." (Rawls 1997, 483).

Overlapping Consensus and Stability for the Right Reasons

To recapitulate, Rawls assumes that citizens typically have to balance two sets of views: one being the particular person's comprehensive doctrine, and the other a political conception. Concerning the broader scale of society, however, we are faced with the fact of reasonable pluralism, and as we have seen, this is what prompted PL to search for ways of bringing about social unity and *stability*. To this end Rawls presents the following definition of an overlapping consensus: "In such a consensus, the reasonable doctrines endorse the political conception, each from its own point of view. Social unity is based on a consensus on the political conception; and stability is possible when the doctrines making up the consensus are affirmed by society's politically active citizens and the requirements of justice are not too much in conflict with citizens' essential interests as formed and encouraged by their social arrangements." (Rawls 2005, 134). It is important to see that Rawls' search for overlapping consensus is internally related to the overall aim of political liberalism, namely "to uncover the conditions of the possibility of a reasonable public basis of justification on fundamental political questions" (Rawls 2005, xix). But how is this possible? On the one hand we have public reason justifying the basic political conception, and on the other hand we have "the many nonpublic bases of justification belonging to the many comprehensive doctrines and acceptable only to those who affirm them" (*ibid*). Rawls, in fact, refers to this constellation as the *dualism* of political liberalism.[81] Again we must ask: Given this dualism, how can one hope to achieve sufficient public justification?

At this point it is necessary to mention what seems to be a tension or a lack of consistent terminology in Rawls' treatment of this central issue. What creates the impression of an unresolved tension is the puzzling fact that Rawls uses different expressions alongside each other, or at least in the same context. On the one hand we find the idea of *justification*. This concept, one would expect, is internally related to 'reason'.

---

81 "The dualism in political liberalism between the point of view of the political conception and the many points of view of comprehensive doctrines is not a dualism originating in philosophy. Rather, it originates in the special nature of democratic political culture as marked by reasonable pluralism." (Rawls 2005, xxi).

Nonetheless, Rawls seems to expect a justification issuing also from the comprehensive doctrines, and even to consider this necessary in order for us to have what he calls a 'full justification'. On the other hand, the more frequent expressions occurring in connection with the treatment of overlapping consensus are words like 'endorse', 'support' or 'affirm'. So how are we to understand the status and function of an overlapping consensus? To approach a possible answer let me begin by noting that the concept of justification is specified quite early in PL, namely in the section 'Fundamental Ideas' where a distinction between three types of justification is introduced. The same distinction recurs later in Rawls' 'Reply to Habermas', and I am going to look closer at this particular context, which is of special interest here, because Habermas has raised a question directly addressing the above mentioned tension. Paraphrased by Rawls the question is the following:

[H]e asks whether the doctrines belonging to the consensus further strengthen and deepen the justification of a freestanding conception; or whether they merely constitute a necessary condition of social stability. By these questions I take Habermas to ask, in effect: What bearing do doctrines within an overlapping consensus have on the justification of the political conception – once citizens see that conception as both reasonable and freestanding? (Rawls 2005, 385).

And this is precisely the issue: If the point of the political conception is that it is 'freestanding', why would it be in need of further justification from comprehensive doctrines? What kind of game is Rawls into here, 'justification' or merely 'stability'? This is ambiguous, at best, but the answer, as we shall see shortly, seems to be: both. Let us look first at Rawls' general reply and then, in turn, explain its major ingredients. The answer to the question/objection posed by Habermas lies, counters Rawls, "in the way in which political liberalism specifies three different kinds of justification and two kinds of consensus, and then connects these with the idea of stability for the right reasons, and with the idea of legitimacy." (*ibid*). But how is this to be understood?

The first kind is called a *pro tanto* justification. By this Rawls refers to the justification in public reason of the political conception, but, and this is the important point, taking into account only *political* values. Hence, this form of justification can never claim to be more than *pro tanto*, since "it may be overridden by citizen's comprehensive doctrines once all values are tallied up" (*ibid*, 386). What is lacking in this first kind of justification becomes clearer when Rawls goes on to introduce the second type: "full justification is carried out by an individual citizen as a member of civil society. (...) In this case, the citizen accepts a political conception and fills out its justification by embedding it in some way into the citizen's comprehensive doctrine as either true or reasonable, depending on what the doctrine allows." (*ibid*). But isn't the concept of justification at odds with speaking more loosely of 'embedding it in some way'? Or, to put it differently: What is the point in claiming 'full justification' when what is going on seems to be just a matter of establishing overlapping consensus? While in 'full' justification the emphasis is on the *individual* citizen, the third and final form of justification (called 'public justification') occurs when "*all* the reasonable members of political society carry out a justification of the shared political conception by embedding it in their several reasonable comprehensive views." (*ibid*, 387; emphasis by me).

Part of the confusion here stems from the question I raised earlier, namely whether the political conception, given its status as freestanding, is in need of further justification. In order to attain stability, a liberal democracy needs to search for the possibility of forming an overlapping consensus, but again that seems to be a different matter. To see that Rawls is ambiguous here, consider the following quotation:

Recall that a political conception of justice is *not dependent* of any particular comprehensive doctrine, including even agnostic ones. But even though a political conception of justice is freestanding, that does not mean that it cannot be *embedded* in various ways – or mapped, or inserted as a module – into the different doctrines citizens affirm. (*ibid*, emphasis by me).

The confusion may to some extent be dispelled by remembering that in some contexts Rawls distinguishes between the *presentation* of a political conception and its *justification*. The implicit point here seems to be that its freestanding character applies to its presentation (only?) which, in turn, does not preclude that it be in need of further justification. But this distinction seems not to apply to the above quotation, and even if it did,

I would still maintain that using expressions like 'embedded', or 'inserted as a module', points in the direction of a pragmatic overlapping consensus and not in the direction of a more ambitious, quasi-Habermasian project of justification. Nonetheless, as the following passage indicates, it seems important to Rawls to be able to hold the two ideas together, for, as he argues, "Only when there is a reasonable overlapping consensus can political society's political conception of justice be publicly – though never finally – justified." (*ibid*, 388).

The second aspect of Rawls' general answer to Habermas consists in distinguishing two kinds of consensus (none of them, incidentally, equivalent to what Habermas understands by consensus). Apparently, what Rawls is getting at here is simply to make it clear that overlapping consensus is not to be confused with the normal, everyday notion of politicians negotiating a compromise and reaching a consensus. In contrast to this, Rawls offers the following characteristic where he seems still to be struggling to hold on to the idea of justification:

The very different idea of consensus in political liberalism – the idea I call a *reasonable overlapping consensus* – is that the political conception of justice is worked out first as a freestanding view that can be justified *pro tanto* without looking to, or trying to fit, or even knowing what are, the existing comprehensive doctrines. It tries to put no obstacles in the path of all reasonable doctrines endorsing a political conception by eliminating from this conception any idea which goes beyond the political, and which not all reasonable doctrines could reasonably be expected to endorse (to do that violates the idea of reciprocity). When the political conception meets these conditions and is also complete, we hope the reasonable doctrines affirmed by reasonable citizens in society can support it, and that in fact it will have the capacity to shape those doctrines toward itself. (*ibid*, 389).

The most frequently word used by Rawls in this connection is 'endorse' or (as a variation) 'support'. But surely this is not the same as 'justify'? Further, in the above quotation Rawls reveals his *hope* that the political conception will be able to 'shape' the comprehensive doctrines 'toward itself'. Besides, 'hope' is a recurrent expression in connection with the idea of an overlapping consensus. But, one might want to ask, how much is covered by the ideal of an overlapping consensus, what is 'the depth and breadth' of it? To this relevant question Rawls answers that "the consensus goes down to the fundamental ideas within which justice as fairness is worked out [...] As for its breadth, it covers the principles and values of a political conception (in this case those of justice as fairness) and it applies to the basic structure as a whole." (*ibid*, 149).

A recurring theme in Rawls is his insistence that it is not sufficient that the adherents of differing comprehensive doctrines tolerate each other just to achieve the minimum of a *modus vivendi*.[82] To put it differently, when he points to the issue of stability as central aim of political liberalism, what he really means is stability *for the right reasons*.[83] Thus, what he contends is that "it is not sufficient that these doctrines accept a democratic regime merely as a *modus vivendi*. Rather, they must accept it as members of a reasonable overlapping consensus." (Rawls 2005, xxxvii f.). In fact, the concept of a reasonable overlapping consensus constitutes the counterpart to what is just a modus vivendi.[84] At the same time, Rawls (2005, 165) is well aware that we should probably assume that "a full overlapping consensus is never achieved but at best only approximated." Instead, he describes it as a *process* consisting of a number of steps. Nonetheless, the main point is that "in the overlapping consensus [...] the acceptance of the political conception is not a compromise between those holding different views, but rests on the totality of reasons specified within the comprehensive doctrine affirmed by each citizen" (170f.).

The fact that those comprehensive doctrines worthy of the predicate 'reasonable' do contain an amount of (non-public) *reasons* may of course point in the direction of non-public justification being necessary in order to achieve stability for the right *reasons*. This makes sense. Nonetheless, the dominant vocabulary used by Rawls ('endorsement') seems to point

---

82 As a historical example, Rawls (1997, 459) points to the strife between Catholics and Protestants in the 16th and 17th centuries "when the principle of toleration was honoured only as a *modus vivendi*."

83 Rawls (2005, xxxvii) reminds us that this phrase "does not occur in the text of PL, but 'stability' should usually be given that meaning in both *Theory* and PL, as the context determines."

84 Cf. Rawls 2005, 134: "I distinguish an overlapping consensus from a modus vivendi." See also pp. 146ff.

in a less ambitious direction. The same is true when he uses the word 'affirmation'.[85] While I cannot dissolve the tension or ambiguity inherent in Rawls' account, I venture instead to present a reading which may serve to make it at least somewhat understandable. My guess is that the emphasis on justification by comprehensive doctrines is partly a residue from *Theory* and partly an attempt to alleviate the concerns raised by Habermas' critique. This reading is corroborated by the fact that in Rawls' later comments on PL (fx the introduction to the paperback edition), and particularly in 'The Idea of Public Reason Revisited', the concept of justification is *not* being used. Here, it is sufficient for Rawls to state that: "A reasonable judgment of the political conception must still be *confirmed* as true, or right, by the comprehensive doctrine." (Rawls 1997, 483; my emphasis). At the end of this chapter I shall return to the matter of a 'Kantian' vs. a 'pragmatic' reading of Rawlsian political liberalism.

The Public Political Forum and Public Reason

With the central idea of *public reason* Rawls, apparently, wants to remind us that in spite of the fact of reasonable pluralism there is something that we do have and should have in common, namely the domain covered by public reason. In presenting this idea he is aware, however, that there may be those who simply reject it:

The idea of public reason specifies at the deepest level the basic moral and political values that are to determine a constitutional democratic government's relation to its citizens and their relation to one another. In short, it concerns how the political relation is to be understood. Those who reject constitutional democracy with its criterion of reciprocity will of course reject the very idea of public reason. For them the political relation may be that of friend or foe, to those of a particular religious or secular community or those who are not; or it may be a relentless struggle to win the world for the whole truth. Political liberalism does not engage those who think this way. The zeal to embody the whole

---

85 As in the following example: "Citizens affirm the ideal of public reason, not as a result of political compromise, as in a modus vivendi, but from within their own reasonable doctrines." (Rawls 2005, 218).

truth in politics is incompatible with an idea of public reason that belongs with democratic citizenship. (Rawls 1997, 441f.).[86]

At the same time, it is important to note that public reason "neither criticizes nor attacks any comprehensive doctrine, religious or nonreligious, except insofar as that doctrine is incompatible with the essentials of public reason and a democratic polity. The basic requirement is that a reasonable doctrine accepts a constitutional democratic regime and its companion idea of legitimate law." (*ibid*, 441). Again, why should this simple willingness to *accept* be tantamount to comprising the necessity of a 'full' or 'public' justification?

As to the *contents* of public reason, Rawls wants us to understand this as a political conception of justice consisting of three elements: "first, it specifies certain basic rights, liberties, and opportunities" [...] "second, it assigns a special priority to these rights, liberties, and opportunities" [...] "and third, it affirms measures assuring all citizens adequate all-purpose means to make effective use of their basic liberties and opportunities." (Rawls 2005, 223). In the somewhat later development of his thinking, I believe it's important to appreciate that Rawls becomes increasingly open and broad-minded when reflecting on the contents of public reason and political liberalism. Thus, if we turn to 'The Idea of Public Reason Revisited' and look at the section on 'The Content of Public Reason', we find the following statement:

[T]he content of public reason is given by a family of political conceptions of justice, and not by a single one. There are many liberalisms and related views, and therefore many forms of public reason specified by a family of reasonable political conceptions. Of these, justice as fairness, whatever its merits, is but one. The lim-

---

86 And in the same vein: "Of course, fundamentalist religious doctrines and autocratic and dictatorial rulers will reject the ideas of public reason and deliberative democracy. They will say that democracy leads to a culture contrary to their religion, or denies the values that only autocratic or dictatorial rule can secure. They assert that the religiously true, or the philosophically true, overrides the politically reasonable. We simply say that such a doctrine is politically unreasonable. Within political liberalism nothing more need be said." (Rawls 1997, 488).

iting feature of these forms is *the criterion of reciprocity*, viewed as applied between free and equal citizens, themselves seen as reasonable and rational. [...]

Each of these liberalisms endorses the underlying ideas of citizens as free and equal persons and of society as a fair system of cooperation over time. (Rawls 1997, 450f.; emphasis added).

This is a surprisingly open view, and as we can see, the criterion of reciprocity takes center stage in delimiting this 'family' of political conceptions.[87]

It is important for Rawls to emphasize that he makes a distinction between the *idea* of public reason on the one hand, and its *ideal* on the other. This latter "is realized, or satisfied, whenever judges, legislators, chief executives, and other government officials, as well as candidates for public office, act from and follow the idea of public reason and explain to other citizens their reasons for supporting fundamental political positions in terms of the political conception of justice they regard as the most reasonable. In this way they fulfill what I shall call their duty of civility to one another and to other citizens." (*ibid*, 444).

I believe one should appreciate and grant that this ideal may well exert its influence (not least because it may always be invoked and appealed to), even when at the same time we realize that the actual, day-to-day business of politics (inevitably?) falls short of this ideal. Rawls himself is also fully aware of this. Thus, in a context where he has referred to 'sensible proposals' for remedying things in the social and medical sector, he continues in a way that reveals his dissatisfaction with American politics: "But as things are, those who follow the 'great game of politics' know that none of these sensible proposals will be accepted. The same story can be told about the importance of support for international institutions (such as the United Nations), foreign aid properly spent, and concern for human rights at home and abroad. In constant pursuit of money to finance campaigns, the political system is

---

87 In the same context Rawls (451f.) adds that "For instance, political liberalism also admits Habermas's discourse conception of legitimacy (sometimes said to be radically democratic rather than liberal), as well as Catholic views of the common good and solidarity when they are expressed in terms of political values."

simply unable to function. Its deliberative powers are paralyzed." (*ibid*, 449f.).

Since in its scope public reason is limited to the public political forum,[88] we must surely ask: What about the rest of society? For logically, when public reason pertains only to the rather limited public political forum, there must also be something else. This is what Rawls calls the *background culture* and characterizes as "associations such as churches and universities" (Rawls 2005, 215).[89] In what seems to me an important footnote, he informs us that we should actually conceive of society as consisting of *three* interacting spheres, namely 1) the public sphere of politics, 2) the background culture, and mediating between them 3) the *non-public* political culture:

The background culture includes, then, the culture of churches and associations of all kinds, and institutions of learning at all levels, especially universities and professional schools, scientific and other societies. In addition, the nonpublic political culture mediates between the public political culture and the background culture. This comprises media – properly so named – of all kinds: newspapers, reviews and magazines, television and radio, and much else. (Rawls 1997, 443f.).

Provided that public reason is functioning and doing its 'work of reconciliation' (Rawls 2005, 157) we may regard constitutional democracy as a *deliberative* democracy characterized by the 'the idea of deliberation' itself. What Rawls (1997, 448) assumes here is "the knowledge and desire on the part of citizens generally to follow public reason and to realize its ideal in their political conduct." At the same time, however, he is also aware that "without widespread education in the basic aspects of constitutional democratic government" (*ibid*, 449) this will not be possible to realize.

Finally, in outlining public reason Rawls makes the important point that public reason should be distinguished from 'secular reason' and

---

88 According to Rawls (1997, 443), the public political forum may be divided into three parts: 1) the discourse of judges in their decisions, 2) the discourse of government officials, and 3) the discourse of candidates for public office.
89 He also refers to it as 'the culture of civil society' (Rawls 1997, 443).

'secular values'.[90] This, of course, is yet another way of underlining that PL does not represent a secularist position.

The Role of Religion in the Public

When discussing the role of religion (more specifically: religious arguments) in the public, the basic tenor of Rawls' treatment seems to be 'How open can we be towards religion?' Recall, also, that Rawls has no wish to get 'entangled' with religion – unless this turns out to be absolutely necessary. In spite of this general spirit of openness and impartiality, however, a liberalist position is frequently criticized for as it were relegating and confining religion to 'the private sphere'. In order to counter this widespread prejudice, let us take our point of departure in the fact that Rawls explicitly distances himself from the public-private distinction. Instead, as we have seen, he distinguishes between *public* and *non-public* reasons. Concerning the latter, he specifies that they "comprise the many reasons of civil society and belong to what I have called the 'background culture', in contrast with the public political culture. These reasons are social, and *certainly not private*" (Rawls 2005, 220; emphasis by me). And in a footnote he dispels any remaining doubts on the part of the reader by explicitly stating: "The public vs. nonpublic distinction is not the distinction between public and private. This latter I ignore: there is no such thing as private reason" (*ibid*).

But, as one might expect, openness and impartiality cannot be the whole story. Obviously, there must also be the other side of the coin, namely the degree of constraints and limits imposed on comprehensive doctrines, including religion. Famous in this regard is Rawls' so called *proviso* which he introduces in the following way:

To engage in public reason is to appeal to one of these political conceptions – to their ideals and principles, standards and values – when debating fundamental political questions. This requirement still allows us to introduce into political

---

90 "For I define secular reason as reasoning in terms of comprehensive nonreligious doctrines. Such doctrines and values are much too broad to serve the purposes of public reason. Political values are not moral doctrines, however available or accessible these may be to our reason and common sense reflection. Moral doctrines are on a level with religion and first philosophy." (Rawls 1997, 452).

discussion at any time our comprehensive doctrine, religious or nonreligious, provided that, in due course, we give properly public reasons to support the principles and policies our comprehensive doctrine is said to support. I refer to this requirement as the *proviso*, (…) (Rawls 1997, 453).

But will religious people settle for this? Rawls is aware that this may present a problem, and therefore he poses the following variation on his formulation of the basic problem for political liberalism: "How is it possible for citizens of faith to be wholehearted members of a democratic society […]? Expressed more sharply: How is it possible – or is it – for those of faith, as well as the nonreligious (secular), to endorse a constitutional regime even when their comprehensive doctrines may not prosper under it, and indeed may decline?" (*ibid*, 458f.). The addition 'or is it?' clearly signals that in actual fact the overlapping consensus needed may be difficult to achieve. But of course Rawls believes that there is in fact a solution; this lies in the assumption (or hope?) that the religious citizens will realize that their liberty depends on their granting the same liberty and opportunities to all other members of society. And thus we get the following response: "Here the answer lies in the religious or nonreligious doctrine's understanding and accepting that, except by endorsing a reasonable constitutional democracy, there is no other way fairly to ensure the liberty of its adherents consistent with the equal liberties of other reasonable free and equal citizens." (Rawls 1997, 460).

And Rawls even offers a concrete proposal as to how a given religious doctrine could perhaps square this constraint in relation to its transcendent source of authority: "In endorsing a constitutional democratic regime, a religious doctrine may say that *such are the limits God sets to our liberty.*" (*ibid*, 460; emphasis by me).[91] Will this be possible? Yes, I believe it will (albeit probably not for the 'Abrahams' of this world), remembering that the only forms of religion that PL engages are the *reasonable* comprehensive doctrines. Furthermore, we might recall here Rawls' assumption that these are not *fully* comprehensive, and therefore should be able to accommodate and accomplish a balance with the political conception of a democratic society.

---

91 Cf. also Rawls 1997, 484 where this expression is repeated.

The *proviso* is the central element in what Rawls has come to call the 'Wide View' of public political culture, and this expression is in itself indicative of his concern to be as open as possible.[92] But how should we more specifically understand the *proviso*, – what does it imply? First, Rawls (1997, 463) makes it clear that "the introduction into public political culture of religious and secular doctrines, provided the proviso is met, does not change the nature and content of justification in public reason itself."[93] It may change *something*, however, for the wide view "recognizes that the roots of democratic citizens' allegiance to their political conceptions lie in their respective comprehensive doctrines, both religious and nonreligious. In this way citizens' allegiance to the democratic ideal of public reason is strengthened for the right reasons." (*ibid*, 463). This, I believe, should be considered an important recognition on the part of political liberalism. Returning for a moment to the discussion above regarding the ambiguity in Rawls (justification vs. pragmatic endorsement), I take this as further evidence that he ought to be talking about *motivation* ('roots of allegiance') rather than justification. If this is a correct interpretation, we would have something parallel to Habermas' distinction between justification and motivation.

More or less in the same vein, Rawls points to the fact that there may be *positive* reasons for introducing comprehensive doctrines into the sphere of public reason. What citizens should appreciate here, is that they all benefit from being 'forced' (under the proviso) to recognize and

---

92 As an example of the wide view Rawls (1997, 456) points to the story of the Good Samaritan. This is in itself interesting, since this story is often invoked by religious people wanting to urge the point that constitutional democracy in reality has Christian roots. To this story Rawls comments: "Are the values appealed to properly political values and not simply religious or philosophical values? While the wide view of public political culture allows us, in making a proposal, to introduce the Gospel story, public reason requires us to *justify* our proposal in terms of proper political values." (emphasis by me).

93 Also, it deserves to be noted that "there are no restrictions or requirements on how religious or secular doctrines are themselves to be expressed; these doctrines need not, for example, be by some standards logically correct, or open to rational appraisal, or evidentially supportable. Whether they are or not is a matter to be decided by those presenting them, and how they want what they say to be taken. They will normally have practical reasons for wanting to make their views acceptable to a broader audience." (*ibid*).

better understand each others comprehensive doctrine.[94] Nonetheless, Rawls is, of course, well aware that there may be a host of possible questions and objections to the proviso. As far as the questions are concerned (*when* must the proviso be satisfied, and *who* has the obligation to do it?), his answer is that details like this "must be worked out in practice and cannot feasibly be governed by a clear family of rules given in advance" (*ibid*, 462). Regarding the objections ('Does it not unreasonably limit...' or 'is it not too restrictive'?), he points to the example of school prayer and says that those who assume that PL would automatically reject this practice are actually wrong. What he finds, however, is that this example "serves to emphasize that the principles that support the separation of church and state should be such that they can be affirmed by all free and equal citizens, given the fact of reasonable pluralism." (*ibid*, 476). And, immediately following, he makes a comment on the reasons underlying the separation of church and state:

The reasons for the separation of church and state are these, among others: It protects religion from the state and the state from religion; it protects citizens from their churches and citizens from one another. [...It is] a grave error to think that the separation of church and state is primarily for the protection of secular culture; of course it does protect that culture, but no more so than it protects all religions. (Rawls 1997, 476).

If we look at the ideal of an overlapping consensus in terms of the *values* at stake, Rawls engages in an interesting thought experiment regarding the ranking of values in a religious, comprehensive doctrine:

Thus, suppose we call *transcendent* such values as salvation and eternal life – the *Visio Dei*. This value, let's say, is higher, or superior to, the reasonable political values of a constitutional democratic society. These are worldly values and therefore on a different, and as it were lower, plane than those transcendent values.

---

94 "These benefits of the mutual knowledge of citizens' recognizing one another's reasonable comprehensive doctrines bring out a positive ground for introducing such doctrines, which is not merely a defensive ground, as if their intrusion into public discussion were inevitable in any case." (*ibid*, 464).

It doesn't follow, however, that these lower yet reasonable values are overridden by the transcendent values of the religious doctrine. In fact, a *reasonable* comprehensive doctrine is one in which they are not overridden; it is the unreasonable doctrines in which reasonable political values are overridden. (*ibid*, 483).

As is easy to discern, this quotation is of considerable relevance to the investigation of this book. For what we have here is something like a litmus test of religious doctrines and positions. And if we apply it to the Abraham of Genesis 22, it is clear that part of the appalling character of his deed stems from the fact that *by our standards*, and by the test proposed by Rawls, Abraham clearly acts according to an unreasonable comprehensive doctrine. Furthermore, we may deduce that those who interpret Islam to the consequence that a religiously based *sharia* law overrides the political values of a democratic society also represent an unreasonable comprehensive doctrine. In fact, what Rawls demands of the religious, namely *separating* their views (into 'political conception' and 'comprehensive doctrine) and then *balancing* them, seems to go directly against those religious manifestations, of a more or less fundamentalist nature, that insist on seeing religion and politics as one, integrated world-view.

And apparently, Rawls has felt this a hard bullet to bite for a great many religious people, for he immediately continues by repeating his soothing admonition: "Recall that it was said: In endorsing a constitutional democratic regime, a religious doctrine may say that such are the limits God sets to our liberty." (*ibid*, 484). And on closer scrutiny I think we may conclude that this is more than just a proposal on Rawls' part, for when all is said and done, this seems to be the *only* avenue for those among the religious who have problems aligning their political and religious commitments. For we can well imagine that many of them would be inclined to react like this: 'Well, we do not *like* the political system, but we *tolerate* it and live by it, because (at least for the time being) this is what seems to be in the best interest of our religious community. But as we know, this option is ruled out by Rawls, since it (at best) qualifies only as a *modus vivendi* and falls short of the desired stability (based on endorsement) 'for the right reasons'. At the same time, one is led to wonder whether the interpretation 'Such are the limits God sets to our liberty' does in fact meet the requirement of stability for the right reasons.

Is it more than a half-hearted, luke-warm endorsement? Maybe it is, and maybe it's not.

In concluding, however, Rawls (1997, 486) assures us that "[t]here is, or need be, no war between religion and democracy." In addition, I would like to point to some statements in a letter (printed in Rawls 1997, 438f.) which in July 1998 he wrote to his publisher. Here, Rawls talks about his work in progress for a revised edition of *Political Liberalism* and reveals that he has "incorporated at various places almost all of 'The Idea of Public Reason Revisited'" (*ibid*, 438) which he himself considers "by far the best statement I have written on ideas of public reason and political liberalism" (*ibid*). Most people would no doubt agree. But then he continues with what seems to me an interesting comment on the contents of this important article:

It contains a number of new ideas and alters greatly the nature of the role of public reason. In particular, I stress the relation of public reason and political liberalism to the major religions that are based on the authority of the church and sacred text, and therefore are not themselves liberal. Nevertheless, I hold that, except for fundamentalism, they can support a constitutional democratic regime. This is true for Catholicism (since Vatican II) and much of Protestantism, Judaism and Islam. Thus, public reason and political liberalism have considerable relevance to highly contested questions of our contemporary world. (*ibid*).

Suffice it to say that in the years since Rawls' death (in 2002) their 'considerable relevance' has not diminished and the questions have not become less contested. Besides, I find it interesting that Rawls himself clearly states that his 1997-article ('The Idea', etc.) "alters greatly the nature of the role of public reason". And I take this as indicating a development in his thinking from a more 'Kantian' to a more 'pragmatic' position.

Habermas: Deliberative Democracy and Religion
In 2005 when Jürgen Habermas was once again awarded a prize, this time the prestigious Holberg Prize (also known as the 'Nobel Prize of the Humanities'), the Norwegian organizers had prior to the event itself placed a 5-minute sample of an interview on the internet, so that everyone would have the chance of getting a 'live' impression of Habermas. In this

interview he was asked what he himself considered the common theme of his work, and in answer to this he pointed to the idea of democracy as the 'red thread' (German: 'roter Faden') of his sociological and philosophical thinking. This of course has biographical reasons: Born in 1929, Habermas has experienced the rise and fall of Nazism, and in 1944, when he was only fifteen years he was enrolled in the military – just like so many other German boys his age.

Democracy and Its Foundation
In considering democracy and its foundation, Habermas makes a comparison between a liberal and a republican version of democracy. Whereas the *liberal* conception regards politics as a battle for positions fought by parties acting strategically, the *republican* conception focuses on public communication and parties aiming to reach mutual understanding. In each case a different paradigm forms the basis: For the liberal version of democracy it is the free market, and for the republican version it is that of a conversation. Now, in light of Habermas' theory of communicative action one is hardly surprised to find that he tends to favour the republican model – and of course in a Kantian version.[95] This notwithstanding, he acknowledges that there are both pros and cons to this model. The advantage he sees in the fact that it incorporates a vision of democratic self-organizing through a bond of communicating groups and individuals; the backdrop, on the other hand, is that it may be considered too idealistic. Why? For one thing because it makes the democratic process dependent on the virtues of citizens having the common good as their primary concern (cf. Habermas 1996, 282f.).

Therefore, Habermas proposes a third model, that of a *deliberative* democracy which should also encompass the whole of civil society.[96] Its

---

95 Cf. also the following statement, "Political liberalism (which I am defending in the special form of a Kantian republicanism) understands itself as a non-religious and post-metaphysical justification of the normative foundations of the democratic, constitutional state." (Habermas 2005, 107; my translation). To the distinction between political liberalism (Rawls) and Kantian republicanism (Habermas), see also Habermas 1996, 126.

96 Concepts like 'deliberative democracy' and 'civil society', obviously, are extensively debated within political philosophy and in need of further clarification. For a helpful discussion see Hendriks (2006).

starting point is the recognition that the important thing is to institution-alize forms of communication enabling the widest possible participation in deliberating political issues. The normative core, in other words, is the 'procedural' way of reaching consensus which we also find in Habermas' version of moral theory, i.e. that of discourse ethics. Habermas offers the following comment on the relation of deliberative democracy to the liberal and the republican conception: "Discourse theory adopts elements from both sides and integrates them into the concept of an ideal procedure for consideration and decision-making. This *democratic procedure* establishes an internal connection between *negotiations* and *discourses of self-understanding* and *justice,* and it provides grounds for the assumption that under such conditions it may be possible to reach reasonable and fair results." (*ibid,* 285f.; my translation). In particular, it is necessary to institutionalize democratic, communicative procedures in order to enable 'solidarity' to maintain itself vis à vis the media of money and administrative power (*ibid,* 289). Also, the constitutional institutionalization of democracy presupposes basic liberal and political rights. In other words, democracy and human rights cannot be regarded independently of one another.

One question that concerns Habermas (and is important for under-standing his position towards religion) is whether the democratic state can provide its own legitimation. In fact, this was the subject which Habermas chose for his discussion with Cardinal Ratzinger (now pope Benedict XVI) in January 2004. The answer seems to be yes and no. Yes, because the communicative rationality and the procedure of discourse are sufficient to ensure that laws and political decisions are justified and being accepted as legitimate by the citizens. But the answer tends to be 'No', if we look at the *motivational* side and take into account the attitudes (Rawls: 'civic virtues' and affirmation/endorsement from within one's comprehensive doctrine) that citizens should display. The point here is that these virtues must be socialized into each and every citizen, and this fact alone makes democracy dependent on its citizens' ethical and cultural forms of life (life-world and background culture). In short, as Habermas (2005, 9) puts it, "In the long run, the liberal state is dependent on mentalities that it is unable to produce from its own resources" (my translation).

What is Implied in 'Secularization'?

At this point we have the opportunity to return to the discussion about secularization in the previous chapter, albeit now in relation to Habermas' later thinking with its more positive approach to religion. On the more general level, we may say that the notion of 'secularization' implies giving an account of how 'the sacred' or 'religion' is related to the historical process which in the West is often understood as 'rationalization' or 'modernization'. There are at least two elements here: One is the possibility that religion may itself have been conducive to the process of secularization, and the other is to understand how the present manifestations of religion have themselves been decisively shaped by this process. In other words: where are we, and how did we get there? To Habermas, it is obvious that the signature of *modernity* is to be found in the 18th century Enlightenment project which in turn is epitomized in Kant's philosophy with its distinction between theoretical and practical reason. To this corresponds the differentiation between three distinct value spheres: 1) science (cognitive rationality), 2) morality and justice (moral rationality), and 3) art and self-representations in general (aesthetic-expressive rationality). But what about *religion* which seems nowhere to be found in this tri-partite account of the different value spheres of cultural modernity? This question effectively spurred the development of philosophy of religion in its modern sense. Kant's answer, having cut the ground beneath the traditional proofs of God's existence, was to present 'God' as a necessary postulate arising from the aporias of practical reason.[97] Let us take a look at how Habermas in his more recent works reacts to this important question.

A good place to start is the interview entitled 'Ein Gespräch über Gott und die Welt' (Habermas 2001a). Here, Habermas makes it clear that in his opinion religion (i.e. Christianity) has in more than one respect exercised a formative role in the cultural modernization of the West. Already the idea of a monotheistic God is an expression of a cognitive level of abstraction which, according to Habermas, enabled the human mind to entertain two important idealizing moves: On the one hand to regard

---

97 Other reactions and answers are to be found in Hegel, Schleiermacher, and Kierkegaard (cf. Habermas 2005, 238ff.)

'nature' as an entire object for investigation, and on the other hand to view the social world as a potentially universal community of persons created in the image of God.[98] More specifically, Habermas (2001a, 175) speaks in this context of an 'egalitarian universalism' that derives directly from ancient Jewish and Christian ideas of justice and brotherly love.[99] To sum up, Habermas gives Christianity and the church credit for having performed, with a German phrase, 'bedeutende Schrittmacherdienste', i.e. having set the course for the mentality which was conducive to cultural modernization. Whether this development is to be seen as irreversible and evolutionary or not, is a question to which we shall return shortly.

Concerning the effects of the historical process of secularization on religion, Habermas is quite clear that in modern society religion can no longer serve as the normative foundation of a public morality shared by all citizens. Instead, as emphasized by Rawls, what we find is the fact of pluralism. For Habermas (1996, 20), this thoroughgoing devaluation of metaphysical core concepts necessarily implies that moral philosophy must be content with relying on a *post-metaphysical* level of argumentation. Recognizing that there is a certain amount of loss connected to this, Habermas encourages us to accept the profound change in what it means that something is normatively binding. Under post-metaphysical conditions, normativity can only be 'produced' or be the result of a process of impartial judging and weighing of arguments. When the perspective has once and for all shifted from God to man, 'validity' becomes a predicate we apply to those moral norms that are accepted by all that are affected by it (cf. *ibid*, 51f.).

Within this development there also took place what Habermas calls a modernization of faith itself. Going on since the Reformation and Enlightenment, this modernization may be seen as a response to three challenges: "the fact of pluralism, the emergence of modern science, and the spread of positive law and a profane morality" (*ibid*, 14; my translation). These challenges require that an "arduous work of hermeneutic

---

98 Clearly, what Habermas points to here is a markedly *positive* feature of monotheism which Jan Assmann (cf. Chapter One) did not recognise.

99 Habermas (2001a, 187) is also prepared to admit that his own theory of communicative action – with its implied *telos* of mutual understanding – may be considered a late product of a Christian heritage.

self-reflection must be undertaken from within religious traditions. In our culture, it has essentially been performed by theology" (*ibid*, 15f.; my translation).

Well aware that religions that rely on revelation are transmitted in the form of dogma and creeds, Habermas nonetheless maintains that "in the West, the Christian teachings have been developed by the conceptual means and in the scholastic forms of philosophy into an academic (German: 'wissenschaftlich') theology. This internal rationalization has paved the way for a cognitive change that – despite the ambivalences of Luther himself – in the wake of the Reformation movement has led to a reflective mode of faith" (Habermas 2001a, 176; my translation).[100] In other words, faith in modernity is a *reflective* faith characterized by the following features:

- Being self-critical;
- Being non-exclusive (accepting pluralism);
- Relativizing one's own point of view.[101]

Immediately following, Habermas compares this reflective mode of faith with the reasonable comprehensive doctrines of Rawls:

The reflective consciousness which has learned to look at itself with the eyes of the others is also constitutive for the rationality of what John Rawls has termed 'reasonable comprehensive doctrines'. This carries the important political implication that the believers are able to know why they must forsake violence, in particular violence organized by the state, as a means of establishing the truth of their religion. As far as this is concerned, what we might call the 'modernization of faith' is a necessary cognitive condition for enforcing religious tolerance and establishing a neutral state power. (Habermas 2001a, 177; my translation).

---

100 Obviously, Habermas has been the subject of extensive debates among theologians. See Arens (1989), and more recently Adams (2006) and Henriksen (2007).

101 For a slightly different formulation see Habermas (2001b, 14) where it is said that believers in a pluralistic society must reflect on their position in three steps: First, they should be able to cope with the cognitive dissonance arising from their encounter with other confessions and religions. Second, they must adjust to the authority of science, and, finally, they must accept the premises of the constitutional state.

Thus, on the one hand what we have in modern societies is a reflective and reasonable faith which should have no particular problems in adjusting to the demands of a democratic, pluralistic society. But this is not all, for on the other hand we encounter the face of a fundamentalist religion (be it Christian, Muslim or any other). Habermas, who repeatedly displays his awareness that fundamentalism is a *modern* phenomenon, offers the following definition: "Fundamentalist is the label we apply to religious movements that, existing under the cognitive limitations of modern conditions, nonetheless propagate or even practice the return to the exclusivity of pre-modern attitudes of faith" (*ibid*).[102] Note in this connection the words 'return' and 'pre-modern': there is an irreversible development at work here. In another context where he comments on the founding father of modern, protestant theology, Friedrich Schleiermacher, Habermas further notes that Schleiermacher has paved the way for "the consciousness of a post-secular society that is adjusting itself to the continued existence of religion in a continually secularizing environment" (Habermas 2005, 251; my translation). In other words, secularization continues.

From a Theory of Evolution to Historical 'Learning Processes'
In the now famous debate with former cardinal Ratzinger, Habermas (2005, 107) proposes to regard the continuing secularization of culture and society as 'a double learning process' which has forced both religion and the Enlightenment tradition to reflect on their respective borders. Below, when we turn to focus on Habermas' perspective on the current role of religion, we shall see what this entails for his view on the relation between religious and secular citizens, and the role of religious arguments in the public sphere. In fact, whereas the 'early' Habermas spoke of the logic and dynamics of evolution (cf. last chapter), he now speaks more cautiously of 'historical learning processes'. We shall see shortly that this

---

102 Consider also the following characterization: "Fundamentalist movements may be understood as the ironic attempt – with restorative means – to accord ultra-stability to one's own life-world. The irony consists in a traditionalism that misunderstands itself. Although it arose from the process of society's modernization, it nonetheless imitates a collapsed substantiality. As a reaction to the overwhelming drive toward modernization, fundamentalism represents a completely modern movement of renewal." (Habermas 1996, 261; my translation. Cf. also Habermas 2001b, 10).

change in perspective is internally connected with his more positive and sympathetic stance towards religion in general.

To get the broader picture, we may begin by noting that Habermas has realized (much like Rawls and Audi) that the democratic state relies on an ethic of civic virtues. Far from being something that we may take for granted, the realization of this civic ethic presupposes that religious and secular citizens have gone through complementary learning processes. This, basically, involves two things. One is that a sufficient number of citizens have reached the reflective and self-critical mentality inaugurated by philosophical modernity; if this is not the case, the political integration of society will, according to Habermas, be in danger. The other assumption connected to the idea of a 'learning process' is that we are dealing with a cognitive process with a specific direction. Now, Habermas is aware that these two premises of a learning process rest on a specific self-understanding of modernity. And this, in turn, can (only?) be defended as a theory of societal evolution (cf. Habermas 2005, 151). Realizing, however, that this kind of theory is likely to cause controversy, Habermas offers another kind of argument why he has, apparently, given up all arguments based on the evolution of society. The important point seems to be that we have no right to imply that citizens of a liberal state "should describe themselves from the perspective of a theory of religious evolution, and, if that were the case, in light of this label themselves as cognitively 'backwards'. Only those involved, and their religious organisations, should decide the question whether a 'modernized' faith may still qualify as 'true' faith." (*ibid*, 152; my translation). What matters now (in contrast to the 'early' Habermas) is that political theory must proceed under a double self-limitation. Says Habermas, "If political theory must leave it an open question whether the functionally necessary mentalities can be achieved at all by way of learning processes, it must also recognize that its normative conception of the public use of reason will remain 'essentially controversial' among citizens themselves" (*ibid*; my translation).

What has replaced Habermas' earlier conviction that western rationalization has followed a path marked by a certain evolutionary logic is the picture of a 'genealogy of reason' with embedded learning processes. What is important here is to realize that religion and philosophy have a common origin in the revolution of world-views that took place in the so called 'axial age'. Habermas summarizes the consequences of this as follows:

> If religious and metaphysical world-views have initiated similar learning processes, both modes, faith and knowledge, with their traditions based in Jerusalem and Athens, belong to the history of the origin of secular reason in whose medium the sons and daughters of modernity today are coming to terms regarding their position in the world. This modern reason will only learn to understand itself, when it clarifies its position toward the contemporary, reflective religious consciousness and realizes the common origin of both complementary forms of spirit from the thrust of the axial age. In speaking of complementary forms of spirit, I turn against two positions – on the one hand against a narrow-minded Enlightenment that denies religion any reasonable content, but also against Hegel for whom religion represents a form of spirit well worth remembering, but only in the manner of an 'imaginative thinking' subordinate to philosophy. (...) Secularization has not so much the function of a filter constantly excluding traditional contents, but rather that of a transformer constantly changing the current of tradition. (Habermas 2007, 2; my translation).

The Distinction between Faith and Knowledge

In 2001, at a ceremony where Habermas was awarded the peace prize of German book-sellers, he chose to speak on the classic subject of faith vs. knowledge.[103] Shortly after the fateful event of 9/11, Habermas makes no secret of his dismay and concern that the announced 'war on terror' will imply the return of politics in the neo-Hobbesian version of a globalized security-state where police, secret intelligence agencies, and the military take center stage. The important point, according to Habermas, is that in order to avoid a war between cultures we, in the West, must recognize our own ambivalences toward secularization and realize the proper meaning of secularization in a post-secular society. What is important for handling disagreements concerning political issues is that citizens meet the fact of

---

103 Looking back, Habermas (2007, 2) states that "The motivation behind my being occupied with the theme of faith and knowledge is the wish to mobilize modern reason against the defaitism lurking in itself" (my translation).

value pluralism on the basis of a *fallibilistic* consciousness, i.e. knowing that you could be wrong – and your opponent right. To this corresponds a notion of the state which, being strictly neutral towards differing world views, harbours a public reason willing to learn from both sides. So what does it mean that the dynamics of secularization continue, as we have noted above? It means that although open and willing to learn, the communicative rationality of public reason as the end result ('im Ergebnis') forces citizens to distance themselves from strong traditions and the content of world-views (cf. Habermas 2001b, 15).

Thus, as intermediary between the traditional adversaries of religion and science, faith and knowledge, Habermas places the common sense of everyday language. Obviously, this is far from being a fixed entity. On the contrary, it is continually being enlightened and rationalized by the discoveries of science. However, it is important for Habermas to emphasize that it will never be possible to scientifically 'naturalize' the linguistic common sense rationality. (Examples of this kind of scientist 'faith' Habermas dismisses as simply bad philosophy.) The reason for this is that this rationality has its basis in each individual's freedom to say 'yes' or 'no' to the communicative claims made by one's interlocutor. Despite the necessary distance that public, communicative reason upholds toward religious traditions, it acknowledges at the same time that even a post-secular society saps into the normative contents of religion. More than this, Habermas (2001b, 22f.) recognizes that the moral foundations of the liberal state are religious in origin. Further, Habermas (2001a, 192) speaks of the 'philosophical program of translation' (of the semantic contents of religion).

It is no coincidence that Habermas' recent book is entitled *Zwischen Naturalismus und Religion*, for this is precisely where he wants to position his social philosophy of communicative rationality. It remains open and willing to learn from both naturalistic science and religion, but at the same time it insists on maintaining a necessary distance. This question of a sensibility for 'borders' reflects Habermas' awareness that both science and religion have a potential for reductionism or totalitarianism. But at the same time it signals his attempt to secure a central role for a post-metaphysical and fallibilistic philosophy which renders society the important service of *interpreting* insights from both science and religion.[104] This favoured type of philosophy is characterized by Habermas in the following way:

The secular counter-piece to a religious consciousness that has become reflective is a post-metaphysical thinking which demarcates itself in two directions. On the one hand, on agnostic premises it refrains from judging about religious truths and insists (without any polemical intentions) on maintaining strict borders between faith and knowledge. On the other hand it opposes a positivistic reductionism in the concept of reason as well as the exclusion of religious teachings from the genealogy of reason. (Habermas 2005, 147; my translation).

The Role of Religion Revisited

In Chapter Four we got acquainted with the 'early' Habermas of the 70ies and 80ies who tended to see religion either as embedded in the evolution of world-views or as evaporating into communicative rationality. Since then the picture has changed, and what we find (and have already encountered above) is a Habermas who is much more sympathetic and sensitive not only to the historical and contemporary role of religion, but also to the demands of the 'believers' themselves. What may be able to account for this seeming change of heart as regards religion? Should we, in effect, distinguish between a 'Habermas 1' and a 'Habermas 2'? In order from the outset to preclude the easy way to answer this question, let me emphasize that Habermas himself has not 'turned religious'. In fact, he has more than once characterized himself as 'religiös unmusikalisch' (i.a. as having no sense of music in the religious domain). Now, as one would expect, this apparent change in his attitude towards religion has not gone unnoticed among his interpreters and commentators. To give one example, during the interview mentioned earlier, Habermas' interlocutor, Eduardo Mendieta, quotes two passages on religion belonging to

---

104 This philosophical program was launched by Habermas already in the 1980ies when he published the article 'Die Philosophie als Platzhalter und Interpret' (Habermas 1983, 9-28). Two decades later his position has become more positive and seems to involve more than mere translation: "In short, the position of post-metaphysical thinking toward religion is that of being willing to learn and agnostic at the same time." (Habermas 2005, 149; my translation).

the 'early' and 'late' Habermas respectively, and then adds the following comment:

These two quotations reveal two opposing tendencies in your works. Either religion is made 'fluid' by and evaporates into communicative rationality and is *aufgehoben* in discursive ethics; or religion is accorded the function of containing, and even nourishing semantic contents that are deemed indispensable for ethics and morality, and for philosophy itself. These two ideas do not fit together. (Mendieta in Habermas 2001a, 190; my translation).

Habermas, however, is not willing to see any contradiction here. And perhaps one might in fact regard it as a (at least partly) natural development in light of the fact that what we have witnessed during the last decade is by many called a 'return of religion'.[105] Perhaps this is what has prompted Habermas to talk about the 'post-secular society' and to invoke the idea of a 'genealogy of reason' where religion has played an important part. In fact, the overall thrust of his later writings is to stress that both parties (religious and secular citizens) need each other, and, first of all, need to understand and respect each other. Thus, in one of his latest publications, an essay in *Neue Zürcher Zeitung*,[106] he makes the following

---

105 According to Cooke (2006, 189), Habermas has himself mentioned "two reasons for his shift in position. The first is that recent developments in biotechnology (particularly in the field of genetic engineering) threaten an instrumentalization of human nature that fundamentally endangers our understanding of ourselves as members of the human species. (...) The second is that the terrorist attacks by fundamentalist Islamic militants from September 11th 2001 onwards (...) raise the question of whether a process of modernization that is in danger of de-railing can be rescued with purely secular means." It should be added, however, that Cooke (correctly) recognizes that "Habermas has not changed his mind regarding the philosophical evaluation of religious truth claims: as in his previous writings, philosophy and religion are deemed to constitute separate universes of validity" (*ibid*, 195).

106 The essay was published Feb. 10, 2007. The title ('Ein Bewusstsein von dem, was fehlt') is explained by reference to a deeply Kantian motif: the insight that the morality of reason is unable, finally, to accomplish its own demands. In the same vein, but with an unmistakable added twist of Benjamin's 'anamnetic solidarity', Habermas continues: "Still, practical reason misses its own destination, when it no longer has the power to awaken, and keep awake, in the minds of profane people a consciousness of the damaged solidarity world-wide, a consciousness of what is needed, of that which cries out to heaven." (Habermas 2007, 3; my translation).

observation: "It makes a difference whether you talk to each other or just about each other. For the former to happen, two conditions must be met: The religious side must recognize the authority of 'natural' reason, i.e. the fallible results of institutionalized science and the basic principles of a universalistic egalitarianism in law and morality. On the other hand, secular reason should not be allowed to position itself as the final arbiter regarding the truths of faith, even though, in the end, it may only accept as reasonable what can be translated into its own discourses which are in principle accessible to everybody." (Habermas 2007, 1; my translation).

Habermas is of course well aware that these two conditions are far from trivial. Granting that dialogue and mutual understanding is what we should strive for, we may still wonder whether his vision of a balanced relation between faith and knowledge, between religionists and secularists is perhaps not too idealistic. In order to see where the problem arises for a democratic, well-ordered society ('Rechtsstaat'), we need once more to return to the issue of fundamentalism. Habermas writes,

As the case of Rushdie reminded us, a fundamentalism which leads to an intolerant practice is incompatible with the legal state ('Rechtsstaat'). This practice is based on religious or historical-philosophical interpretations of the world demanding exclusivity for one privileged form of life. Conceptions like these lack the consciousness of the fallibilism of their own validity claim and the respect for the 'burdens of reason' (John Rawls). [...] In contrast, the subjectivized faiths of the modern world are characterized by a reflective attitude which not only allows (...) a modus vivendi. The non-fundamentalist world-views which Rawls calls 'not unreasonable comprehensive doctrines' further allow – in the spirit of Lessing's tolerance – a civilized dispute of convictions, in which one party, without sacrificing its own validity claim, is able to recognize the other parties as co-contestors for authentic truths. In multicultural societies, the legal constitution can tolerate only those forms of life that articulate themselves in the medium of such non-fundamentalist traditions. This is so, because the equally justified co-existence of these forms of life demands the mutual recognition of different cultural memberships: A person must also be able to be recognized and accepted as member of a community which is integrated around a different notion of the good. In other words, the *ethical integration* of groups and sub-cultures with their respective collective identity must be kept separate from the level of the more abstract, *political integration* encompassing all citizens. (Habermas 1996, 261f.; my translation).

As this passage clearly reveals, Habermas is in basic agreement not only with Rawls' notion of reasonable comprehensive doctrines but also with his attempt to attain integration and loyalty by way of formulating a *political* (i.e. not philosophical or religious) basis. What both Rawls and Habermas have realized is that complex societies can no longer be held together by a consensus on substantial values but only on the sheer procedure of legitimate jurisprudence and the exercise of power (cf. Habermas 1996, 263). The point, as mentioned in my earlier treatment of Rawls, was that citizens subscribing to different comprehensive doctrines might endorse and remain loyal to the political basis without thereby compromising their own moral and/or religious convictions. But again, this will only work when we are dealing with comprehensive doctrines that are *reasonable*, or with what Habermas calls the reflective and 'subjectivized' versions of faith. And we should not forget that we have another possible, in fact very real, reaction to secularization and the process of modernization, namely fundamentalism. Rawls' *proviso* we may regard as *his* way of dealing with the problem that not all comprehensive doctrines are reasonable. But what, we must ask, is the solution that Habermas advocates?

Here we must be aware that Habermas has been impressed by the many critical arguments that have been raised against Rawls' proviso (fx from Nicholas Wolterstorff, cf. next chapter). One of his comments to these objections goes like this: "The most serious one is that many religious citizens would not be able to undertake such an artificial division [sc. between 'secular' and 'religious' arguments] within their own minds without destabilizing their existence as pious persons" (Habermas 2006, 8). Or as he says a little later: "Put differently, true belief is not only a doctrine, believed content, but a source of energy that the person who has faith taps performatively and thus nurtures his or her entire life." (*ibid*, 9). This admission on Habermas' part may cause us to wonder, for so far we have heard of only two versions of religion in post-secular society, namely fundamentalism and reflective faith. And for a person of reflective faith it would hardly be considered an 'artificial division' to separate one's personal religious outlook from the political concerns and common good of society. So the urgent question we need to ask is: Who is Habermas referring to with the phrase 'many religious citizens'? Fundamentalists? – Maybe, but again probably not. Conservative Christians in the US, however, might be a good candidate. Now, given Habermas' diagnosis of the process of modernization and secularization, what we could generally say about both fundamentalists and conservative Christians are, basically, two things:[107] 1) they represent an ironic self-misunderstanding, and 2) they haven't learned what they ought to have learned from the historical learning processes, namely, again, two things:

- "to put their own faith convictions in a reflective relation to the fact of a pluralism of religions and world-views" and
- "bringing the knowledge-privilege of the institutionalized sciences, and the primacy of the secular state and the universal morality of society in accordance with their own faith" (Habermas 2005, 10; my translation).

If this is the case, wouldn't the proper strategy be a *pedagogical* one, namely for a democratic society to organize the required learning processes in order to remedy the fact that some citizens have apparently not learned what they ought to?[108] Somewhat curiously, Habermas backs off here and seems content to say that philosophy should not interfere in a task which falls to theology. But surely to rely on theology will solve nothing. For one thing, it is (at least to my knowledge) only within Christianity that a truly critical and reflective theology has developed. And despite this, what we have witnessed in recent years is the resur-

---

107 I am aware that by generalizing here I am in danger of drawing a skewed picture of many conservative (or 'traditional' or 'evangelical') Christians. Within contemporary Christianity 'fundamentalists' and 'conservatives' may to some extent be overlapping groups who (particularly in the USA) seem to join forces on controversial issues like homosexuality and abortion. What separates them, however, seems to be more important: Whereas fundamentalists dream of returning to a golden age prior to modernity, conservative Christians are more aptly characterized as being post-modern.

108 In this perspective, the Mohammad cartoons, published by the Danish newspaper *Jyllands-Posten*, may be considered a shock-treatment meant to instigate a learning-process that some Muslims have apparently not gone through. No doubt, however, dialogue is a more adequate way to achieve this.

gence and strengthening of fundamentalist, traditionalist or conservative versions of Christianity.

Furthermore, if we go back and take a closer look at the two quotations cited earlier, we will see that they are not really addressing the same religious people. As regards the first quotation (and provided we think of conservative Christians), it is probably true that they would find the distinctions between religion, secular state, and science 'artificial', and also that it would tend to 'destabilize' their religious identity. But what about the second passage where Habermas asserts that 'true belief is not only a doctrine, believed content, but a source of energy that the person who has faith taps performatively and thus nurtures his or her entire life'? Yes, I agree that this may serve as an adequate description of the religiosity of many contemporary citizens. What I fail to see, however, is how having religion as a source of energy that nurtures your entire life would prevent you from living up to the standards required by Habermas from democratic citizens. In other words, we need to realize that there are different *types* of religiosity, each more or less compatible with democracy.

Nonetheless, Habermas seems willing to accept the objections voiced against Rawls and Audi (cf. next chapter). In particular, he finds it to be a 'compelling objection' that true belief is a source of energy which nurtures the believer's entire life. This, in turn, leads him to make the following concession: "the liberal state, which expressly protects such forms of life in terms of a basic right, cannot at the same time expect of *all* citizens that they also justify their political statements independent of their religious convictions or world views." (Habermas 2006, 8). But what, we must ask, does 'protect' entail in this passage? How is the *quid pro quo* between liberal democracy and conservative religion to be conceived? The answer, as far as I can see, remains less than entirely clear, because Habermas seems more intent on painting a harmonious picture of the relation between democracy and religion.

At this point, let us take stock of the general outline of the relation between religion and deliberative democracy: Habermas, as we have seen, accords religion an important, historical part in the 'genealogy of reason', and he speaks very positively about the important values and normative ideas inherent in religious traditions. Still, like Rawls he maintains the notion of an *institutional threshold* separating the *informal* public domain from the *formal* institutions of parliament, the courts, and public administration in general.[109] The crux of the matter, of course, is what consequences are to be drawn from this, and here, I believe, one must closely follow Habermas' line of reasoning.

The background, as we have just seen, is that Habermas has been much influenced by the argument that it is totally alien, and almost impossible, to (most?) religious people to split up their identities in a 'religious' and a 'secular' part, or to make a distinction between which arguments may count in their public and private lives, respectively. Faith, so the argument goes, is integral to the believer's entire existence. Habermas (2005, 133) refers to this as the 'central argument' and later calls it a 'striking' argument.[110] The first consequence he draws from this is that the liberal state cannot expect of *all* believers "that they should also justify their political decision-making independently of their religious convictions. This stringent demand can only be directed at politicians." (*ibid*).[111] Or as he later phrases it, the liberal state has no right to transform the necessary *institutional* separation into a *mental and psychological* burden for its religious citizens (*ibid*, 135). However, even Habermas must uphold *some* constraints vis à vis religious citizens:

---

109 The institutional threshold works as "a filter that from the Babel of voices in the informal flows of public communication allows only secular contributions to pass through" (Habermas 2006, 10).

110 On this important issue I fully agree with Thomas M. Schmidt who has given the following reply to Wolterstorff's complaint which Habermas seems to have uncritically adopted: "Hierauf ist zu erwidern, dass die liberale Idee des öffentlichen Vernunftgebrauchs Menschen, die ein Leben im Sinne des religiösen Integralismus führen wollen, in der Tat bestimmte Lasten auferlegt. Aber nicht alle religiösen Personen wollen oder müssen ihre Religiosität im Sinne des Integralismus verstehen, um konsequente Gläubige zu sein. Religiöser Integralismus ist nicht identisch mit authentischer religiöser Existenz überhaupt. (...) Der Untergang eines bestimmten Milieus oder Lebensstils als solcher ist noch kein Anzeichen für Ungerechtigkeit oder Intoleranz. Religöse Überzeugungen können ein Recht auf 'Artenschutz' in einer pluralistischen und säkularen Gesellschaft jedenfalls nicht prinzipiell als eine Forderung der Gerechtigkeit begründen." (Schmidt, 2001, 254).

111 The relation between *empirical* and *normative* semantic content is ambivalent here. It is clear (empirically) that the liberal state *cannot* expect all religious citizens to make independent justifications, but from this Habermas slides into the normative statement that it *ought to* be expected only of politicians. The missing link here is Habermas' acceptance of the argument that to expect otherwise would imply a threat to the very identity of many religious people.

Everyone must be aware and accept that only secular reasons count beyond the institutional threshold that separates the informal public from parliaments, courts, and administrative bodies. Sufficient for this is the epistemic ability also to reflectively regard one's own religious convictions from the outside and to combine them with secular opinions. Religious citizens may very well recognize this 'institutional proviso of translation' without having to split their identities into public and private elements every time they participate in public discussions. Therefore, they should be allowed to express and justify their convictions in religious language, when they are unable to find a secular 'translation'. (Habermas 2005, 136; my translation).

What is going on here? Habermas seems to be in perfect agreement with a Rawlsian position, but his argument seems less clear. First, because he assumes the existence of reflective, epistemic abilities that some religious people apparently lack. And, second, because he now seems to assume that religious people must not, after all, experience a split identity – provided they are able to find 'secular' citizens willing to perform the job of translation for them. But again: Who exactly are the 'religious people' referred to in the above quotation? If they have acquired reflective, epistemic abilities it is hard to imagine what their problem might be. And if not, one wonders whether they would be truly interested in a) contributing to a public reasoning about democratic matters, and b) having their contributions translated into a secular language.

Habermas (2001b, 20f. and 2006, 11) wants to see a 'cooperative' translation of religious contents. On the one hand, this is due to his conviction that the religious traditions contain semantic resources that we haven't so far utilized for the common good. On the other hand, the idea of a cooperative translation is supposed to remedy the fact that, according to Habermas, the pluralism of world-views entails unequal *burdens* for religious and secular citizens (cf. Habermas 2001b, 21f.). Thus, in his recent writings on religion and democracy Habermas more than once touches upon what he sees as an *asymmetry* between religious and secular citizens, the point being that democracy demands more from and puts a heavier burden on the religious citizens: "The translation requirement (…) demand[s] of the religious citizens an effort to learn and adapt that secular citizens are spared having to make." (Habermas 2006, 13). Habermas, therefore, is adamant to counter-balance this asymmetry. Thus, as he points out, if secular citizens are to be able to cooperate with their religious counterpart, they must stop regarding religion as "archaic relics of pre-modern societies" and to regard "freedom of religion as the cultural version of the conservation of a species in danger of becoming extinct." (*ibid*, 15).

We may conclude, then, that like Rawls, Habermas emphasizes that "Every citizen must know and accept that only secular reasons count beyond the institutional threshold that divides the informal public sphere from parliaments, courts, ministries and administrations." (Habermas 2006, 9). At the same time, Habermas sees religious speech as "a serious candidate to transporting possible truth contents, which can then be translated from the vocabulary of a particular religious community into a generally accessible language." (*ibid*, 10).

Conclusion: Rawls or Habermas?

This chapter has dealt with the two major theorists of contemporary political liberalism. Rawls and Habermas may even be said to belong to the same family of social philosophy, since they both conceive of society on a broadly Kantian basis, although in the case of Rawls I have been able to trace a development, where the Kantianism of *Theory* gives way to the more pragmatic, 'political' approach of PL. Still, the idea of *public reason* figures prominently in the deliberative democracy envisioned by both thinkers. When it comes to the role of religion in public life, however, two different pictures begin to emerge. It should not be overlooked, however, that the background to these divergent strategies and opinions vis à vis religion is a substantial agreement on a number of important points. Thus, they both emphasize the liberal state's neutrality toward religion as well as the important corollary that only *secular* reasons count beyond the institutional threshold. As a consequence, and in order to implement the 'wide' view of public reason, both Rawls and Habermas endorse a program of 'translation' – in order to make it possible (and probably also more attractive) for religious citizens to participate in public, political debates.

Before Rawls died in 2002, he and Habermas had a chance to meet and exchange views on more than one occasion. Both men had a lot of sympathy and respect for each other, something which is clearly reflected in the published interchanges, where Habermas (1996, 65f.) insists that his on some points dissenting views be regarded as belonging within the borders of a 'family quarrel'. Unfortunately for our purposes, however, the relation between democracy and religion was never treated in the debate between Rawls and Habermas. And yet, in the years since Rawls' death, the urgent need to tackle this subject and its surrounding issues has only increased. Habermas, of course, has followed the debate between Rawls (and Robert Audi) and their critics, and in turn he has, in particular since 2005, developed his own position.

With this background in mind, let me turn to where I see Habermas differing from the position of Rawls. First of all, one major difference has to do with their basic self-understanding as theorists of democracy. Whereas in *Political Liberalism* Rawls has turned more 'pragmatic' and endeavors to establish, as it were, a 'minimal' political theory without the heavier burden of philosophical commitments, Habermas (and this despite his allegiance to post-metaphysical thinking) clearly wants to retain a central role for philosophy as responsible for maintaining the proper balance between religion and science.[112] Besides, having abandoned his earlier, broadly evolutionary perspective, Habermas now refers to a somewhat sketchy notion of the 'genealogy of reason' where religion has played an important role. This, in turn, serves as an argument for his current position that philosophy should be open and willing to learn from religion, because our religious tradition harbours important (and otherwise inaccessible) normative ideas.[113] In line with this, Habermas

---

112 This important difference is also manifest in Rawls' 'Reply to Habermas' (in: Rawls 2005, 372ff.). Here, Rawls (with a Wittgensteinian twist?) refers to his own basic position in the following way: "The central idea is that political liberalism moves within the category of the political and leaves philosophy as it is" (*ibid*, 375). In contrast, "Habermas's position, on the other hand, is a comprehensive doctrine that covers many things far beyond political philosophy" (*ibid*, 376).

113 For a deeper understanding of this, see Brunkhorst (2007, 101f.) who argues that already from the early 1970ies the development of Habermas' theory of communicative action was heavily influenced by Walter Benjamin's idea of 'the weak messianic power'. In an essay from 1972 Habermas distinguished between two forms of criticism: the *consciousness-raising* critique of ideology and the *redemptive criticism* (German: 'rettende Kritik'). Says Brunkhorst, "The point that Habermas makes with Benjamin is that the sources of radical reinterpretation and public solidarity *can be dried out through the*

more than Rawls stresses the point that the moral foundations of a liberal democracy are religious in origin. Thus, according to Habermas, the liberal state even has an *interest* in unleashing religious voices in the political public sphere. But does 'religious' here not refer only to Christianity having passed through a historical process of self-reflection? Is Habermas taking the 'fact of pluralism' (Rawls) seriously, and can we really believe that he wants to see the whole pluralist specter of religious voices being unleashed?

What, we should ask, may account for these differences which Habermas himself acknowledges by noting that his position toward religion is 'less restrictive' than that of Rawls? Apart from what has already been mentioned above, I believe that the difference in national, political and religious context should be considered a major factor. Rawls comes from a background where the constitutional fathers, although arguing from a Christian heritage, established 'a wall of separation' between church and state. At the same time, and somewhat paradoxical, Rawls has witnessed since the 1980ies how conservative, 'evangelical' Christians have spared no means in trying to influence the political process and the decisions of the courts. Habermas' context, on the other hand, is a more homogeneous religious culture, where an established majority Church (be it Lutheran or Catholic) and its academic theology still play a widely accepted role as the 'moral conscience' of society.

Which of the two positions should we prefer, then, as the best way to deal with the thorny issues of democracy and religion? And is Habermas correct in judging his own position as being less restrictive than that of Rawls? Before reaching a final verdict, it is worth looking into some of the current critical debates on political liberalism and the role of religion.

---

repression of validity claims which are related to the semantics of our tradition" (*ibid*, 102). Hence, in light of this we may interpret Habermas' recently more positive stance toward religion as being partly a return to a position of 'redemptive criticism'.

Chapter Six

CRITICAL DEBATES ON POLITICAL LIBERALISM AND RELIGION

In most countries of the Western world, the relation between religion and politics, as well as the role of religion in the public square, are hotly contested issues. Indeed in my own country, Denmark, the so called 'Cartoon Controversy' in 2006 almost flooded newspapers with contributions from deeply concerned citizens. Interesting in this regard, was the fact that the controversy divided the 'intellectuals' into two opposing camps: One (probably the majority) took the 'multicultural' position and demanded equal respect for all cultural and/or religious sensibilities, and found this to be more important than demonstrating the right to freedom of speech. The other camp considered it more appropriate, faced with the enraged masses of most Arab countries, to staunchly defend the democratic liberties and thus, albeit indirectly, encourage the Muslims to demand the same liberties of their more or less autocratic rulers. In this connection I should perhaps also add that the Danish Prime Minister (who, incidentally, is also Secretary of the press) came out as an unwavering defender of the freedom of expression. Later, however, when the controversy had faded away, the Prime Minister did not refrain from telling the Danish public that in his opinion religion 'ought not take up too much space in the public', but 'should rather be kept within the private sphere'.

As I reflect on it now, all three levels of the debate have, albeit in different ways, prompted me to write this book. As far as the newspaper contributions are concerned, they were of course of a rather superficial nature, but precisely because of this they demonstrated to me the need to present a more complex picture of the contested compatibility of religion and democracy. Regarding the division among the intellectuals, my personal sympathies leaned toward what seemed to me the minority camp. At the same time, however, I felt that the division reflected a false alternative, and that a more nuanced position was called for. And finally, I was dissatisfied with the Prime Minister's somewhat rigid distinction between 'public' and 'private'.

In order to hopefully remedying this, I have selected for this chapter a number of recent contributions, particularly from the American debate. Obviously, as one would expect, Rawls is the main target of criticism. However, I have also chosen to paraphrase the interesting debate (which, incidentally, has also influenced Habermas) between philosopher Robert Audi and theologian Nicholas Wolterstorff.

Interpreting Liberalism

The purpose of this first section is to take a closer look at the way in which political liberalism (and in particular: its position *vis à vis* religion) is presented and discussed by some of the participants in the debate on religion and democracy. An interesting contribution comes from Harvard-theologian *Ronald F. Thiemann*, who has provided a useful account of the political philosophy underlying the U.S. constitution.

The core values of the constitution are *freedom*, *equality*, and *tolerance*. Thiemann reminds us that for the fathers behind the constitution these values were ultimately derived from a *theological* philosophy, i.e. from a Christian conception of man as created in the image of God. Nonetheless, contemporary political liberalists believe that these core values are best protected and maintained when religion is kept out of public affairs. In other words, religious arguments should be excluded from the public arena. Thiemann, who deplores this allegedly liberalist position, quotes Ronald Dworkin for saying that a government "must be neutral in one particular way: among conceptions of the good life" (Thiemann 1996, 76).

The demand for separation between church and state follows logically from this principle of neutrality. But, Thiemann asks, "how can government adjudicate controversial moral or political issues while prescinding entirely from all notions of 'good' or 'value'?" (*ibid*, 77). The fact that a government claims neutrality conceals this and may contribute to social unrest once people discover that the government's decision on controversial matters, despite claims to neutrality, rests on certain normative conceptions. Thiemann, of course, is aware that political liberalists will deny this and claim that the courts have only followed the demand for 'the priority of the right over the good' (which is also an important maxim of Rawls). Thiemann, in other words, wants to get beyond what he calls 'the myth of neutrality', for what is 'right', he argues, is always based on an implicit idea of 'the good'. Hence Thiemann's objection: "The notion of liberty is not enhanced by the assertion that governmental decisions must be (...) independent of any conception of the good life, or of what gives value to life." (*ibid*, 79). With specific reference to Rawls, Thiemann commends him by complaining that few "have adopted his nuanced and subtle stance on religion. Most defenders of political liberalism continue to assert that religious and theological arguments cannot meet the conditions of publicity." (*ibid*, 89). In a later section of this chapter we shall return to the question whether Thiemann, in the end, is able to agree with the position of Rawls.

Another theologian, *Nicholas Wolterstorff*, starts out with the admission that liberalism is often misunderstood, and he therefore throws in a plea for basic fairness: "Let's be fair to liberalism!" (Wolterstorff 1997, 165). In light of this, it strikes the reader as odd, however, that Rawls, being generally accepted as the major representative of political liberalism, is dealt with in a presentation which is highly selective, and at best sketchy. Instead, and even more pronounced in another contribution (cf. Audi & Wolterstorff 1997, 8off.), Wolterstorff spends much energy on Locke, but in the end only to dismiss him on the grounds of being guilty of 'epistemological foundationalism'. As far as Rawls is concerned, Wolterstorff fails to mention his explicit distancing political liberalism from both 'comprehensive' and Enlightenment versions of liberalism. In fact, as we saw in the previous chapter, Rawls makes an important point of constructing a version of liberalism that is *political* – and not philosophical, metaphysical, or constituting a comprehensive doctrine.

The result of this is that Wolterstorff generally operates with a rather broad (and not very precise) notion of 'liberalism', and my guess is that he makes this choice because this is what serves his interests best. It is not, however, helpful in engendering a constructive debate. To see this, let me offer a few quotations. In outlining the definitive traits of liberalism, Wolterstorff claims that "[t]he view is that those members [sc. adult members as free and equal] are neither to base their political debate in the public space, nor their political decisions, on their own particular religious convictions, nor on such religious convictions as they might all share. When it comes to such activities, they are to allow their religious convictions to idle." (Wolterstorff 1997, 166). This, however, is not the position of Rawls. To this, of course, Wolterstorff might counter that what he has in mind here is the broader concept of liberalism.[114] Be that as it may, but only a few pages later he turns the same complaint directly on Rawls: "What Rawls tells me is that if I step outside my own religious community and enter the public debate about the treatment of the poor in our society, I must at no point [sic! TN] appeal to my religious convictions." (*ibid*, 172). However, as we saw in the last chapter, this is emphatically *not* Rawls' position.

In his general description of liberalism, Wolterstorff focuses first on what he sees as the 'common theme' uniting those who have theorized about liberal democracy, namely the imposing of epistemological restraints: "a common theme has been that a good citizen of a liberal democracy will refrain from allowing religious reasons to be determinative when deciding and/or debating political issues of certain sorts." (Audi & Wolterstorff 1997, 69). In commenting directly on Rawls, it should be noted that Wolterstorff does acknowledge it to be 'one of the great merits' that under 'comprehensive doctrines' "he includes not only religions but comprehensive philosophies." (*ibid*, 90). Apart from this, however, we do not hear much about comprehensive doctrines (Wolterstorff focuses almost exclusively on what he sees as the unfair constraints on religion) or overlapping consensus. On the contrary, (consciously?) overlooking that the point of this idea lies in the possibility of overlap between differing sources of commitment, Wolterstorff instead imposes on Rawls a *consensus populi* viewpoint (cf. *ibid*, 91f.),[115] which allegedly implies the

---

114 Cf. also the following statement: "What unites this buzzying variety of positions into one family of liberal positions is that they all propose a restraint on the use of religious reasons in deciding and/or debating political issues. That is the heart of the matter." (Audi & Wolterstorff 1997, 75). This, of course, is a correct observation, but Wolterstorff fails to present the arguments why this is deemed a necessary step.

115 Cf. also Wolterstorff 1997, 171 and 179.

idea (Wolterstorff asks us to imagine a Quaker meeting) that we must continue debating until no one disagrees. Habermas (2006) has correctly noted that this analogy makes a travesty out of Rawls' position.

Perhaps a more harmful misrepresentation occurs in a context where Wolterstorff is referring to current controversies in American society on issues such as homosexuals and school prayer. Seeing these as illustrative examples he continues:

On these particular issues, the Idea of liberal democracy yields clear conclusions: homosexuals should enjoy equal freedom under law to live their lives as they see fit, and state sponsored schools should not include prayers as an official part of the school program.[116] Yet large numbers of Americans see otherwise. They do not accept the Idea of liberal democracy at these points. Rawls works with an extraordinarily idealized picture of the American political mind. One can see why: If the Idea of liberal democracy is not identical with the shared political culture of American society, then the prospect of extracting, from that political culture, principles of justice that are both *shared* and *appropriate to a liberal democracy*, is hopeless. (Audi & Wolterstorff 1997, 97).[117]

I shall refrain from commenting on the contents of this quote other than noting that what seems to be going on here is that Wolterstorff mistakenly confuses Rawls' political liberalism with *liberal politics* which, at least in the US, everyone is supposed to know is bad.

The Separation between Church and State

Why should a liberal democracy be committed to the separation between church and state? What is at stake here, and how might the separation be interpreted? Thiemann has put a good deal of energy into scrutinizing this

---

116 Unfortunately for Wolterstorff, Rawls (1997, 476) has explicitly addressed the controversial issue of school prayer and emphasized that political liberalism is not necessarily against this.

117 In this quotation it is clear that Wolterstorff criticizes the 'Idea of liberal democracy' (which for some reason he writes with a capital 'I'). In other contexts, fx in outlining his own so-called 'consocial' position, he makes a strategic distinction between something called 'the liberal position' (which he is against) and 'the Idea of liberal democracy', which he claims to embrace. See to this distinction Audi & Wolterstorff 1997, 115.

theme. He begins by noting that a certain ambiguity seems built into the constitution, and in particular the Bill of Rights. An important concern for the constitutional fathers was to protect the freedom of conscience. This is the basic principle behind the Bill of Rights and it also informs the famous non-establishment clause: 'Congress shall make no law respecting an establishment of religion or prohibiting the free exercise thereof'. And in a similar spirit Jefferson coined the equally famous metaphor of a 'wall of separation between church and state'. This, notes Thiemann, seems to imply that Christianity cannot claim a special position, not least because of the concern to protect the rights of minorities.

The problem today, according to Thiemann, is that the expressions used in the constitution ('separation' and 'neutrality') have been interpreted differently by judges in a number of cases. Generally speaking, the courts have tried to explicate state-church separation through the concept of 'governmental neutrality'. Yet, in practice, claims Thiemann, government and religion have often been 'deeply entangled with one another'. Hence the need to introduce a third concept, that of *accommodation*; its purpose is to indicate how and when the state may accomodate religion without thereby violating the non-establishment clause of the first amendment. However: "Since the nonestablishment clause forbids any governmental assistance to religion, and the free exercise clause mandates governmental accomodation of religion, the two clauses can easily work at cross-purposes." (Thiemann, 1996, 57).

As a means of further clarification, Chief Justice Burger developed, in connection with a specific case (Lemon vs Kurtzman, 1971), a test consisting of three criteria. All actions and decisions by the government should: a) have a secular purpose; b) have a primary effect that neither promotes nor hinders the exercise of religion; and 3) avoid 'excessive governmental entanglement' with religion (cf. *ibid*, 59). Thiemann, however, finds the conceptual basis for the courts' decisions flawed due to "fundamental problems in the liberal political philosophy on which the Court regularly draws" (*ibid*, 60). This relates particularly to the concept of 'neutrality' which, according to Thiemann, has been interpreted in at least three different ways:

1) As *strict neutrality* requiring a "consistent no-aid to religion policy" (*ibid*, 61).

2) As *nondiscriminatory neutrality*: This is a 'softer' variant of the first, opening the door to at least some space for religion in public.

3) And, finally, as *benevolent neutrality*: This position "seeks to broaden the framework within which religion might be freely exercised by expanding the doctrine of accomodation to include public sphere accomodation". This interpretation prohibits only "governmentally established religion or governmental interference with religion" (*ibid*).

In Thiemann's evaluation, the first position may well be logically consistent, but it will not be possible to make it work in a democracy "in which government regulation affects virtually every aspect of individual and corporate life" (*ibid*, 62). And as concerns the third position, it can be criticized for not being an expression of neutrality at all. Says Thiemann, "In particular, defenders of this position have failed utterly to address the question of the possible discriminatory effects of a broadened view of accommodation." Since none of the proposed versions of neutrality really work, Thiemann ponders if not "the time has come to jettison the concept altogether" (*ibid*, 64).

Another issue for Thiemann is to point out that the constitutional fathers had a too limited and narrow understanding of the role of religion in society. They were silent as to whether religion could foster the virtues necessary to promote justice and equality. In other words, the founders "failed to address the question of the sources and function of public virtue in American society" (*ibid*, 27). Hence, the result was a vacuum "that was quickly filled by a civic piety derived from *Christianity*" (*ibid*, 28). Civil religion, however, can no longer be considered alive and well. Thiemann points to several studies documenting that the historic American civil religion no longer functions as provider of symbols of public life. In light of this, Thiemann is convinced of the pressing need to define "an appropriate place for religion within a pluralistic democracy" (*ibid*, 37). But what, we might ask, is implied in 'religion' here? No doubt Thiemann has in mind Christianity, but in that case he fails to address the fundamental problem which was the impetus behind Rawls' political liberalism: the fact of pluralism.

Returning to the debate between Audi and Wolterstorff, Audi (1997, 39) argues that the theory of separation implies three principles held together by the ideal of religious liberty:

The first principle – which I shall call *the libertarian principle* – says that the state must permit the practice of any religion, though within certain limits. The second principle – *the equalitarian principle* – says that the state may not give preference to one religion over another. [...] The third principle – *the neutrality principle* – is less commonly affirmed, but also belongs to any full-blooded liberal account of separation of church and state. It says that the state should neither favor nor disfavor religion (or the religious) *as such*, that is, give positive or negative preference to institutions or persons simply because they are religious.

Wolterstorff, at first glance, may seem to generally agree with Audi. Thus, when describing his understanding of liberal democracy, the principle of neutrality is clearly included: "*Equal protection* under law for all people, *equal freedom* in law for all citizens, and *neutrality* on the part of the state with respect to the diversity of religions and comprehensive perspectives – those are the core ideas." (Audi & Wolterstorff 1997, 70). Later, however, when arguing that the principle of neutrality allows for two different interpretations, he insists on neutrality understood as *impartiality* among religions on the part of the state, and he criticizes Audi for preferring a *separation* interpretation – and taking this for granted (cf. *ibid*, 149). Audi's reply to Wolterstorff on this issue, reveals, though, that he sees the disagreement somewhat differently:

He [sc. Wolterstorff] sees impartiality *among* religions as crucial for liberal democratic governments; I favor impartiality *regarding* religion, and I contend that it implies neutrality toward religion. I grant, however, that the freedom to practice one's religion is central for liberal democracy. I hold, then, that governmental *indifference* toward religion is inappropriate to a liberal democracy. I believe this is a point of strong agreement between us (Audi & Wolterstorff 1997, 167).

I suppose that what Audi has in mind in finding governmental *indifference* 'inappropriate', might be something like the French 'secularist' version of liberal democracy (*laicité*), to which also Habermas distances himself. Contrary to a secularist position, Audi emphasizes that his idea of 'impartiality *regarding* religion' may well make government see it as its obligation to facilitate the free exercise of religion. In his own words, he regards this "a legitimate, if secondary, aim of government under liberalism" (*ibid*, 128).[118]

In debating this whole issue, the basic tenor is that the themes of separation, neutrality, and constraints is a problem for religion – and may be unacceptable to a good many religious persons. In this light, I find it interesting that Audi (1997, 38) also reminds us that religions (and their adherents) may *themselves* have internal reasons for preferring to exist in a liberal democracy. Says Audi, "They might, for one thing, religiously endorse a moral case for a liberal state. But they might also see such a state as best for their own flourishing, especially in a world of inescapable religious pluralism." And 'flourishing' here could also be understood as encompassing the best possible guarantee that one's religion will not be dominated by the norms and ideals of another religion.[119]

Perhaps one of the most interesting and provocative questions raised by Audi in the context of church-state separation is the following: "And if there should be a measure of separation between religious institutions and the state, *should there be, in our conduct as citizens, a related separation between religious and secular considerations?*" (Audi & Wolterstorff 1997, 2; emphasis added). This is surely worth pondering, and I believe that Audi is basically correct in establishing this parallel. In point of fact, his principle of *theo-*

---

118 A further, clarifying comment by Audi is the following: "I believe, then, that it is best for government in a free and democratic society to be not only *neutral among* religions but also *neutral toward* religion. I cannot say too emphatically, however, that this does not require abstaining from adopting policies that have the *effect* of advancing religion." (*ibid*).

119 Audi makes the following observation in this regard: "For any of us who are religious, the prospect that we might be coerced by preferences based on some other religion is generally loathsome. Few have a similar reaction to coercion plausibly imposed for purposes of maintaining law and order or public health or a minimal level of education. Liberalism is in part a response to the intuitive difference nearly everyone feels in such cases." (Audi & Wolterstorff 1997, 134).

ethical equilibrium (cf. below) speaks directly to this point. The morale, we might say, is that where there are rights and benefits, there must also be obligations. In this light, it is difficult not to leave the debate between Audi and Wolterstorff with the overall impression that the religious position tries to achieve as many rights and benefits as possible, but at the same time opposing all forms of constraints as infringing, as it were, on their religious liberty and freedom of expression. Wolterstorff, albeit in a sophisticated manner, seems to me representative of this tendency. But let me close this section with Audi's plea for a 'double' separation:

My effort has been to show that, and to some extent how, a liberal democracy should separate church and state institutionally and how individuals should separate religious and secular considerations in their conduct as citizens. But separation need not create a gulf that is never crossed by communication. There need be no unbridgeable gulf either between governmental and religious institutions or between individuals of differing religious positions.[120] Nor need there be a split within individuals who are considering both religious and secular reasons for political conduct. (Audi & Wolterstorff 1997, 143).

The Nature of Religious Obligations

Before looking closer at the constraints which liberal democracy imposes on reasons deriving from an individual's comprehensive doctrine, we would do well, I think, to reflect on the nature of religious reasons and obligations. In this regard Audi (1997, 42ff.) has made a helpful contribution reminding us that religious obligations have "at least five kinds of evidential grounds" (*ibid*, 43): 1) scripture, 2) non-scriptural authority (clergy and theological community), 3) tradition, 4) religious experience, and 5) natural theology. Since these sources are 'logically independent', the important possibility occurs "that a religious obligation can be aligned with a secular one [...]. We should now expect that there is sometimes not only a *plurality of obligational grounds* for a kind of conduct, but also religiously and secularly *mixed obligational overdetermination*, the kind that occurs when there are both sufficient religious reasons *and* sufficient secu-

---

120 One is reminded here of Rawls' *dictum*, 'there need be no war between religion and democracy'.

lar reasons for a kind of conduct, for instance being honest." (*ibid*, 45f.). Having established this, Audi then goes on, much like Rawls, to emphasize the fair chances of *overlap* between religious and secular reasons:

If we think of the Hebraic-Christian tradition, it is clear that there is much overlap between religiously and secularly grounded obligations. Nor is this tradition opposed to taking secular grounds seriously, or even to looking to them for purposes of, say, better understanding the conduct required by both sets of grounds, or of enhancing one's motivation to produce that conduct. Granting that a person's faith can and should inform aspects of secular life, including especially the treatment of other people, reflective secular living can also lead to enhanced understanding of one's faith. (Audi 1997, 46).

On this basis then, Audi proposes that each individual should seek to establish a *reflective equilibrium* (i.e. working out a balance between the religious and secular sources of one's views) and adopt an attitude of *fallibilism*. For, as he sees it, "both an effort to achieve reflective equilibrium and an attitude of fallibilism are appropriate to mature, rational practitioners of a religion for which, as is typical, there are multiple, independent, and sometimes unclear or ambiguous sources of authority regarding human conduct." (*ibid*, 47). In emphasizing the ideal of a reflective faith, Audi comes remarkably close to the picture of the reflective mode of Christianity outlined by Habermas in the previous chapter. It goes almost without saying, of course, that no religious fundamentalist would subscribe to this.[121] And to Abraham we may assume that such a requirement would be simply incomprehensible.

The Constraints on Religious Reasons

In his opposition to the (so far: misunderstood) constraints that political liberalism imposes on religious comprehensive doctrines, Wolterstorff

---

121 Cf. also the following statement: "Religious commitment is not, in its mature embodiments, a monolithic position of blind obedience, but a complex, multi-layered fidelity to a multifarious array of texts, traditions, authoritative directives, religious experiences, and people in and outside one's own religious community. A mature religious commitment may require sensitivity, reflection, self-renewal, and, often, the practical wisdom to reconcile conflicting elements." (Audi 1997, 74).

puts forward a number of criticisms. In a first move he argues that the restraint "appears, on the face of it, to violate the equal freedom component within the Idea of liberal democracy" (Audi & Wolterstorff 1997, 77). His choice of words here seems to suggest that he is not quite sure about it, or that there may be some other interpretation. Later in the same text, however, whatever doubts that Wolterstorff might have had, have vanished. Thus, reminding the reader that it "belongs to the *religious convictions* of a good many religious people in our society that *they ought to base* their decisions concerning fundamental issues of justice *on* their religious convictions", he concludes: "Accordingly, to require of them that they not base their decisions and discussions concerning political issues on their religion is to infringe, inequitably, on the free exercise of their religion." (*ibid*, 105).

Wolterstorff's second move consists in pointing out that liberalism's ideal of public reasoning "is patently unrealistic as a proposal. Most people who reasoned from their religion in making up their mind on political issues would lack the intellectual imagination required for reasoning to the same position from the independent source." (Audi & Wolterstorff 1997, 78). To bolster this scepticism, he also argues that the "pervasiveness of disagreement and controversy in our society constitutes overwhelming evidence for the conclusion that, on such issues, there simply are not any considerations that all adult citizens who are fully rational and adequately informed on the matter at hand will find persuasive and can identify with." (*ibid*, 154). Commenting on this point, Audi counters Wolterstorff's pessimism: "I think that if one notes the plethora of secular considerations for and against various political positions in a modern Western democracy, the evidence is against this pessimism." (*ibid*, 127).[122]

But how is the constraint to be understood? Audi emphasizes its *inclu-*

---

122 Also on this issue, Audi makes the following observation: "In addition to differing with Wolterstorff on the likely and extensive alignment between religious and secular reasons, I would ask for examples of cases in which, first, no such overlap can be found and, second, the law or policy in question is supported *only* by religious reasons yet is still one that informed, reflective citizens would wish to defend as appropriate for a religiously and otherwise pluralistic democracy. I am inclined to think that there are few if any such cases." (*ibid*, 127).

sive nature saying that "it is the advocacy and support of laws and public policies that are constrained, and the constraint is *inclusive* rather than *exclusive*: the chief point is not that one cannot have and be motivated by religious reasons but that one should have and be motivated by least one set of evidentially adequate secular reasons." (Audi & Wolterstorff 1997, 138). At the same time he believes that in this respect he is probably less restrictive than Rawls, although stressing that his position is close to that of Rawls.[123] Wolterstorff, on the contrary, fails to see why we should differentiate between types of reasons in the first place: "What difference does it make what reasons citizens use in making their decisions and conducting their debates, if the positions they advocate do not violate the Idea of liberal democracy? And in particular, why should *religious* reasons (which are not derived from the independent source) be singled out for exclusion?" (Audi & Wolterstorff 1997, 77).[124]

As is clear from this quotation, Wolterstorff holds fast to his interpretation of the constraint as implying an *exclusion* of religious reasons.[125] On his own part, in a section aptly entitled 'No Restraint on Religious Reasons', he does, however, propose *some* kind of restraints on citizens in a liberal democracy:

---

123 Cf. Audi & Wolterstorff 1997, 135 and 138. See also Audi (1997, 61) where Audi mentions Rawls' restriction on the reliance on comprehensive views, and continues, "My position is, on this count, less restrictive than his; mine allows that they may figure crucially both evidentially and motivationally, and both in general public discussion and in advocacy and support of laws and public policies, provided (evidentially) adequate secular reasons play a sufficiently important role." But what is 'a sufficiently important role'? Be that as it may, in both Rawls and Audi we find the *proviso* in place and maintained.

124 In outlining the need for a *translation* of religious contributions in the public political sphere, Habermas (2006, 11) remarks on how critics like Paul Weithman and Nicholas Wolterstorff "wish to jettison even this proviso. In so doing, contrary to their own claim to remain in line with the premises of the liberal argument, they violate the principle that the the state shall remain neutral in the face of competing world views."

125 Stephen Macedo has tried to correct this wide-spread misunderstanding: "Politcal liberals do not, as some argue, seek to exclude religious people from the public realm or to curtail their political speech." (Macedo, 2003, p. 150). In contrast, (and admirably simply stated): "What political liberalism asks of us is not to renounce what we believe to be true but to acknowledge the difficulty of publicly establishing any single account of the whole truth." (*ibid*, 149).

In the first place, restraints are needed on the *manner* of discussion and debate in the public square. In our manner of argumentation, we ought to show respect for the other person. Our discussions ought to be conducted with *civility*. The virtues of civility belong to the ethic of the citizen. [...]

Second, the debates, except for extreme circumstances, are to be conducted and resolved in accord with the rules provided by the laws of the land and the provisions of the Constitution.[...]

Third, there is a restraint on the overall goal of the debates and discussions. The goal is political justice, not the achievement of one's own interest. Here I side with the liberal position, against the competition-of-interests position. (Audi & Wolterstorff 1997, 112f.).

As becomes clear in this quotation, there is at least *something*, on which Wolterstorff is able to agree with 'the liberal position' he otherwise criticizes. This point of convergence is reiterated as he puts forward his own alternative called the *consocial* position. But perhaps 'alternative' is not the correct word, for it is somewhat difficult to discern its positive content. Instead, in outlining the consocial position, Wolterstorff hits on the two issues that are undoubtedly the most provocative to a good many religious representatives: "First, it repudiates the quest for an independent source and imposes no moral restraint on the use of religious reasons. And second, it interprets the neutrality requirement, that the state be neutral with respect to the religious and other comprehensive perspectives present in society, as requiring *impartiality* rather than *separation*" (*ibid*, 115). Earlier on in the same text (p. 81) Wolterstorff assures us that he 'firmly embraces' the idea of liberal democracy, and he contends "that the consocial position is fully harmonious with the Idea of liberal democracy."

Concrete examples are often helpful, and it deserves to be noted that one particular example (brought forward by Wolterstorff) is commented on by both contributors. I include it here, because I believe it is useful in order better to understand what separates the two positions. Wolterstorff relates how a group of Christians ('Christian Environment Council') turns up in Washington and addresses the national media in support of endangered species. The reason they offer is that "according to the Scriptures, the earth is the Lord's and all that dwells within it (Psalm 24:12), and the Lord shows concern for every creature (Matthew 6:26)."[126] To this, Wolterstorff then adds the following comment:

I fail to see that those Christians, in offering, in the public square, those reasons for their position, were violating the ethic of the citizen in a liberal democracy. Let it be added that if they wanted to persuade those who do not accept the Hebrew or Christian Bible as authoritative, they will of course have to find and offer other, additional reasons for their position. Whether or not a reason is *appropriate* depends not only on the position but on one's purpose. Reasons are used for doing different things. (Audi & Wolterstorff 1997, 112.).

In his reply, Audi first remarks that whereas some versions of liberalism might want to exclude such a use of religious reasons, his own view is that "these reasons are not excluded; the main point is to *include* some sufficient secular reason." (*ibid*, 140). But then, in a second move, he remarks, "For my part, I would be at best reluctant to compel non-religious citizens – and disagreeing religious ones – to spend limited tax dollars for a purpose I could not be sufficiently motivated to pursue by secular reasons. If the only reasons that move me are religious, and if I would not want to be coerced on the basis of religious reasons playing a like role in someone with a conflicting religious perspective, I would want to abstain from coercion." (*ibid*, 141).

Civic Virtue: The Ethical Role of Citizens

Both Audi and Wolterstorff agree that civic virtues are important, and not only this: The question of the ethical role of citizens plays a major role in their debate. This theme, it seems to me, is important, not least because it serves implicitly to make clear that democracy suffers considerable damage, if citizens only claim (and act upon) what they see as their *rights*. Thus, Audi, "I will contend, however, that there are ideals of moral virtue which require of us more than simply acting within our moral rights. In particular, there are *ideals of civic virtue*, which arguably derive from moral ideals [...] and demand of us more than simply staying within our rights." (Audi 1997, 43).

---

126 Quoted from Audi & Wolterstorff 1997, 112.

From this, Audi goes on to investigate the relation between civic virtue and religious commitment. This, obviously, depends on the nature of religious authority, and to clarify this Audi assumes what he calls 'a broadly Western theism' where "we can take God to be omniscient, omnipotent, and omnibenevolent", and then he continues, "Might we not, then, expect God to structure us and the world so that there is a (humanly accessible) *secular path* to the discovery of moral truths, at least to those far-reaching ones needed for civilized life?" (*ibid*, 49). I think we can appreciate, what Audi is getting at here: Having established the possibility of bridging the gap between the religious and the secular from the human side, so to speak (cf. his account of the nature of religious obligations above), he now wishes to demonstrate a similar possibility when looked at from God's side. Similar to Rawls' argument that transcendent values (although considered 'higher') should not necessarily 'override' more worldly and secular values, it is a major point for Audi to convince us that there need be no conflict between an individual's religious and secular obligations. And on this background, it is understandable that he has felt the need to directly address the challenge stemming from the situation of Abraham in Genesis 22:

What then of the case of Abraham and Isaac? Does it not present a religious obligation (to sacrifice a son) as taking precedence over a moral one? This is one reading, but even if we knew that God placed (one or more) religious obligations over moral ones, we could still have better reason for believing that God commands, say, protection of one's children than for believing that God commands any particular action inconsistent with this. Should Abraham, however – insofar as he (reasonably?) believed that it was God requiring the sacrifice – have believed that sacrificing his son was inconsistent with protecting him? That is not clear: God's ways of protecting us are infinite. Note, too, how the story ends: the morally prohibited action is not required after all, perhaps suggesting that despite appearances, there cannot be an inconsistency between religious and moral obligations. (Audi 2000, 129).

What is one to think of this line of reasoning? Well, for one thing I believe that Audi deserves credit for having so clearly perceived the challenge to political philosophy inherent in Genesis 22. Quite another matter, of

course, is whether one finds his reading of the story plausible. Personally, I must confess that I find it seriously flawed. The impression I am
left with is that in order to reach his desired result ('there cannot be an
inconsistency between religious and moral obligations') Audi proposes
a reading of Genesis 22 which trivializes Abraham's dilemma (not to
mention Isaac's situation). It's a devout ('God's ways of protecting us
are infinite') and overly harmonizing interpretation which, incidentally,
is worth comparing to Kant's interpretation in Chapter One.

A major point in Audi is to argue that civic virtue implies (for the religious person) a commitment to seeking 'theo-ethical equilibrium'. Before
going deeper into this, however, we must take a look at the two basic
principles that he attributes to civic virtue.[127] First, the *principle of secular
rationale* which says "that one has a prima facie obligation not to advocate
or support any law or public policy that restricts human conduct, unless
one has, and is willing to offer, adequate secular reason for this advocacy
or support (say for one's vote)." (Audi 1997, 55). Second, the *principle of
secular motivation* which "adds to the rationale principle that one also has
a (prima facie) obligation to abstain from advocacy or support of a law
or public policy that restricts human conduct, unless one is sufficiently
motivated by some (normatively) adequate secular reason." (*ibid*, 56).[128]
On this basis, Audi then introduces a 'second-order' principle specially
addressed to citizens of a religious persuasion, namely the *principle of theo-
ethical equilibrium*: "where religious considerations appropriately bear on
matters of public morality or of political choice, religious persons have a
prima facie obligation – at least insofar as they have civic virtue – to seek

---

127 As to the purpose, the two principles, says Audi (1997, 73), "simply aim at preventing
    a certain kind of domination by religious reasons in contexts in which they should
    be constrained; and adhering to the principles makes it much easier to speak with
    an appropriate civic voice. To be sure, in public advocacy of laws and policies that
    restrict human conduct it seems *generally* best to conduct discussion in secular terms;
    but there may be special contexts in which candor or other considerations require
    laying out all of one's main reasons."
128 Later Audi (1997, 73) adds that the motivation principle "allows that one may *also*
    have religious reasons and be motivated by them. The ideal for religious citizens is
    indeed a cooperation between the religious and the secular, not the domination of
    the former by the latter."

an equilibrium between those considerations and relevant secular stand-ards of ethics and political responsibility." (*ibid*, 62). One could consider this, I suppose, an attempt on Audi's part to translate Rawls' overlapping consensus to the level of the (religious) individual.

On the contrary, Wolterstorff insists that the ideal of civic virtue entails *no* restraints other than the three mentioned above:

[T]he ethic of the citizen imposes definite restrictions on the *manner* in which citizens conduct their discussions and debates. But the ethic of the citizen imposes *no restraint on the reasons* citizens offer for their positions – except such restraints as may be implied by the restrictions on position and manner. To the contrary: it implies that there are no such restraints. At this point, citizens are free to live their lives as they see fit.

Let religious people use what reasons they wish, and offer them to whomever they wish. Let non-religious people do so as well. (Audi & Wolterstorff 1997, 164; emphasis added).

In connection with the issue of civic virtue, there is in particular one feature which receives special attention by Wolterstorff, i.e. the theme of showing each other proper *respect*. It seems he has a valid point here, when he argues that "we must consider the situation not only from the speaker's perspective but also from the hearer's." (*ibid*, 159). Respect, so Wolterstorff, entails that you really *listen* to the other with the inten-tion, not only to persuade the other, but also of *learning* something from him or her. To this Wolterstorff then adds what strikes me as a revealing comment:

Is the situation different if coercion is in the background? I fail to see that it is. Suppose that some law or policy with coercive import is under consideration. We each state our view on the matter – saying whatever we want to say. We each listen to the other and make our final decision in the light of what we have heard. Then we vote. If I lose in the vote, then, though I do not agree, I *acquiesce* – un-less I find the decision truly appalling. I do not like the decision; I prefer that it have gone the other way. But I have been allowed to say whatever I wanted to say, and I have been heard, genuinely heard. Is there anything more that I can ask of you by way of respect? (Audi & Wolterstorff 1997, 160).

Rawls, of course, would immediately object to this, since 'acquiescence' is, when all is said and done, just another term for *modus vivendi* and lacking 'overlap'.[129] And Audi, as we would expect, reacts in a similar way. Having credited Wolterstorff for his description of an 'empathic civility', he says, "My position is designed in part to reduce the chance that those who are outvoted will merely acquiesce or, especially, that those who are coerced in some important matter will find the majority decision truly appalling. I think it is not likely that this will happen when both they and those enforcing a law or policy are fully rational and adequately informed." (*ibid*, 172).

Interpreting Historical Background and Current Problems
During the decade that has passed since the publication of Audi & Wolterstorff (1997), it has become increasingly clear that we live in a 'world of terror' where many forms of religious fundamentalism make no secret of their hostility toward liberal democracy. This fact, and the many concerns it raises, is already touched upon by Audi in the opening remarks of his contribution to the co-authored volume. Religious fundamentalism, he notes, "is a powerful force in many parts of the world, and, in some of its forms, it is hostile to democracy"; and, he continues, "There is much division of judgment regarding how much (if at all) fundamentalism may be undermining democracy in the United States, but there is little disagreement on the growing influence of the 'religious right', as it is often called, in American political life." (Audi & Wolterstorff 1997, 1). Disagreement or not, the fact is that one looks in vain for concern over the influence of the religious right in Wolterstorff's contribution to the

---

129 Earlier, I touched upon the difference between Audi's optimism and Wolterstorff's pessimism or scepticism. What is the source of this difference? Perhaps a clue to this may be found in the fact that Wolterstorff, in continuation of the above quotation, adds the following remark: "That I am coerced by a law that I oppose – is that not, per se, an indication that I am not being accorded full respect as a free and dignified individual? In a way, yes. But here we have to be reminded of the Augustinian point: we are talking about the politics of earthly cities, not about the politics of the heavenly city." (Audi & Wolterstorff 1997, 160). This may lead the reader to speculate: Does Wolterstorff's theology make him regard man and society as being in a fallen, sinful state, and is *this* a major reason for his rejecting the liberalist ideal and being content with majority vote?

debate. Instead, he complains that religious voices are being 'silenced' and that in public political debate they are allegedly forced to leave their religious convictions to 'idle'.[130]

More generally, what we find is that points of historical background and current problems are interpreted markedly different, and apparently this is something that we need to be mindful of when following the debate on religion and democracy. Thus, in Wolterstorff's book, all that is negative ("the slaughter, torture, and generalized brutality of our century") stems from 'a secular cause', whereas he is happily and elaborately telling us that "Many of the social movements in the modern world that have moved societies in the direction of liberal democracy have been deeply and explicitly religious in their orientation." (Audi & Wolterstorff 1997, 80). As the following passage suggests, however, Wolterstorff thinks that all these societal blessings of religion do not get all the credit they deserve:

These movements are often analyzed by Western academics and intellectuals as if religion were nowhere in the picture. The assumption, presumably, is that religion plays no explanatory role in human affairs and thus does not require mentioning. It is only an epiphenomenon. [...] Thus does ideology conceal reality and distort scholarship! Even the free and equal doctrine, which lies at the very heart of liberal democracy, had religious roots – in Protestant dissent of the seventeenth century. (*ibid*, 80).[131]

It is correct that 'religion' (Wolterstorff no doubt means: Christianity) has been a motivating factor behind many social movements for positive social change. But why is it apparently so much more difficult to reach agreement that religion, and particularly in some of its manifestations,

---

130 In commenting on Wolterstorff's 'idling' metaphor Audi replies that "it is clear that at best it describes highly restrictive versions of liberalism" (*ibid*, 123), i.e. neither Rawls' nor his own.

131 In another contribution Wolterstorff (1997, 167) mentions the same secular causes of societal evil, and adds, "The common denominator is that human beings tend to kill and brutalize each other for what they care deeply about. In seventeenth century Europe, human beings cared deeply about religion. In our century, most seem to have cared much more deeply about one and another secular cause. Liberalism's myopic preoccupation with religious wars is outdated."

is also causing problems?[132] Or, to formulate the question differently, why is it so difficult for many religionists to acknowledge the need for a Rawlsian *proviso* or Audi's plea for reaching reflective equilibrium between religious and secular values?

Perhaps there is reason to suppose that psychological factors play an important role here: Confronted with the demand for 'constraints' on religion, and being taught that secular reasons have a broader, more universal appeal than religious reasons, the (more or less) religiously conservative people are being reminded that secularization has tended to marginalize them. Or, to be more precise, they are reminded that

- No matter how much religion has *historically* influenced society and the development toward democracy, *today* liberal democracy rests on a basis which is independent (in terms of rational justification) of religion and/or other comprehensive doctrines; "the political order is not God-given, but a result of human effort" (Andersen 2005, 103).
- Today we find the Genesis 22 story of Abraham's willingness to sacrifice deeply problematic and disturbing, because we no longer assume that the demands of religion, and religious authority, automatically take precedence over moral obligations.

Recent Criticisms of Political Liberalism

In this section I have chosen to present three different contributions to the debate on Rawls and political liberalism. The purpose, of course, is to introduce and evaluate some recent interpretations in order to broaden the picture before trying to present a conclusion to this chapter.

Jeffrey Stout

An important contribution to the issue of the compatibility of religion and democracy has come from Princeton philosopher Jeffrey Stout who

---

132 In commenting on what is covered by the word 'religious', Audi (1997, 39f.) makes an interesting observation: "I cannot here try to define 'religious', but it must for our purposes be taken sufficiently narrowly to permit a distinction between the moral and the religious, and the cases that most concern us are those presupposing that religion is theistic. Non-theistic religions pose – other things being equal – far less serious church-state problems."

in 2004 published a book entitled *Democracy and Tradition* (Stout 2004). The title itself is important in that it has at least two meanings relevant to the contents of the book. First, American democracy is interpreted as being in a severe crisis.[133] To remedy the crisis and save democracy for the future, all people of good will must join forces, according to Stout. Alas, what he finds is that 'democrats' (secular liberalists like Rawls and Rorty) and 'traditionalists' (philosophers and theologians like McIntyre, Hauerwas, and Milbank) have entrenched themselves in opposing camps, not willing to engage one another. Second, in order to correct one-sided interpretations and enable a dialogue Stout endeavours to *bridge* democracy and tradition, and not only this, for in fact he makes a point of seeing democracy *as* tradition. In doing this, he labels himself a 'pragmatic expressivist' drawing on American thinkers such as Emerson, Whitman, and Dewey.

From a European perspective, then, one must emphasize the degree in which Stout's book reflect *American* tradition and current affairs, and in fact it is perhaps best seen as a contribution to a rather *internal* debate between Stout and (among others) his friends and colleagues Richard Rorty and Stanley Hauerwas. In this set-up, however, Rawls is seen by Stout as having played a very important, albeit also unfortunate role. This is due to the fact that his *A Theory of Justice* (1971) has gained enormous influence by being standard reading in law schools and departments of philosophy. Soon everyone in this camp would be a contractarian believer in liberal democracy, whereas in the traditionalist camp, in the theological seminaries, the students would be exposed to the anti-modern and anti-secularist theologies of Hauerwas or Milbank. Applied to the current situation in the U.S., Stout makes the following assessment:

---

133 In one of his latest contributions where Stout wants to make a plea for democracy as a 'spirited, passionate affair', the pessimistic diagnosis is even more pronounced: "Unless citizens wake up, and take responsibility for the condition of their society, democracy will be completely eviscerated and the economically powerful will no longer be answerable to anyone else. In that event the correct name for our political system would indeed be *plutocracy* – a government of the people, by the wealthy, and for the wealthy. (...) Whenever economic power is both concentrated in the hands of a few and easily convertible into unconstrained political power, it makes no sense to speak of political life as democratic." (Stout 2007, 6).

We are about to reap the social consequences of a traditionalist backlash against contractarian liberalism. The more thoroughly Rawlsian our law schools and ethics centers become, the more radically Hauerwasian the theological schools become. (...) Liberalism, according to Hauerwas, is a secularist ideology that masks a discriminatory program for policing what religious people can say in public. The appropriate response, he sometimes implies, is to condemn freedom and the democratic struggle for justice as 'bad ideas' for the church. Over the next several decades this message will be preached in countless sermons throughout the heartland of the nation. (Stout 2004, 75 and 76).

This is the unfortunate *polarization* between contractarians and traditionalists that it is Stout's ambition and goal to overcome. The overall purpose, in other words, is to get 'beyond secular liberalism and theological traditionalism' (headline from Stout's book, p. 294). But since the traditionalist camp is reluctant to enter into dialogue, it is clear that Stout, basically, has dedicated himself to a project requiring *persuasion*. Thus, looking back in the 'Conclusion' he comments: "I have sought to persuade seriously committed religious citizens, especially those members of the Christian majority who have half-acknowledged democratic commitments in their hearts, that identifying with the civic nation in a democratic republic like ours need not conflict with their theological convictions." (*ibid*, 297). Let us see, then, how he proceeds in order to meet the traditionalists half-way – or perhaps even more than that.

The first move, as we would expect, consists in a critique of Rawlsian liberalism.

Stout can, of course, agree with Rawls that citizens in a democratic society should always do their best to give reasons (when participating in public debate) that others may be able to accept. However, he finds that Rawls' demands on public reason and 'reasonableness' go too far: "In short, to be reasonable is to accept the need for a social contract and to be willing to reason on the basis of it, at least when deliberating in the public forum on basic constitutional and political matters." (*ibid*, 67). Hence, if citizens opt out of this project they are classified as 'unreasonable'. Stout does not agree and wants to embark on a different route: "I want to explore the possibility that a person can be a reasonable (socially cooperative) citizen without believing in or appealing to a free-standing conception of justice." (*ibid*, 68).

Stout paraphrases Rawls to the effect that only if the demands of public reason and 'reasonableness' are met "can we redeem the promise of treating our fellow citizens fairly in matters pertaining to the use of coercive power. And this conclusion leads, in turn, to a restrictive view of the role religious reasons play in the public forum." (*ibid*, 68). This allegedly restrictive view is what he later (p. 295) calls 'the sticking point' making it necessary to criticize Rawls. And in fact, we find Stout joining the opposition leveled by Wolterstorff: Rawls' constraints on religious arguments are seen as going against 'the spirit of free expression'. Stout acknowledges of course that a modification has occurred with 'the wide view' outlined by Rawls in 'The Idea of Public Reason Revisited', but this is not enough to satisfy his concerns. Says Stout, "I find this version of the position slightly more plausible than the original, simply because it is less restrictive. It makes a bit more room for such instances of exemplary democratic reasoning as the religiously based oratory of the Abolitionists and of Martin Luther King, Jr." (*ibid*, 69).[134] And he continues: "I see it as a strong count against Rawls' current position that these particular speakers will barely squeak by on his criteria, if they manage to do so at all. The alleged need to satisfy the proviso in such cases suggests to me that something remains seriously wrong with the entire approach Rawls is taking" (*ibid*). The following passage, however, makes one wonder how much really separates Rawls and Stout, after all: "It seems more reasonable to suppose that one should try to argue from universally justifiable premises, whenever this seems both wise and possible, while feeling free nonetheless to pursue other argumentative strategies when they seem wise. This would be to treat the idea of public reason as a vague ideal, instead of reifying it moralistically into a set of fixed rules for public discussion." (*ibid*, 75). But again, in order for Stout's project of persuasion to succeed he is pressed to 'soften' political liberalism by turning it into 'a vague ideal'.

---

134 Also Troy Dostert (cf. below) points to Martin Luther King as an example of a 'prophetic discourse' which has been of great importance in achieving positive change in the political culture of American society.

The traditionalists not only regard Rawls as a 'secularist' (despite his repeated refusals to accept this label), they also vehemently oppose 'enlightenment' accounts of secularization and modernity. Therefore, Stout's second move consists in "an account of the benign sense in which our political discourse is secularized. Hence, one can participate in it wholeheartedly without implicitly discounting one's theological convictions." (*ibid*, 298). To get at this 'benign sense', Stout makes an important point of distinguishing between the purely descriptive notion that modern society is 'secularized' and a more normative commitment to 'secularism':

There is a sense in which the ethical discourse of most modern democracies is *secularized*, for such discourse is not "framed by a theological perspective" taken for granted by all those who participate in it. But secularization in this sense is not a reflection of a commitment to *secularism*. It entails neither the denial of theological assumptions nor the expulsion of theological expression from the public sphere. And it leaves believers free to view both the state and democratic political culture as domains standing ultimately under divine judgment and authority. That believers view the political sphere this way does not entail that others will, of course. But this just means that the age of theocracy is over, not that anti-Christ has taken control of the political sphere. (*ibid*, 93).

The last part of this quotation reveals, it seems to me, how far Stout is willing to go in order to pacify the 'believers'. For the same purpose, commenting on the development regarding the authority of the Bible, he introduces a distinction between a) the Bible's authority over an individual's conscience, and b) its 'public discursive authority'. And on this basis he continues: "I want to recommend putting more weight on the second than on the first in telling the story of secularization in general and the story of the Bible in seventeenth-century English politics in particular." (*ibid*, 95). Stout is probably correct in assuming that these two aspects of secularization have developed in different 'rhythms' so to speak; but certainly they must be seen as inter-related developments? Stout, however, goes against the view of secularization that I argued for in Chapter Four of this book:

Secularized discourses, as I am defining them, do not necessarily involve or produce participants who lack religious commitments. Most U.S. citizens profess some sort of belief in God, but their public ethical discourse is secularized in the sense I am trying to specify. This is a major advantage of my account over accounts of secularization that focus on an alleged loss of religious belief or on "disenchantment" of the world. The theory I offer is an account of what transpires between people engaging in public discourse, not an account of what they believe, assume, or presuppose as individuals. It has nothing to do with their experience of the world as a disenchanted universe, emptied of divine intentions and spiritual meaning. (*ibid*, 98).

Be that as it may; what is important to see is that there is an *internal* connection between this conception of 'secularization' and Stout's opposition to any restrictions on the use of religious arguments in public.

Finally, I wish to comment on Stout's general interpretation of Rawls. I must confess that I find it skewed because of the marked tendency of Stout to identify Rawls with *A Theory of Justice* and its ensuing influence on American intellectuals. Thus, framing the controversy in light of Hegel's critique of Kant, Stout (pp. 77ff.) casts Rawls in the role of Kant, while he himself supports Hegel's 'expressivism'. Obviously, Stout acknowledges that in *Political Liberalism* Rawls "does depart from Kant in a number of ways" (*ibid*, 78), but the conclusion is clear: "Rawls remains a Kantian" (*ibid*). I believe that this is a mistaken reading. In order for Rawls' project (and the goal of 'overlapping consensus') to work or just to have some success, it *must* be interpreted in the 'political' (not philosophical) and pragmatic spirit in which Rawls himself clearly intended it.[135] If one

---

135 See also Young (2003, 21), who comments that "Rawls rejects the impulse to develop a political vision and design institutions so that everyone in the polity is ultimately part of a single community. Such a strong sense of unity will suppress or oppress reasonable ways of life incompatible with the dominant values of the community. Mutual commitment to a set of public institutions that can justly regulate cooperation among individuals and groups, moreover, does not require this degree of unity. It nevertheless requires more unity than the merely negative agreement to live and let live." At the same time, however, she finds Rawls' idea of a comprehensive doctrine "too thin a concept to cover the fact of pluralism in ways of life in modern societies." (*ibid*, 23). Hence, Young predicts, a "theory that took account of this plurality and depth of the role of value commitments in people's lives would find more overlap but less

needed to be a Kantian to endorse it, the whole point would be lost. In fact, Rawls' pragmatism is much closer to Stout than he is willing to allow for. Further, in attacking Rawls' 'restrictive view' Stout seems to overlook the fact that the *proviso* applies only to the public political forum and not to civil society (what Rawls calls 'the background culture').

Stout's project of struggling to bring liberalists and traditionalists together is certainly a noble one. I wonder, however, whether he has not laboured in vain. Softening political liberalism and preventing 'secularist' connotations may not be what religious traditionalists or conservatives are looking for. Why? Simply because opposition to what is perceived as being 'secular' is what they thrive on and what may therefore be considered a precondition of their existence in the first place.[136]

J. Judd Owen

In his book *Religion and the Demise of Liberal Rationalism* J. Judd Owen, political scientist at Emory University, is airing the postmodern skepticism toward theories of liberal democracy. And thus it is no coincidence that the target of his criticism is labelled 'liberal *rationalism*'. Owen's investigation may be said to test Rawls in relation to two versions of post-modern 'anti-foundationalism', namely neo-pragmatist Richard Rorty and deconstructionist Stanley Fish. There is a marked difference between the two, however. Whereas Rorty believes that it is possible for liberalism to break away from its rationalistic origins, the critical perspective of Fish is far more radical: if we follow his perspective, the project of liberalism is self-defeating, because it purports to be more tolerant and neutral than it really is. In Owen's paraphrase of Fish: "In the guise of neutrality, liberalism has managed to replace all other partisan agendas with its own partisan agenda. Liberalism claims to stand above the partisan struggle but necessarily takes part in it. Therefore, according to its own self-understanding, 'liberalism doesn't exist'." (Owen 2001, 133). Owen's personal intention, however, is "to offer a limited defense

---

consensus possible among them." (*ibid*, 24). For an elaborate and strong defense of political liberalism on this count (and the related issues of 'culture' and 'diversity'), see Macedo (2003).

136 For a more elaborate treatment of Stout, see Clanton 2008, pp. 107-121.

of liberalism against Fish's critique", partly because Fish "has underestimated the conceptual and moral power of liberalism" (*ibid*, 131).But what is the import of this critique for the view of religion and the role of religious arguments? Rorty, the laid-back pragmatist, is famous for having charaterized religion as a 'conversation stopper'. In this respect, however, Owen faults Rorty for 'trivializing' religion.

Despite his critical distance to 'liberal rationalism', Owen (in contrast to Stout) recognizes that the Rawls of *Political Liberalism* has left rationalism behind. And were this not the case, we could hardly imagine seeing Rorty positioning himself near the 'late' Rawls "seizing hold of Rawls' claim that his theory of justice is 'political not metaphysical'." (*ibid*, 72). Still, it is clear that Rorty takes Rawls further than he himself would want to go. To Rorty, liberalism is secular and non-theistic (if not even atheist), whereas Rawls has repeatedly made it clear that he does not see political liberalism as being against religion. Owen expresses the difference quite aptly: "Rawls seeks a nonmetaphysical doctrine of liberalism but not a 'postmetaphysical culture'." (*ibid*, 103). Hence, Rawls and Rorty may well agree on banning metaphysics from political theory, but they are doing so for very different reasons: Rawls makes this move in order to turn the ideal of overlapping consensus into a realistic hope, and precisely in doing this he positions himself (much like Habermas) as being in basic solidarity with the overall project of modernity. In contrast, Rortys motives stem from a postmodern attitude. And in fact, Rorty's attempt to enlist Rawls as support for his own positition cannot hide the fact that a core concept of political liberalism is public reason. In the final analysis, then, Rawls must in *some* sense be a rationalist, and this is just what Fish emphasizes in his critique. Which of the two interpretations is the more accurate, then, Rorty or Fish? If one bothers to (re)read Rawls' presentation of his project in PL, there can be no doubt (and Owen agrees here) that Rorty's reading is more to the point than that of Fish. As we recall, Rawls made it clear that his version of liberalism is 'political' and has no intentions of being a comprehensive doctrine.

Apparently, Owen is sympathetic towards the intention behind political liberalism: "Rawlsian liberalism will respect and embrace to an unprecedented degree a radical plurality of metaphysical/theological doctrines and, it would appear to follow, ways of life." (*ibid*, 99). And yet, he suspects "that the pluralism that political liberalism will comprehend is not so very deep. In fact, the boundaries of that pluralism, the boundaries of the 'reasonable', I will argue, are defined by the willingness to accept Rawls' solution." (*ibid*, 100). On a similar note, Fish's basic objection against the entire Rawlsian project is that Rawls' *proviso* is in reality equivalent to demanding of the fundamentalists that they relinquish their fundamentalism. The upshot of this is, according to both Fish and Owen, that the real message of PL is a *transformative* agenda: "One must come to believe that it is consistent with God's will that it be set aside in politics. Liberalism depends on religion's being substantively transformed, not bracketed. Liberalism cannot simply preserve the private realm intact." (*ibid*, 117). Following from this, Owen's critique of Rawls may be summarized in two points: 1) Rawls is incorrect in claiming that it is possible to keep questions of justice (the 'political') separate from the question of comprehensive doctrines. 2) The spirit of openness and neutrality in PL is not what it looks like; in reality, Rawls' pluralism is "a Trojan horse of conformity" (*ibid*, 127). Owen formulates this criticism in the following way:

Rawls seems to ask very little indeed. No comprehensive doctrines are in themselves out of bounds, and therefore no fundamental change of belief is sought. But Rawls asks more than he knows. Bracketing so very much of one's comprehensive view from consideration in the political realm requires a radical transformation of that comprehensive view. 'Bracketing' is not simply bracketing; it is transforming. (*ibid*, 126).

I believe that Owen is exaggerating the consequences here. Having said this, however, there is no reason to hide that, although probably not intended or planned by Rawls to be a 'program', political liberalism *may* have as a long-term effect that some people's convictions may undergo some kind of transformation. But why is that supposed to be a bad thing?

Troy Dostert

With the publication of his PhD thesis entitled *Beyond Political Liberalism* Troy Dostert, a Lutheran political theorist, has made a noteworthy contribution to the debate on Rawlsian political liberalism. One interesting aspect of the book is that it is intended to be a theologically oriented alternative to Rawls. Still, much like Stout and Owen, Dostert is sympathetic towards the basic intentions of *Political Liberalism* (PL). Rather, his criticism is directed at the *way* in which Rawls carries out these intentions. The crux of the matter is that, according to Dostert, the dominating tendency of PL is to *control* and trying to 'contain' religion in the public square.[137] In Dostert's view, however, this is not the more adequate strategy: "Stated simply, my argument is that it is through engaging our diversity directly, rather than seeking to control it, that we stand the best chance of negotiating public space successfully" (Dostert 2006, 3). Similarly, Dostert finds that in PL Rawls "assumes a hegemonic secular stance" (*ibid*, 9), which in turn leads to a negative attitude towards religion and religious people.

On this background Dostert poses the following question: "How can we envision a politics in which our particular perspectives, religious or otherwise, are not seen in a suspect or threatening light, but instead are welcomed as part of a process of political discovery?" (*ibid*, 166). And a little later he offers the answer that "Only if our 'comprehensive doctrines' are perceived as having real value in probing the limits of present political arrangements can we hold open the possibility of arriving at mutually acceptable solutions to the challenges of moral diversity" (*ibid*, 167). This call, one might say, is met by Habermas' recent positive approach to the value of (reflective Christian) religion.

But again, what is the background of this allegedly negative attitude on Rawls' part? According to Dostert it is a consequence of Rawls' strong commitment to what he (Dostert) considers the founding *myth* of PL, namely the narrative of how liberalism emerged as a saving reaction to the destructive religious wars of 17th century Europe.[138] As a conse-

---

137 In a similar vein Hauerwas, who incidentally served on Dostert's dissertation committee, has complained about what he calls 'the liberal policing of religion'.

138 This critique, as we have seen, was also levelled by Wolterstorff. Dostert raises his critical counter-question: "why should we continue to rely on a narrative that essentially ends once the liberal solution is put in place"? (*ibid*, 82) – Shortly afterwards he elaborates: "Of course, Rawls is not incorrect in noting that there are plenty of coercive appeals made these days in public discourse. But it does not thereby follow that comprehensive doctrines pose the central danger or that religious doctrines are particularly prone to this impulse." (*ibid*, 83).

quence, religion is regarded as divisive and creating problems, and not as a positive, perhaps even necessary contribution to the political culture of a democratic society.

Dostert, who should be commended for his generally fair description of PL, also touches upon Rawls' 'wide view' which allows religious citizens to present their religious arguments not only in the background culture (where no constraints apply), but also in the public, political forum. Dostert admits that this "can be seen as embodying attempts to modify public reason in a more inclusive direction." (*ibid*, 65). Also, it has not escaped his attention that "Rawls even allows that on some occasions religious argument might not simply be acceptable in public debate but in fact helpful." (*ibid*, 67). On this basis, then, Dostert summarizes the self-understanding of PL in the following manner:

With these qualifications in view, political liberals are able to make a plausible claim that in proposing this conception of public reason, they are not seeking to banish religion from public life or confine it to the realm of personal belief, strategies that have been favored by less circumspect liberals. (...) [P]olitical liberals are merely attempting to work out an amicable arrangement whereby reasonable religious viewpoints can converge, as part of the overlapping consensus, on a political conception of justice that all citizens, regardless of their religious or philosophical convictions, can embrace on the same grounds. The restraint in reason-giving political liberalism requires of citizens is on this reading to be seen merely as the price we must pay for securing a mutually acceptable basis for social unity consistent with each citizen's rationality. (*ibid*, pp. 68 and 69).[139]

---

139 This positive reading, which I regard as an accurate picture of Rawls' intentions, is countered, however, by Dostert's persistent tendency to interpret 'public reason' as a secularist project: "It thus seems fair to say that the telos animating political liberalism entails the attempt to achieve a society in which religion eventually comes to have no significant role to play in shaping the norms of the political order. Until we reach that point, it may be tolerated in a functional sense as a necessary evil of sorts, but only if it ultimately serves to work toward the cause of its own public irrelevance, by pointing to the adequacy of purely political values. Herein lies the fundamental secularity of Rawlsian public reason." (Dostert 2006, 87). Note in this connection that Chapter 3, where this quotation stems from, is entitled 'The Secularity of Liberal Public Reason'.

Still, Dostert finds, the question is whether Rawls does not go too far. In elaborating on this, he raises at least three points of criticism. First, Rawls' distinction between the public political forum and the background culture (civil society); this separation is problematic, argues Dostert, and in practice it proves impossible to maintain. To illustrate, he offers the example of a statement from a bishop's conference; the purpose of such a statement is, surely, to influence both kinds of public realm. Second, Dostert poses what he himself considers the central, normative question: "Is it defensible to regard religious arguments as only *conditionally* public, subject to their meeting the criteria of the reasonable?" (*ibid*, 74). And, finally, Dostert criticizes what he sees as "the categorization of *citizens* into reasonable and unreasonable camps" (*ibid*, 182). Here, however, a misunderstanding seems to be at work: the main tenor of Rawlsian PL is *not* to evaluate or classify citizens. Instead, Rawls (wisely it seems) sticks to the level of comprehensive *doctrines*. That, in my opinion, is a very important difference. Here, as always, it is crucial to be able to distinguish between subject matter (fx political or religious views) and person.

A fascinating aspect of Dostert's book is his survey of three American proposals for a 'public theology' (David Tracy, Richard John Neuhaus, and John Howard Yoder). What is interesting about this is the extent to which it becomes clear just how much a theologian's attitude to religion and politics (and to Rawls for that matter) is predetermined, as it were, by his or her general theological outlook.[140] For liberal theologian David Tracy it is not all that difficult to accept PL's account of public reason, and Dostert comments that "[i]n certain key respects, Tracy's understanding of the preconditions of public discourse closely parallels the assumptions that animate political liberalism's conception of public reason." (*ibid*, 97).

Matters are quite different, however, when we turn to neo-conservative Neuhaus who is adamant to stress that democratic society is based on Jewish-Christian values. Moreover, he sees an important *political* role for religion (read: Christianity) in making sure that the political power is kept within its rightful place: 'under God'. Personally, though, Dostert's sym-

---

140 Considering myself a liberal theologian, I am, of course, no exemption from this rule.

pathies lie with Hauerwas' mentor and major source of inspiration, John Howard Yoder. Like Hauerwas, Yoder emphasizes the role of the church as counter-culture and as an 'alternative polity'. Still, although Dostert's somewhat sketchy proposal for a 'post-secular politics' is strongly influenced by Yoder, in the end he sees the need to "place a greater emphasis on the search for shared aims in political life." (*ibid*, 126).

Finally then, what does Dostert's critical alternative to Rawls look like? This, alas, never becomes quite clear, but like the proponents of political liberalism (Rawls, Audi, Habermas) Dostert chooses to focus on the *virtues* that citizens in a democratic society should practice. Unlike the proponents of political liberalism, however, in Dostert's case there are only virtues, and no constraints. According to Dostert, the following four virtues must be regarded of crucial importance for public debate: *sincerity, discipline, dialogic creativity*, and *forbearance* (cf. *ibid*, 168ff.). As a reader, one is easily persuaded that if these virtues were broadly manifested in society things would look a whole lot better. Only, the question is how realistic this scenario is? And in fact, towards the end of his book Dostert seems to be somewhat on the retreat regarding the criticism of political liberalism: "Here too, then, my alternative to political liberalism does not reject its core intuition as much as it challenges the way in which that intuition is actualized politically." (*ibid*, 187). Moreover, Dostert seems to realize that one would be entitled to question whether the norms inherent in his four virtues would be acceptable to other religions than Christianity. This is an objection, however, that Dostert never really answers, – or to be more precise: he evades it by saying, "Whether and to what extent the particular practices I have defended can be embraced by a wide range of citizens and moral communities are empirical questions that I cannot take up here." (*ibid*, 196).

Public Religion in a Pluralistic Democracy?

An important part of Ronald Thiemann's book, to which we have already referred above, consists in a proposal for "a proper 'public theology' [that] can make an essential contribution to the reconstruction of a public philosophy that reaffirms the central constitutional values of liberty, equality, and toleration." (Thiemann 1996, 90). Before we can test the soundness of this argument, however, we must briefly look at Thiemann's conception of liberalism and his criteria for presenting arguments in the public sphere.

Like our previous theological commentators, Thiemann finds political liberalists too restrictive in their attitude towards religion, and therefore he makes a plea for a more 'virtuous' liberalism. With respect to liberal political theory in general, Thiemann distinguishes between 'real' (classical) liberalists, communitarians, and, finally, what he terms 'revisionists' (Rawls is placed in this category). The revisionists, according to Thiemann, occupy a middle-position which "provides the basis for a reconception of the place of religion in American public life." (*ibid*, 98). Or, as he later puts it: "The central challenge of revisionist liberal politics is to develop a polity that honors personal freedom and yet appeals to a sense of common obligation freely offered by the citizenry." (*ibid*, 109). Rawls, no doubt, would fully agree.

In order to pave the way for a more public role for religion, Thiemann, again similar to Rawls, argues that churches and mosques are free associations that do not differ in kind from fx trade unions or other voluntary organizations. Thus, there should be no reason to exclude them "from participating fully in the persuasive forum of democratic politics" (*ibid*, 135). Moreover, Thiemann regards it as misguided to define, in advance, particular 'threshold requirements' which arguments must meet in order to be allowed to enter the political debate. "Rather", he argues, "we should seek to define those virtues of citizenship that we seek to instill in all participants in our pluralistic democracy." (*ibid*). Again, as we have encountered above, it is characteristic of theological participants in the debate that they agree to virtues but reject constraints or 'burdens' (Habermas) on religious citizens. But is Rawls guilty of setting up a 'threshold requirement'? I don't think so. I understand the proviso of his 'wide view' simply as a reminder to *all* comprehensive doctrines that *eventually*, in order to count in the final political process, religious arguments should also be accessible in a more secular language.

Anyway, what Thiemann offers, in order to foster the desired virtues, are meant to work as norms of plausibility, i.e. "criteria that democratic citizens should employ to evaluate arguments in the public domain." (*ibid*, 135). Thiemann presents us with the following three norms:

First, *The norm of public accessibility* requires that arguments (and their premises) should be "open to public examination and scrutiny" (*ibid*). Having said this, however, Thiemann immediately softens the norm by adding that it cannot be demanded but only encouraged: "Persons are free to offer public arguments that appeal to emotion, base instincts, and private sources of revelation, but democratic societies should encourage citizens to resist such appeals as incompatible with the fundamental values of liberal polity." (*ibid*, 136). Second, *The norm of mutual respect* "goes beyond mere toleration in that it requires of citizens that they grant to those with whom they disagree the same consideration that they themselves would hope to receive." (*ibid*). This norm, however, seems already covered by Rawls' 'principle of reciprocity'. Finally, *The norm of moral integrity* entails three aspects: consistency of speech; consistency between speech and action, and integrity of principle.

What connects Thiemann's constructive plea for more acceptance of religion in public life to his earlier treatment of constitutional principles is his realization that the fathers of the American constitution argued for the basic values on the basis of their Christian convictions. Thiemann draws particular attention to James Madison and finds it a striking fact "that the argument through which he discerns these core values is explicitly theological." (*ibid*, 150). In order better to assess the importance Thiemann attributes to this, the following, somewhat longer quotation may be useful:

[T]he theological character of Madison's argument raises a basic challenge to John Rawls' assertion that the core values of democracy constitute a "free standing conception", derived independently of the comprehensive schemes that might serve to confirm these values. As my analysis of Madison shows, the core values can in fact be derived from a particular comprehensive scheme and yet be inclusive of the beliefs of those who do not share that scheme. (. . .) If that is the case, then it surely follows that religious beliefs should not be prohibited from providing public justifications within a democratic polity, as long as those beliefs genuinely contribute to the building of an overlapping consensus. Still, as history clearly demonstrates, not all religious beliefs can or ought to function in public life, but the recognition that some religious beliefs can and do function in that manner should set aside, once and for all, the argument against religious arguments per se in the public sphere. The question is not whether religious arguments qualify as genuinely public, but what kind of religious arguments so qualify. (*ibid*, 150).

What is at stake here? Perhaps we can start out with agreeing that the core values of a constitution *can* be formulated independently of a comprehensive doctrine (i.e. 'freestanding') and that they *can* also be 'derived from a particular comprehensive scheme and yet be inclusive'. Which way of proceeding should be preferred? Judging from a highly relevant example, the debate on how to formulate the new, constitutional treaty of the European Union, the majority of the politicians seem to point in Rawls' direction. Or to be more accurate: Precisely *because* the issue of whether the constitution should have a preamble referring to God proved so controversial and divisive, the planned preamble had to be given up. This may well be considered a shame, but at the same time one should not overlook the fact that there is a deeply Rawlsian lesson to be learnt here: In order to avoid controversy and attain the acceptance of everyone involved, it may sometimes be necessary 1) to 'keep it simple', and 2) to formulate the common core in a language accessible and agreeable to all.

Going back to the above quotation, what is it that Thiemann derives from Madison? Is it anything but good old Bible-based civil religion? I should think not. This has certainly in many respects served us well, but the pertinent question, which Thiemann fails to address, is whether civil religion is an adequate response to the (seemingly) growing pluralism of our globalized times. I can think of several U.S. court cases pointing in the direction that particular elements and instances of civil religion are not perceived by all citizens to be 'inclusive'. If this is our current situation, surely something has been lost, and instead of just grieving we should reflect on how we might be able to compensate for this loss. Habermas' perspective seems to me pertinent here, for he has an acute sense of two points that ought to please any theologian and all those in favour of religion. One is his awareness that in the long run democratic societies are probably dependent on normative foundations that they themselves are not capable of producing. Second, I am thinking of his acknowledgement that something is lost when religious arguments are translated into a more secular language. In other words, Habermas seems to put forward a valid argument as to why a democracy should welcome arguments stemming from a religious context; if not, society risks cutting itself off from the rich symbolic sources of religious tradition. In this regard, Rawls might be open to critique for not sufficiently recognizing the possible *positive* contribution from religious world-views. But again, the crux of the matter is the brute fact of pluralism: Some of us may well like our Jewish-Christian heritage, but would we (or Habermas for that matter) be equally forthcoming toward public arguments from Islamist quarters or from, say, Witnesses of Jehovah?

Returning to Thiemann, he also seems, in the end, to retreat somewhat from his plea for the public relevance of theological arguments. For although some religious beliefs may be publicly accessible, it "does not follow, however, that all religious warrants should be accorded the same welcome in public debate. The important issue is not whether an argument appeals to a religious warrant; the issue is whether the warrant, religious or not, is compatible with the basic values of our constitutional democracy", and so, to further elaborate, "the argument proposes that within the public realm the values of liberty, equality, and mutual respect function as the ideals toward which our political actions should strive. Precisely because these notions are general principles, they function heuristically to orient our society to a set of common goals." (*ibid*, 156).

I detect a valid point here in that Thiemann makes a plausible argument for not singling out *religious* arguments as the only trouble-maker. Nonetheless, with his finally implying that warrants (religious or not) are subservient to what he later calls our 'fundamental democratic values', I find it difficult to see that he differs substantially from Rawls.

Must Faith Be Privatized?

This question, the subtitle of a recent book called *Religion in Public Life*, has given British philosopher *Roger Trigg* cause to reflect and advocate an opposing view. Basically, Trigg may be said to argue from a comprehensive philosophical doctrine of *realism* and commitment to a common rationality. Hence, the main target of criticism is *relativism* in general as well as its manifestations in multiculturalism and postmodernism in particular. In addition, Trigg is wary of the dangers of removing religion (and in particular Christianity) from the public life of Western democracies.

The genre of Trigg's book is that of a passionate essay, and one of its chief merits is that it is a veritable treasure of concrete examples (historic and contemporary) of the highly complex relations between religion, democracy, and public life, including church-state relations. The downside of this, however, is that one searches in vain for more substantial analyses of political liberalism. Thus, Rawls, Audi, and Habermas are treated in a cursory manner. Still, for Trigg this is sufficient to make it clear to the reader that he sides with those commentators who see in political liberalism an implicit secularist program. Says Trigg (referring to Rawls' 'veil of ignorance'):

This suggests the issue is not pluralism, but the divide between a religious and an explicitly secular way of looking at the world. The apparent liberal solution is to side with the secular against the religious. It may seem like neutrality, but it becomes a much more substantial position, dedicated to divorcing religion from any official context. The pretext is the alleged divisiveness of religion. The result appears to many to be a determined opposition to any public religious expression, and that itself sets up great tensions in a society. (Trigg 2007, 115).

As regards pluralism, Trigg sees it neither as an important challenge, nor as something desirable, for as he cautions, pluralism "can quickly degenerate into relativism" (*ibid*, 1). Moreover, Trigg's general attitude to the problem of religion in public life becomes more understandable, once one realizes that he is not exactly a strong believer in secularization: "Not long ago it was assumed that the ebbing of faith, when confronted with the insights of modern science, would soon deprive religion of all its influence; 'secularization' was assumed to be an inexorable trend. Those living in many Western European countries may find that still confirmed in their everyday experience, but Western Europe can be very untypical of the rest of the world." (*ibid*, 190).

It is integral to Trigg's realist position that he sees religion and science as being on a par in terms of rationality;[141] religious reasons, referring to an 'objective reality', are similar to other kinds of reasons (cf. p.30); therefore, why would one want to exclude them from public scrutiny?

---

141 Trigg notes in passing (p.4) that he has published two books on this subject (*Rationality and Religion* and *Rationality and Science*).

Claims Trigg, "Countries which try to keep religious controversy off the public stage are simply restraining forces which will eventually burst forth in some way or other. It is much healthier if religion is allowed to play its part in public, rational, debate about matters of common concern. Religious reasoning is a branch of human rationality. It has as much right to be heard as any form of scientific reasoning, and is sometimes in as much need of critical scrutiny." (*ibid*, 9).

But in Trigg's perspective, the real danger of removing religion from the public sphere lies in the double fact that nations need an *identity* and that basic democratic rights and constitutional principles are in need of a *metaphysical* grounding.[142] In this connection, Trigg makes no secret of his preference for Locke who lived in a time where explicit references to Christianity were the norm rather than the exception. Christianity was the basis, and the "crunch question is how far a reliance on reason, and beliefs in equality and freedom, can survive if that basis is removed." (*ibid*, 80). This, in turn, prompts Trigg to the following interesting reflection:

How much should we rely on theological justification? We can certainly ignore it, and hope that we can keep the superstructure without the historical foundation. That is probably not very feasible, and, in that case, we may have to change other beliefs about the importance of human beings, seeing, for example, no principled distinction between humans and animals. Some welcome that, but if we wish to retain our belief in the importance of humanity, and the 'sanctity' of human life, we may have to stress the role of religion in educational systems, and in the public sphere generally. So far from being privatized, it would turn out that it was explicitly required to explain our intuitions about how our society should be organized. To say that in the current Western world this is controversial would be an understatement. (*ibid*, 83).

Yes, Trigg's position is controversial, but that would be irrelevant if it were also plausible and well-argued. Unfortunately, in an important sense

---

142 Claims Trigg, "We depend on prior metaphysical and religious beliefs about human nature. If freedom and rights, even children's rights, become the only measure of an educational system, it begins to operate in a dangerous vacuum. Little remains to keep a society together." (*ibid*, 189).

it is not. In fact, a major part of his argument is but yet another example of the profound misunderstanding of political liberalism which, having read Trigg, I am beginning to think may be impossible to root out. I am thinking here, of course, of the unfortunate distinction between 'public' and 'private'. The overall argument of Trigg's book hinges on the assumption that liberalism (and probably other evil forces as well) are deliberately endeavoring to 'privatize' religion. Trigg, however, reveals himself as being a poor interpreter of Rawls here. To substantiate this point, let me refer to a section, where Trigg directly quotes Rawls' distinction between 'public' and 'non-public' bases of justification. Immediately following, however, he comments: "Once again, a distinction is introduced between public and private with religious views epitomizing the kind of view which has a 'non-public' basis of justification." (*ibid*, 198). Here, Trigg clearly interprets it as 'private' while still retaining the Rawlsian concept of 'non-public', but just one page later Trigg happily refers to "Rawls' dichotomy [sic!] between public and private [sic!] bases of justification." (*ibid*, 199). Recalling Rawls' explicit and repeated statements that he is not buying into the public-private distinction, this is a grave misinterpretation. Finally, I believe that Trigg completely overlooks the point that in the Rawlsian 'background culture' (which is equivalent to what we would normally call 'the public square') there are no constraints on religion whatsoever.

Conclusion

This chapter has demonstrated that virtually all aspects of political liberalism and its relation to the role of religion in public have been the subject of controversy and debate. In a certain sense, though, it is somewhat strange that the controversy should focus particularly on *religion*, for in PL, as we recall, religion is not 'singled out', as it were, but treated as one possible kind of comprehensive doctrine. Moreover, what is of interest to Rawls is not, as we have seen, whether a comprehensive doctrine is *religious* or not, but whether it is *reasonable* or not.

Turning to the criticism leveled at Rawls from religionists or theological commentators, it is not difficult to identify the recurrent complaints: PL is generally perceived as unduly constraining the use of religious arguments in public. Further, it is accused of implicitly pursuing, under the guise of 'neutrality' and 'impartiality', a secularist program aiming to privatize religion. In order to assess whether this wide-spread opinion is justified, I shall briefly summarize my reading of Rawls and discuss it in relation to the standard objections from religious quarters.

As already indicated in the first part of this chapter, I read Rawls as intending a pragmatic, political solution to the problem of how citizens in a contemporary society, characterized by a plurality of comprehensive doctrines, may find sufficient common ground in order for basic legislature and constitutional essentials to be accepted 'for the right reasons'. Second, from this follows two demands on the citizens of a liberal democracy: 1) to accept the need for a political conception based on the principle of reciprocity, and 2) being willing to reason on the basis of this principle when deliberating in the public, political forum. Personally, I find these demands to be modest, indeed, – or to put it in another way: If you feel compelled to protest against these two demands, could that not *only* be due to the fact that you have a bad case? Third, Rawls advocates certain criteria for the use of public reason; the demands of public reason, however, are limited to the public, political forum. And since this is kept as narrow as possible, Rawls is actually *less* restrictive than he is generally presented. Besides, we have the entire civil society (what Rawls calls the 'background culture') consisting of associations like churches or universities. And mediating between these two parts of society we have all kinds of media comprising what Rawls labels 'non-public political culture'.

This terminology, obviously, goes directly against the standard distinction between public and private. Belonging to civil society, churches and religious debates are certainly regarded by PL as as public as can be. There is thus no sense in which Rawls may be accused of relegating religion to the private sphere. Why all the opposition, then? As hinted at earlier in this chapter, I believe that at bottom we are dealing with a psychological problem: A good many religious people take offense because they 'hear' Rawls (and liberalism in general) as saying that religious arguments are of lesser value than secular ones.[143] This, of course, is not Rawls' position. Having established this, however, it is time to grant that the whole point of the proviso is, in the final event, to assert the priority of 'the secular' over 'the religious', at least in the public, political forum. The contemporary priority of the secular, by the way, is consonant with the general view of cultural evolution and religion which I presented in Chapter Four. In this sense, as noted earlier in this chapter, it may be correct to ascribe to political liberalism a 'transformative' agenda. Moreover, I believe that one should grant to the critics that political liberalism's 'guise of neutrality' should be relinquished. What I mean by this is that *trying* to be neutral is not the same as actually *being* neutral, for this is impossible and (at best) a regulative idea. Instead, it should be recognized openly, by politicians as well as political philosophers, that establishing a proviso is in itself an exercise of discursive power.[144] But, I would like to add, it's a good and necessary way of exercising power.

Despite all the criticism, however, what strikes you is how difficult it apparently is for theological commentators to construct a plausible and viable alternative to Rawls' version of political liberalism. The usual strategy is first to give sketchy and imprecise presentations of Rawls and then to present your own, Christian view as being more adequate (fx Wolterstorff's 'consocial position').[145] For at least two reasons, however, this is hardly convincing. One is that the theological critique generally fails to address the challenge that set Rawls' project of PL in motion in the first place, namely the fact of pluralism. Second, by indirectly saying that '*We* (as Christians) have so much to offer in publioc politics, so *we*

---

143 Obviously, the fact that Rawls is offensive to some need not in itself be perceived as a problem or a grave objection; in fact (to borrow an expression from Rawls) it might be the case that PL were offensive 'for the right reasons'.

144 I owe this insight to my colleague, Lars Albinus.

145 This also applies to Stephen Carter (Carter 1993) who proposes as 'the ultimate solution' "that liberalism develop a politics that accepts whatever form of dialogue a member of the public offers." (*ibid*, 230). As he elaborates: "For unless liberal theory and liberal law develop ways to welcome the religiously devout into public moral debate without demanding that they first deny their religious selves, the caricature of liberalism offered by the radical right will more and more become the truth, for liberalism will continue its slide from a pluralistic theory of politics to a narrow, elitist theory of right results." (*ibid*, 232).

should be heard much more', these critics are in fact (albeit against their own intentions) making a strong case for Rawls' point that it is necessary to distinguish between public reason and comprehensive doctrines. And at the same time they fail to acknowledge the importance of secularization and the fact of pluralism.

Hence, as a general framework for defending democracy and tackling the challenges of pluralism I believe that Rawls' political liberalism is the best we have and that it stands vindicated before a vast specter of criticisms which have proven to be, alas, often based on mistakes or misinterpretations. Having said this, there may well be problems following from political liberalism that calls for further debate, and let me just mention three important themes: One relates to the issue of 'translation', or the requirement that 'in due course' religious arguments must be formulated in a secular vocabulary accessible to all citizens. Although we know that 'prophetic discourse' (like that of Martin Luther King) may be alive and well in the background culture, I believe that we (and Rawls) should be sensitive to the fact that in the very process of translation something valuable might get lost. Anyway, Habermas is clearly more aware of this problem than is Rawls. On the other hand, the weakness of Habermas' position consists, in my opinion, in two things: a) that he moves from the level of comprehensive doctrines to that of individual believers;[146] and b) that his sympathetic proposal for secular and religious citizens to join in a cooperative effort of translation will remain, no doubt, a utopian vision. The strength of Habermas, i.e. that he has developed a theory of communicative action by which it can be rendered philosophically plausible that citizens develop democratic sensibilities, may at the same time be considered a weakness, because it forces him to develop a less than realistic picture of the mutual, cooperative translation between religious and non-religious citizens. On the other hand, Rawls may be criticized

---

146 The problem with addressing the sensibilities of individual believers is that it raises the large issue of recognition and respect which I cannot take up in this context. Suffice it to say that McBride (2005) reminds us of the inherent tension between a commitment to deliberative democracy and the wide-spread call for a 'politics of recognition'. Whereas the former "requires a public sphere which is maximally inclusive of diverse beliefs and perspectives", the latter "typically seeks to insulate such identities from challenge." (McBride 2005, 497).

for leaving the question as to how the proviso is actually to be carried out more or less in the dark. And, finally, both Rawls and Habermas may be criticized for clinging to a too normative and idealistic idea of democracy.[147] However, I do not believe that this kind of criticism should be taken too seriously. After all, an ethics or a theory of democracy is not falsified by the empirical fact that many people do not live up to its standards. Be that as it may (and in order to arrive at the conclusion regarding 'Rawls or Habermas?' which I promised earlier in this chapter), my personal opinion is that Rawls' version of liberal democracy is the more adequate to deal with the multiple challenges of religious pluralism.

A second theme concerns the *scope* of public reason. Although Rawls has strong reasons to limit it to the political forum, it may still be too narrow a view. At the same time, as Jonathan Quong reminds us in an interesting paper arguing for a broader view (cf. Quong 2004), we should be aware that widening the sphere of public reason would be likely to arouse even *more* discomfort in religious quarters. A final theme relates to a question that was raised by Roger Trigg: Is political liberalism not overlooking that the principles and values of public reason may have a religious foundation? Perhaps, but we should make a distinction here. That the basic values of (most) Western constitutions are of Jewish-Christian origin is a historical fact. From this fact it does not follow, however, that they also need a religious or metaphysical foundation *today*.[148] This might well be advantageous in order to secure motivation or promote national identity, but given the plurality of comprehensive doctrines it is just not an option anymore. Thus, at the end of the day, what we must realize as Christians (or as committed to any other religious comprehensive doctrine) is that something like the Rawlsian proviso is quite simply the *price* we must pay for living in a pluralistic

---

147 For an interesting critique along these lines, see Stepan (2000, 45) who advances the following evaluation of Rawls: "Rawls' argument is both powerful and internally consistent. Yet he devotes virtually no attention to how *actual* polities have consensually and democratically arrived at agreements to 'take religion off the political agenda'. Almost none of them followed the Rawlsian normative map." In an elegant way of summarizing his point, Stepan claims that Rawls "give[s] great weight to *liberal arguing*, but almost no weight to *democratic bargaining*." (*ibid*).

148 Stepan (2000, 44) refers to this way of reasoning as *the fallacy of 'unique founding conditions'*.

society. Some may not *like* this, as we have seen above, but this is as good as it gets.

And where, then, is Abraham in all this? Actually more present that the reader might think, for references to Genesis 22 are to be found more that once in the literature reviewed above.[149] If we think of the Abraham-Isaac story as a test-case, Rawls would no doubt see Abraham's action as based on an unreasonable comprehensive doctrine. Is this verdict from political philosophy all there is to say? I believe that there is in fact more to say, but this raises the task to which I now turn in the final chapter: that of integrating political philosophy and philosophy of religion.

---

149 To mention just two examples: In an earlier context than the quotation already cited above, Robert Audi (1997, 51f.) once again comments on Abraham's sacrifice of Isaac and in continuation remarks on the relation between ethics and theology (*ibid*, 52). And Jeffrey Stout refers to a book by theologian Robert Merrihew Adams called *Finite and Infinite Goods*. In this book, according to Stout, "Adams forthrightly denies in chapter 12 that the killing of Isaac is something that a loving God would actually command Abraham to do (Genesis 22:1-19). So anyone who believes himself to have received such a command from God is not thereby licensed to obey it, but rather required to change his mind about what the true God commands. Would that all believers subjected their assumptions about divine commands to this sort of testing!" (Stout, 2004, 260).

Chapter Seven

INTEGRATING POLITICAL PHILOSOPHY AND PHILOSOPHY OF RELIGION

"In endorsing a constitutional democratic regime, a religious doctrine may say that *such are the limits God sets to our liberty.*" (Rawls 1997, 460; emphasis added).

Setting oneself the task of integrating political philosophy and philosophy of religion may well look strange, perhaps even suspicious, when regarded from the perspective of political philosophy. In fact, in the case of Rawls there seems to be nothing to integrate, since political liberalism is claimed to be a 'freestanding' position.[150] And yet, we should not forget that the whole point of Rawls' project is epitomized in the expression 'overlapping consensus'. From the standpoint of theology and philosophy of religion, however, Rawlsian political liberalism presents a serious challenge and an impetus to reflect on some of the implications for religion, in this case: contemporary Christianity.[151]

But still, there may be more to say – even from the perspective of political liberalism. For one thing, it clearly matters to Rawls whether or not religious citizens endorse liberalism's political conception 'for the

---

150 I am aware that this claim is rejected by some critics (fx Wolterstorff 1997). My own position on this is that in terms of history and tradition the claim probably does *not* hold, but that given the fact of ongoing cultural evolution it is possible, even plausible, to argue PL as freestanding *today*.

151 In order to avoid confusion, let me emphasize that in the present context I conceive of philosophy of religion as a sub-discipline of systematic theology. Thus, in what follows, I may use 'theology' and 'philosophy of religion' as interchangeable concepts.

right reasons'. And some of these reasons might well be religious or at least be the result of religious reflection. Second, if we look at Rawls' piece of advice, which I have elevated to a kind of motto for this chapter, I believe that the implication is clear: Rawls (whether he is aware of it or not) is in effect prompting religious people to do some *religious* reflection, i.e. to find a way of balancing their religious commitments with their commitment to be fully participating members of a democratic society.[152]

To be sure, this is not a new subject for Christian theology. Indeed, ever since the time of Jesus himself it has been considered nothing less than a matter of salvation how to reconcile the demands issuing from two different realms, that of Caesar and that of God. Even in current debates, many theologians are looking back to Augustine or Luther for answers to this conundrum. A truly *contemporary* solution, however, requires in my view that we engage the best available contemporary understanding of the society in which we live, rather than versions of society as it was in the 5th or the 16th century. It is not least in this sense, then, that I take the political philosophy of Rawls and Habermas to be a timely and highly relevant subject for systematic theology. But this is only one half of the story; the other half goes in the opposite direction, so to speak, since here philosophy of religion appears not only as a source of inspiration, but also as putting the major points of political philosophy into perspective. Thus, the overall purpose of the following chapter is to serve as an exercise in conducting this kind of constructive dialogue.

What *is* the issue, then? As I see it, the major challenge may be divided into two parts: One is drawing the consequences stemming from Rawls' (or God's?) 'limits', and the other is sketching an interpretation of Christianity where God's freedom and human freedom are at least compatible. Obviously, it would be foolhardy to attempt to solve such a large and complex issue in the context of a final chapter. Nonetheless, in the hope of at least being able to present a few interesting ideas I shall proceed in three steps: First, I take stock of Rawls' limits and constraints regarding the role of religion and ponder their general consequences for theology. Second, I return to Kierkegaard and *Fear and Trembling* in order

---

152 Audi (1997 and 2000) is more explicit here with his call for religious citizens to establish a 'theo-ethical equilibrium'.

to inquire whether his solution to Abraham's dilemma may contain elements of contemporary relevance. And, finally, I import some ideas from a 'Russian connection', namely the social philosophy of Nicolas Berdyaev. However, I wish to make it clear that I would strongly oppose being identified or associated with the thinking or general position of Berdyaev. In other words, he functions in this context just as an example. Hence quite consciously, I treat him in a selective manner bordering on the irresponsible. But as a Christian philosopher he *is* useful in the context of this book for mainly two reasons: He has presented a non-authoritarian concept of God and revelation, and he has given the problem of man's double relation to God and to society some thought.

Theological Consequences of Rawlsian Political Liberalism

In pondering the theological consequences of political liberalism, the overall tendency should be relatively clear, namely that Rawls demands from religious citizens (and all other citizens) two things: A certain degree of self-limitation and a willingness to endorse the basic, political order 'for the right reasons'. But what does this entail and require, more specifically, when considered from the perspective of philosophy of religion? Rawls' demands may, I believe, be summarized in the following four points:

- Recognizing the basic principles of separation between church and state, including state *neutrality* towards religion.[153]
- Recognizing that religious liberty also includes the right to freedom *from* religion.
- Recognizing the proviso and that in *this* sense (and in this sense only) does the secular take priority over the sacred. Not because it is 'higher' or intrinsically 'better', but simply because it is more inclusive, publicly accessible, and commonly acceptable.
- Recognizing basic 'civic virtues' and the need to strive for balancing one's religious and secular bases of judgment.

---

153 As the debate between Audi and Wolterstorff (cf. last chapter) has demonstrated, the demand for neutrality is open to different interpretations.

Theologically, I would argue, this entails recognizing a general, historical trend of secularization (cf. Chapter Four). For unless this is more or less accepted, it is unlikely that the endorsement of society's basic political order will be given for the right reasons. What is more, believers who have not grasped and accepted the historical process of secularization may be prone to regard many elements of contemporary culture as 'Satan's work' or the instrument of 'evil forces'. Hence, in this perspective it should be seen as an important task for theological schools, Christian churches and ministers to teach and preach the basics of secularization (including the 'fact of pluralism') and, at the same time, to encourage believers *not* to think of secularization as the enemy of religion, but, rather, as the *liberation* of religion. Religious citizens should, at least if they are Christian, accept (and hopefully even rejoice in) the fact that the days of theocracy and religious hegemony are over, and that there is no going back. In turn, they are of course free to give this fact a religious interpretation to their liking, be it that secularization has been willed by God, or that it was made possible, in the first place, by certain distinctions of Christian theology.[154] What we have here, I believe, is that we need to finally distance ourselves from the uncomfortable implication of Abraham's intended sacrifice, namely that the model (i.e. Abraham as the 'Father of faith') we are called to emulate is one where what is perceived as God's commands should be unquestioningly obeyed, always. In other words, recognizing both the irreversible process of secularization *and* the continuing relevance of religion (= Habermas' 'post-secular' society) gives us access to a norm or criterion by which to evaluate different manifestations of religion.

In a similar spirit, Christians may regard the separation between church and state as having its origin in the famous saying of Jesus, "Render to Caesar the things that are Caesar's, and to God the things that are God's" (Mk 12:17). Still, I can easily imagine someone objecting that this is just a call for a modus vivendi, and not stability for the right reasons.

---

154 In fact, this way of arguing has been promoted by major theologians of the 20th century like Friedrich Gogarten, Dietrich Bonhoeffer, and Rudolf Bultmann. Although their position rests on a specific theology, it may find find support in other, more historical accounts of Western secularization; cf. most recently Taylor (2007).

To such an objection I would simply reply that in an autocratic, more or less totalitarian society this, of course, is the only realistic possibility. In a constitutional democracy, however, it is possible to expect a good deal more. Part of this 'more', as I discussed in the previous chapter, is contained in Audi's suggestion that the state-church separation be reflected in a similar separation on the side of individual religious believers, i.e. their being able to a) separate religious and secular arguments, and b) balancing them by striving for (and hopefully attaining) a *theo-ethical equilibrium*. I regard this principle of Audi's as one way of specifying the consequences of Rawls' "these are the limits that God has set on our liberty". Or, as in the sarcastic rephrasing proposed by Owen (2001, 117): "One must come to believe that it is consistent with God's will that it be set aside in politics." This twist is at least funny, but as we know, its content is not a necessary consequence of the restraints proposed by Rawls, Audi, or Habermas.

The principle of separation presents a classic theological theme which has traditionally been treated under the heading of 'the two kingdoms', one earthly, the other heavenly. Thus, as a first result of our 'integrationist' dialogue we may conclude that theological reflection can agree with political philosophy on the necessity of *separating* the two realms or 'kingdoms'. It would be a grave mistake, however, to overlook that the whole point of the argument (fx in Luther) has been to assert that it is *God* who governs in *both* kingdoms. We will probably not be amiss in assuming that this was a natural way of looking at things in the 16th century; today, however, I see no way for an honest theology to maintain this interpretation. God's law is no longer the foundation of society. Or as Habermas would phrase it: In modern societies religion can no longer serve as the normative foundation of a public morality shared by all. Religion, in other words, has irretrievably lost its former function as a world-view (German: *Weltbild*) governing the rest of society. What may be left, at best, are vague, symbolic references to 'God' as in civil religion or in preambles to constitutions, where the 'authors' acknowledge to be ultimately answerable to God.[155]

---

155 On this, see the interesting discussion in Graf 2006, 65ff., as well as Trigg's comments on the Canadian charter (Trigg 2007, 160ff.).

And yet, even such symbolic references may have significance and exert a positive influence, for example in instilling in judges and law-makers a healthy sense of humility. I reject, however, the neo-conservative argument (be it from philosophers or theologians) that politics and government need a religious (and, interestingly, by 'religious' these voices always mean 'Christian') foundation in order to be kept on the straight and narrow. Indeed, experience points in the direction that power has a way of corrupting those who exercise it. The more general issue, however, i.e. whether a society is viable without God as its foundation, should not be decided in advance, but rather regarded as an empirical question. Given the process of secularization and the contemporary fact of pluralism, however, the natural starting point *today* would, I believe, for political philosophers as well as theologians, be to think of the political order as 'freestanding'. Another matter, of course, is that philosophy of religion may find cause to remind political philosophers that it is consonant with the spirit of democracy itself that it be considered a *fallibilistic* project. Hence, should a tendency to hypostasize or deify democracy arise, it may be worthwhile to argue that a fallibilistic consciousness is one way of taking seriously the Christian virtue of *humility*.

The principles of state neutrality and religious freedom may cause a lot of complex court cases these days, but I do not see them as presenting any *theological* problems. On the contrary, freedom of religion should be considered a cornerstone of any contemporary theology worthy of its name. Individual believers (or some churches) may not like neither state neutrality nor freedom of (and from) religion, but when faced with the prospect of being controlled by another religion than their own, they will, of course, see the point.

Concerning the *proviso*, it is interesting to note that almost all theological commentators see it as an affront to religion or even (like Wolterstorff) as an intolerable constraint. Rawls, nonetheless, points in a different direction by alerting us to a *positive* effect of the proviso, namely that it forces the many different religious voices to translate their contributions into a common and generally accessible language. The very positive and desirable outcome of this is that different religious traditions and positions get the opportunity to understand each other better than before. Hence, from a theological perspective, Rawls' proviso and its concomitant translation requirement (although perhaps not intended as such) may be perceived as a valuable contribution to inter-religious dialogue. Habermas' more ambitious, and less realistic proposal, as we have seen, is interesting in this connection, because it includes demands on secular citizens as well: According to Habermas, these citizens should (among other things), by way of continuing, communicative 'learning processes', develop a self-critical perspective on the relation between faith and knowledge.

If these are the limitations on religion stemming from political liberalism, the flip-side of the coin is the legitimate function of *religion* vis à vis the political order. Here, in civil society (Rawls' 'background culture') there is ample space and an important role for a 'public theology'. In most Western countries this public role is implicitly recognized by the state, for instance when governments set up special ethics committees where the voice of theology or the church is welcomed. Here, faced with the dilemmas posed by contemporary medical technology, politicians sense that fundamental issues concerning our view of man and what it means to be human are at stake. This, I believe, may be interpreted as a way of recognizing the point which was so forcefully made by Kierkegaard, namely that the individual is always *more* than his role as a citizen. And we shall see shortly that Berdyaev makes a similar point. Hence, in order to counter-balance Rawls' proviso we may invent a *theological* proviso: We will give commitment and loyal support to the political order provided it is (at least implicitly) recognized that man is not reducible to his role as a citizen. In order for this to be generally recognized, however, it should be explicitly mentioned in preambles to constitutions (like the American Bill of Rights).

Still, there may be many situations in the life of a society where *prophetic discourse* (like that of Martin Luther King) or even *civil disobedience* are called for. I just fail to grasp how Rawls' proviso can be interpreted as preventing this or (even worse) violating the right to 'free expression' (Wolterstorff). Its whole point, as I have argued, is not to rid the public sphere of religion, but simply to make it clear that in a pluralistic society of many different comprehensive doctrines, our common platform must be formulated in a secular language accessible and acceptable to all citizens. This is simply the price we must pay for living in a multi-religious society. I really do not see how anyone could object to this. Moreover, I find it significant that the vague alternatives put forward by some critics are generally characterized by taking neither secularization nor the fact of pluralism seriously.[156] How, then, are we to understand the widespread resistance to political liberalism's limitations on religion voiced by theological commentators? First of all, it is understandable that religious citizens of a more or less conservative bent dislike being reminded that religion (Christianity) can no longer dominate society. This, however, should not be blamed on an allegedly 'secularist agenda' of political liberalism, when in reality it is, as I tried to demonstrate in Chapter Four, the product of a cultural evolution marked by a general, secularizing trend. But of course, once this sense of being increasingly marginalized is in place, one can begin to understand why political liberalism is interpreted as intending, as it were, to exclude religion from the public realm. And, finally, it makes sense why some would find it more attractive to attack Rawls than to engage in the kind of critical self-reflection that is actually called for.

Kierkegaard's *Fear and Trembling* Revisited
One would be hard pressed, I believe, to conceive of a more drastic example of a clash between religion and public morality than Genesis 22. And yet, Kierkegaard lets his Johannes de Silentio take the horrific elements of the story to their absolute limits by way of an empathic identification with Abraham's isolation and anguish. The perspective of Isaac, the victim of sacrificial violence, is overlooked in order for Kierkegaard to be able to stage the double dilemma of a father and a citizen who is completely at odds with his moral commitments. Focusing in the present context on Abraham the 'citizen', Kierkegaard emphasizes that Abraham (by way of infinite resignation) has completely left the public order (Danish: *det Almene*) and now stands utterly alone in a 'private' relation to his God.

Is there anything in this situation that may serve to distinguish Abraham from a contemporary religious fanatic about to do something terrible? Kierkegaard may be interpreted as giving two answers. First,

---

156 As a recent example of this, see Clanton 2008.

he tries to highlight the perfect nature of Abraham's love for Isaac, but (particularly from the perspective of our times) this does not seem convincing. Then, second, near the end of Problema II, he offers (as we saw in Chapter Two) some distinguishing marks as a tool for discerning whether someone in a similar situation may be considered a true 'knight of faith'. These criteria are helpful to some degree, but in my opinion they are not nearly sufficient to vindicate Abraham: from a contemporary perspective he still looks suspiciously like a religious fanatic or a suicide-bomber. And this in itself should be enough to arouse second thoughts about him and his God-relation. But, more to the point: In light of the historical process of secularization we may simply say that while Abraham's God-relation may well have been possible, and even plausible, *then*, for *us* it can no longer be a 'live option' – to borrow an expression from William James.[157]

Returning to the issue at hand: Abraham's situation being positioned, as it were, in a no man's land between God and society, what is Kierkegaard's solution to this? As we saw in Chapter Two, the idea of a 'double movement of faith' is apparently intended to explain Abraham's dilemma. First, by a movement of infinite resignation, he gave up Isaac (although still loving him) and distanced himself from society realizing that God wanted the sacrifice carried through; then, second, in a movement of faith 'by virtue of the absurd' he nonetheless believed that Isaac would be given back to him in order for him to return to the public order and continue his daily life.

What is going on here? I believe that the implication of Abraham believing two mutually exclusive things at the same time should already

---

157 In this connection it is somewhat ironic that Charles Taylor, in the context of his account of Western secularization, adopts a rather traditional approach to Gen 22. Taylor wants to see Gen 22 as expressing a 'counter-movement' to the connection between religion and sacrifice (and violence and mutilation). In other words, he interprets Gen 22 as being in line with the Old Testament prophets' rejection of making sacrifices to Baal. Comments Taylor: "This is not what God wants, as he signifies to Abraham on Mount Moriah" (p. 648). Besides, when reading Taylor's book I was struck by the fact that he repeatedly, and in fact right from the very first page of his book, speaks of 'the God of Abraham' (cf. also p. 385: 'the God of Abraham, Isaac and Jacob'). Hence, contrary to my position, Taylor seems to be firmly anchored in an 'Abrahamic' perspective.

alert us to the implausibility of Kierkegaard's solution. And by repeatedly using words like 'paradox', 'wonder', and 'the absurd' Kierkegaard himself makes no secret of this. Things look brighter, however, when we look at the double movement of faith from the perspective engendered by political liberalism. For considered in this light, we may say that the important function of the double movement of faith is, rather, to *mediate* between the (sometimes conflicting) commitments to God and society. Thus, to elaborate, I would characterize it as the theological answer to Robert Audi's call for a 'theo-ethical equilibrium'. The knight of faith should interest us, I would argue, because he is able to inwardly balance the cognitive and emotional instabilities which may arise from the fact of his double citizenship, i.e. simultaneously inhabiting the kingdom of Caesar and the kingdom of God. On this interpretation, then, the core idea of the double movement of faith is that each believer must find a way of *combining* her faith relation to God with all of her worldly affairs. As a means of accomplishing this, the double movement is not only of direct contemporary relevance, it may also serve as a model for integrating the respective concerns of political philosophy and philosophy of religion.

Besides, we should pay attention to the fact that not only are the movements performed *inwardly*, it is also emphasized by Kierkegaard that the knight of faith is 'hidden' and not outwardly recognizable. The example of this is the tax-collector who also serves to make the Kierkegaardian point that Christian faith is a faith for *this* life. The upshot of this emphasis on the hidden and inward character of faith is that it is hard to imagine how it might cause conflicts in relation to society. In this connection it should also be remembered that the purpose of the late Kierkegaard's embittered public conflict was an attack on Christendom, and not on the political order.

We have already more than once stressed the point that each individual is always more than her role as a citizen. It does not follow from this, however, that faith should automatically be regarded as *higher* than the ethical or the political. Faith, so the text of *Fear and Trembling* insisted, is faith for *this* life. Hence, to elaborate, the purpose and function of faith may be seen in bringing an eternal, spiritual perspective into the daily business of our mundane and broadly secular lives. Abraham, in my view, obscures this point, whereas the tax-collector illustrates it. Or to put it differently: In order to make the important point of a Christian's double relation to society we do not need any Abraham on Mount Moriah. Any tax-collector will do just fine.

Whatever one may think of Kierkegaard's solution to Abraham's dilemma, he has certainly (although this was not his intention) illustrated the extent to which a radical monotheism like that of Abraham's may, more likely than not, conflict with the political and moral order. Thus, we have ample reason to turn, in the following section, to a more recent Christian thinker who seems to have been of the opinion that radical monotheism should actually be considered alien to the essence of Christianity.

The Realm of Caesar and the Realm of God: Reconciling Human and Divine Freedom

The religious thought of Russian philosopher Nicolas Berdyaev (1874-1948) is not easily categorized.[158] Berdyaev himself cites as his main sources of inspiration thinkers like Kant, Schopenhauer, Marx, Kierkegaard, and Nietzsche. To this, of course must be added the influence of Russian philosophy of religion, notably Dostoyevsky. And finally, one should not overlook the inspiration stemming from Christian mysticism (Eckehart, Angelus Silesius, and Jakob Boehme).

What emerges from this combination of biographical experience and religio-philosophical inspiration, is the position of a Christian *personalism* which may well be considered outdated by philosophers but has, in my view, a lot to offer to theological reflection. And certainly, in the context of this book Berdyaev is highly relevant, because he directly addresses the following three issues: 1) The relation between God and human freedom; 2) Christianity's relation to Judaism and Islam, and 3) the relation between the two kingdoms: the realm of Caesar and the realm of God.

Before looking somewhat deeper into his thinking on these themes, it should be admitted from the outset, I believe, that Berdyaev is not at

---

158 Banished from the Soviet Union by the bolsheviks in 1922, Berdyaev in 1923 reached Paris where he lived until his death. Readers who may wish to go deeper into the life and work of Berdyaev, I refer to the Berdyaev homepage (http://www.chebucto. ns.ca/Philosophy/Sui-Generis/Berdyaev/.) where many relevant sources are easily accessible.

his best, or most convincing, when commenting on matters pertaining to political philosophy. As a former Marxist, he obviously knows a good deal about socialism (in theory as well as in practice); still, the argument behind his apparent personal sympathies for a 'personalist socialism'[159] is sketchy and has a utopian character. What is more, this political preference seems to be indicative of a fundamental contradiction in his thinking openly acknowledged by Berdyaev himself.[160] And no doubt, Berdyaev had ample reason to be disappointed by and weary of politics, and this may at least partly account for his occasional critical remarks on democracy. The deeper reason, however, seems to lie in his view that compared to the commitments of personalism, democracy recedes to a more relative status. At best, and as the following quotation demonstrates, we may perhaps characterize Berdyaev's stance toward democracy as ambiguous: "Democracy is a relative form of society. Whereas the values of personality and freedom on the other hand has an absolute significance. On one side democracy denotes the sovereignty of the people, the dominance of the majority and in this sense it is on the whole unfavourable to personality and freedom. But on another side democracy means the self-government of man, a man's rights as a man and a citizen, the freedom of man, and in this sense it has an eternal significance." (Berdyaev 1944, 210).

In *The Divine and the Human* (Berdyaev 1949) the overall point is to clear the way for a new understanding of the relation between God and human freedom. This relation, complains Berdyaev, has been wrongly understood due to the dominant *legal* interpretation of Christianity where God is seen as a monarchical ruler who has been offended by the rebellious sins of humanity and must therefore sacrifice his own son as 'ransom' in

---

159 "Personalist socialism starts from the supremacy of personality over society. It is simply the social projection of personalism, in which my belief has grown ever more and more firm." (Berdyaev 1944, 17).

160 "The fundamental contradiction in my thinking about social life is bound up with the juxtaposition in me of two elements – an aristocratic interpretation of personality, freedom and creativeness, and a socialistic demand for the assertion of the dignity of every man, of even the most insignificant of men, and for a guarantee of his rights in life. This is the clash of a passionate love of the world above, of a love of the highest, with pity for this lower world, the world of suffering." (Berdyaev 1944, 9).

order to pay the debt.[161] This traditional conception, according to Berdyaev, is degrading both to God and man. To our good fortune, however, an
ongoing evolution of religious ideas has been accompanied by a gradual
'purification' of Christian consciousness – leaving behind "a monarchical
despotic understanding of God" (Berdyaev 1949, 6).[162] Instead, Berdyaev
emphasizes again and again that God is *spirit* (not being) which in turn
means that he is *personality*, *freedom*, and *love*: "It is impossible to insist
strongly enough upon the fact that God is not a reality like the realities
of the natural and social world. God is spirit. God is freedom and love."
(*ibid*, 7). Or as he puts it in a different context: "God does not exist as
an objective reality found to be necessary by me, as the objectivization
of a universal idea. He exists as an existential contact and meeting, as
the process of transcension, and in that meeting God is personality."
Berdyaev 1944, 39).[163]

Similarly, as we shall see, man, too, is first and foremost personality
and spirit which, again, means freedom and creativity. And in light of this
freedom and creativity Berdyaev can acknowledge an element of truth
in Feuerbach's critique of religion.[164] In fact, to finally think through the
meaning of human freedom and creativity means to realize that man
creates God, but in this very act God Himself comes into existence. Says

---

161 Berdyaev, obviously, is not alone in this critique and comments that "It does great
honour to Russian religious thought of the nineteenth century, that it always reacted
negatively to the legal interpretation of Christianity" (*ibid*, 5).

162 As we shall see, the Christian idea of *incarnation* plays a crucial role in this respect.
At the same time, Berdyaev seems quite clear that the evolution of religious consciousness demands a new interpretation of Christianity: "Humanity has entered on
a stage when the religious ideas, however subtle and sophisticated, of rewards and
retributions, of legalistic transactions, of a moral and eschatological reign of terror
are certainly quite incapable of relieving man's existence, imperilled and torn as it is
by the world." (Berdyaev 1950, 301).

163 And a little later he adds: "And God as personality does not desire a man over whom
he can rule, and who ought to praise Him, but man as personality who answers His
call and with whom communion of love is possible" (*ibid*, 40).

164 "It is true that man creates God in his own image and likeness as sometimes he has
created Gods, but the really important thing is that this human image and likeness
should approximate to the image and likeness which is divine. Here there is a mys-
terious dialectic of two, not the action of one from above in a downward direction"
(Berdyaev 1949, 3). Some pages later he says of Feuerbach that he "was a devout atheist
and through him the human conception of God has been purified" (*ibid*, 13).

Berdyaev, "There is a paradox in the knowledge of God which must be courageously faced and put into words, thus; the affirmation of God by my whole being means that God exists; human freedom creates God, and this means that God is; my creating of God is a divine-human act of creation." (Berdyaev 1949, 185).

To replace the legal interpretation of Christianity Berdyaev advances a *dialectical* and more dynamic view of the God-man relation. God is personality and not 'the Absolute', and "Man is personality because God is personality and *vice versa*" (Berdyaev 1944, 50).[165] By virtue of this emphasis on the essential freedom of both God and man, Berdyaev, logically, also considers *revelation* to be characterized by a similar dialectic: "There are two partners in revelation. It is divine-human. There is the one who reveals himself and there is the one to whom he is revealed" Berdyaev 1949, 3). Thus, he does not shy away from drawing the implication that "in revelation both God and man are active, that revelation has a divine-human character" (*ibid*, 15).[166] Now, having established that Berdyaev not only emphasizes *freedom* as an essential feature of God and man, but also sees the divine and human aspects of freedom as being mutually interdependent, let us turn to the consequences of this for grasping the true spirit of Christianity.

We have seen how Berdyaev criticizes the legal interpretation of Christianity. As an integral part of this critique he also overturns the traditional view of God as a perfect being residing in heaven from where he rules the world. In sharp contrast, Berdyaev (1944, 82) maintains that "God is not a master and He does not dominate." And further: "He determines

---

165 Cf also the following passage: "If God is personality and not the Absolute, if He is not only *essentia* but also *existentia* (...) then suffering is inherent in Him, and there is a tragic principle in Him. Otherwise God is not personality, but an abstract idea or being such as is conceived by the Eleatic philosophers. The Son of God suffers not only as Man but also as God." (*ibid*, 51).

166 One important consequence of this is that Berdyaev must distance himself from the traditional theological emphasis on God's *aseity*, i.e. the notion that God (as the highest and most perfect being) does not need anything outside himself. In marked contrast to this, Berdyaev (1949, 47) notes that "We must be bold enough to recognize God's need of man, and such a need by no means limits God. What actually would not only limit God but also degrade Him is a stony, insensitive immobility and self-sufficiency. There is in God a yearning for the loved one and this confers the highest significance upon the loved one."

nothing. Nor can we think in terms of causality. He is not the cause of anything." (*ibid*, 83).[167] As a consequence, Berdyaev insists on the need for "the purification of the knowledge of God from the ideas of bad earthly theocracy" (*ibid*, 85). And the theological corollary is that he must also relinquish and distance himself from the influential teaching of God's *providence*. Thus, according to Berdyaev, "God is not world providence, that is to say not ruler and sovereign of the universe, not *pantokrator*. God is freedom and meaning, love and sacrifice; He is struggle against the objectivized world order." (*ibid*, 89). This, however, is not all, for Berdyaev even charges the doctrine of Providence for being a form of *idolatry*:

The usual concept of Providence is derived from the government of a state. God is represented as if He were the autocratic head of a state. Emancipation from what remains of the ancient idolatry is what matters, and is of immense importance. Idolatry is a possibility not only in regard to idols but also in relation to God. Such emancipation is the purification of revelation from the base conceptions which the human mind has brought into it, and to set it free from servile religious ideas and beliefs. (Berdyaev 1949, 10).[168]

In other words, what Berdyaev has realized is the important point that monotheism is basically a *political* idea (cf. also Assmann in Chapter One). This seems to me a crucial insight when reflecting on the relation between religion and democracy. For clearly, any religion conceiving of its God as a monarchical ruler (in anything but a purely symbolic or poetic sense) will be likely to come into conflict with the political order. At the same time, the quotation harbours an important implication for the purpose of this book, namely that in Berdyaev's interpretation Christianity must *break away* from traditional monotheism as well as the fellowship of the three Abrahamic religions. And the reason it must do this, is simply that

---

167 In a similar vein he states that "God is certainly not the constructor of the world order, or an administrator of the world whole. God is the meaning of human existence" (*ibid*, 87).

168 Cf also the following passage: "The assertion of God outside divine-humanity, that is, abstract monotheism, is a form of idolatry. Hence the tremendous importance of the doctrine of the Trinity, which must be understood mystically, in the terms of spiritual experience, and not by rational theology." (Berdyaev 1952, 38).

by virtue of the incarnation and God being spirit, love, and freedom, Christianity is essentially *different* from Judaism and Islam:

Christianity is anthropocentric; it proclaims the liberation of man from the power of cosmic forces and spirits. It presupposes belief not only in God but also in man, and this distinguishes it from the abstract monotheism of Judaism and Islam, and from Brahmanism. It must be emphatically said that Christianity is not a monistic and monarchical religion; it is a religion of God-manhood and it is Trinitarian. (*ibid*, 22).[169]

Perhaps the most important basis of this difference is to be found in the fact that the core concept of Berdyaev's interpretation of Christianity is *spirit*. But what is 'spirit'? Spirit, according to Berdyaev (1952, 32), "is not a reality comparable with other realities like material, for example: spirit is reality in quite another sense. It is freedom and not being: it is a qualitative changing of the data of the world, it is creative energy which transfigures the world. Further, there is no spirit without God, as its original source. Man's spiritual experience, on which alone metaphysics can be based, is the only proof of the existence of God."[170] The point, then, in Berdyaev's repeated insistence on the dialectic unity of the *divine-human* is to realize that the spirit, freedom, and love which is revealed in man, all have their original and ultimate source in God.

This, finally, leads us to the third important theme of Berdyaev, namely his Christian, personalist view of man as belonging to two worlds: this world and the kingdom of God. Corresponding to this, Berdyaev (1944, 21) draws a fundamental distinction between man as *personality* and man as *individual*: "Man is personality not by nature but by spirit. By nature he is only an individual." Since personality, as we have seen, is spirit and

---

169 And in a similar vein: "I believe that the greatest revolution brought about by Christianity is the revelation of the humanity of God." (Berdyaev 1950, 301).

170 A few pages later, in a context where Berdyaev accepts Kant's critique of the traditional proofs of God's existence as being 'very convincing', he continues: "What might be called the anthropological proof is much stronger. It consists in the fact that man is a being belonging to two worlds, and for this reason he is not included completely in this world of necessity: he transcends himself as a being of the empiric, revealing a freedom which does not derive from this world. This does not prove, but does show, the existence of God, since it reveals the spiritual element in man" (*ibid*, 35f.).

freedom, it is also that particular aspect of man which is not reducible to society; to elaborate, it means "emancipation from dependence upon nature, from dependence upon society and the state" (*ibid*, 26). Further, he distinguishes between what he calls the *superficial* ego and the *profound* ego. The former may be "capable of various sorts of external communication, but it is not capable of communion" (*ibid*, 25).[171] As we would expect, the superficial ego (socialized and rationalized) is not the personality in man. Therefore, claims Berdyaev, "All the sociological doctrines about man are erroneous, they know only the superficial, objectified stratum in man." (*ibid*, 26).

What, we must ask, are the implications of this Christian anthropology? First of all, it should be emphasized that, ultimately, personality "emanates from God, it makes its appearance from another world. It bears witness to the fact that man is the point of intersection of two worlds, that in him there takes place the conflict between spirit and nature, freedom and necessity, independence and dependence." (*ibid*, 36). This, we may say, is Berdyaev's modern translation of the traditional doctrine of the two kingdoms. And note that as was the case regarding proofs of God's existence, we see also here an *anthropological turn*: the two kingdoms are reflected in man's double nature, and nowhere else.

Also of importance *vis à vis* political philosophy is the fact that Berdyaev, much like Kierkegaard, realizes the necessary implication of man's spiritual nature, namely that it entails a certain *distance* to what goes on in this world: "A person cannot be completely a citizen of the world and of the state, he is a citizen of the Kingdom of God. For this reason personality is a revolutionary element in a profound sense of the word. This is bound up with the fact that man is a being who belongs not to one world but to two." (*ibid*, 37). Moreover, for Berdyaev 'personality' is such an all-encompassing reality that ultimately society can be seen, not as a self-subsisting entity but as a part of personality: "If the distinction we have drawn between the individual and personality is accepted, then it can be said that only the individual is a part of society and subject to it;

---

171 Thus we are introduced here to another important distinction: 'communication' is what goes on in society, whereas 'communion' in love and freedom is what goes on between man and God.

personality, on the other hand, is not a part of society; on the contrary, society is a part of personality. It follows from the fact that man is a microcosm and a microtheos, that society, like the state, is a constituent part of personality." (*ibid*, 103).

Another consequence of the pivotal role of 'spirit' in Berdyaev's thought is that he must oppose the idea of man's basic rights being derived from natural law. Says Berdyaev (1952, 60): "The doctrine of natural law, recognizing the rights of man, independent of political rights fixed by the state, made a theoretical mistake characteristic of the immature metaphysics of that time. In reality, the inalienable rights of man, which fix the limits of society's authority over him, are fixed not by nature, but by spirit. They are spiritual rather than natural rights: nature establishes no rights whatever."[172]

Hopefully, what has emerged from this brief survey of Berdyaev's Christian personalism, is that he has much to offer in terms of resources for a contemporary reflection on theology's relation to the political order. It must be added, however, that two things prevent him from engaging seriously with political philosophy. One is a matter of personal biography, i.e. his early enthusiasm for the Bolshevik revolution which was shortly to be turned into intense disappointment. The other matter seems to follow directly from this, namely that he appears to have developed a profound dislike for politics, and he appears not to have been interested in political philosophy. Thus, in the end, we find in Berdyaev no *integration* of political philosophy and philosophy of religion.

In theory, the necessary implication of his personalist religious thinking is nothing more than what might be characterized as a healthy distance toward taking the business of this world too seriously. In practice, however, Berdyaev seemingly wanted to go further than this. At least this is the impression that follows from one of the passages where he comments

---

172 Berdyaev concludes from this that the honour of having truly liberated man belongs to Christianity: "Once Christianity made a supreme spiritual revolution: it made man spiritually free of the unlimited powers of society and the state, which in the antique world included religious life as well. Christianity disclosed a spiritual element in man which depended not on the world or nature or society, but only on God. This is the truth in Christian personalism, unknown to the pre-Christian world." (*ibid*).

on the relation between the two kingdoms: "'Render unto Caesar the things that are Caesar's and unto God the things that are God's.' This is commonly interpreted in a sense which reconciles the kingdom of Caesar and the Kingdom of God; it is given a meaning which abolishes the conflict. But the life of Christ was precisely this conflict carried through to the utmost limit of intensity." (Berdyaev 1944, 140). Clearly, what we see here is neither modus vivendi nor harmony but Berdyaev insisting on a necessary conflict between the Kingdom of God and the kingdom of Caesar. Interestingly, this may be due to inspiration from Kierkegaard and his attack on Christendom.[173] At the same time, and related to this, it cannot be denied that there is a certain 'tragic' or pessimistic element in Berdyaev's thought.

Conclusion

The purpose of this chapter has been to consider the implications of political liberalism from the perspective of philosophy of religion, and to argue for the possibility of more integration and dialogue between the two fields of inquiry. As a consequence, I have called for theological reflection to 'integrate' political philosophy in order to correctly understand the role and possible functions of religion and public theology in contemporary society.

In a first step, I looked at the theological consequences of the Rawlsian limitations on religion and found them *not* to conflict with the concerns of a contemporary understanding of Christianity. If we adopt the perspective from theology, however, what specifically *religious* reasons might there be for endorsing the basic political conception of a constitutional democracy? To this I answered that secularization and religious freedom should be regarded cornerstones of any contemporary theology. Moreover, a more profound answer may be given by arguing, in line with Berdyaev, that God as spirit is essentially freedom. Hence, God as freedom and human freedom constitute a dialectical unity.

Second, I returned to Kierkegaard and his solution of a 'double movement of faith'. My point here was to interpret it as a possible answer to the

---

173 Incidentally, Berdyaev (1949, 12) refers to a passage from Kierkegaard's *Practice in Christianity*.

problem of balancing religious commitments to the commitment of being a fully participating member of society. Given the fact that, theologically speaking, every Christian is the inhabitant of *two* kingdoms, a believer's relation to society is likely to be characterized by a certain *distance* to the existing political order. This is an 'inner' (or inward) distance however, and it may even be considered healthy for two reasons: One is that it serves as a reminder that 'the political' is not the final (and sometimes not even the most important) word about our human situation. Another is that by maintaining a certain distance and not attributing to the realm of Caesar more than timely and finite significance, it may often prove possible to be of more service to society.

In a third and final step, I turned to Berdyaev and found it to be of particular importance that by purifying Christianity of the idolatry of a monarchical image of God, he has effectively removed a good deal of the potential for a clash or conflict between religion and politics. Moreover, by breaking away from the ideological constraints of an 'abstract monotheism' and by insisting, further, that the specificity of Christianity consists in the combined ideas of incarnation and a Trinitarian conception of God as spirit, Berdyaev may be considered, in my opinion, as effectively taking leave of Abraham.

CONCLUSION

This book, to invoke its subtitle, has been an essay on religion and democracy. There are at least two sides to this overall theme: One is the individual struggling to balance the kingdom of God and the 'realm of Caesar'. The other is without a doubt one of the most pressing issues of contemporary societies, namely how a democracy should relate to the plurality of religions (and other comprehensive doctrines) all striving to achieve influence, recognition, and respect. My tool for keeping these distinctive aspects of the theme together has been the story of Abraham who was commanded by God to kill his own son. And at the same time, the double nature of our subject has been mirrored in the two parts of the book.

In *Part One*, I wanted to display a variety of examples of how Genesis 22 has always been a troubling and disturbing story. From the broader perspective, however, the interpretive history reveals a certain division between on the one hand pre-modern typological or allegorical readings, and on the other hand modern interpretations which have generally displayed a more critical distance to the story. Kierkegaard, whose interpretation of Genesis 22 in *Fear and Trembling* is in my view unsurpassed, is of special interest in this respect, since he may be said to combine insights from both sides of the dividing line. Thus, Kierkegaard, although we may with Habermas characterize him as a post-metaphysical thinker, is pre-modern in his eulogy of Abraham as the 'Father of faith', but at the same time he is markedly modern in offering a solution deriving from and focusing on subjectivity and the related issue of self-realization, i.e. the 'double movement of faith'.

Nonetheless, this should not lead us to forget that by demanding unquestioning obedience to an autocratic and capricious God, the message of Genesis 22 is as pre-modern as can be. In spite of this apparent fact, modern theologians (with Donald Capps as a notable exception) and some philosophers have gone to great lengths in order to save and sanitize not only the God portrayed in Genesis 22, but also Abraham and Kierkegaard. As an inner-theological (or philosophical) exercise this may in itself be innocent enough. But in the contemporary situation of Western democracies threatened by acts of terror, things may begin to look different. Or to state the matter more directly: The contemporary combination of a resurgence of conservative (or even fundamentalist) religion and the terrorist threat to democracy implies, in my view, a call to all religious people of good will to engage in critical self-reflection and to demand of their representatives (whether in churches or in the academia) an immanent critique of authoritarian structures in their respective religions. And although in starting to heed this call I may have to part ways with some theologians, I can at least enjoy the good company of Bob Dylan and Leonard Cohen.

On the background of Abraham's near-sacrifice of Isaac holding the first three chapters together, a core issue of Part One is the question of the relation between religion and morality. Can (and should) they be separated, or are they necessarily interconnected? Here, I believe Kierkegaard provides us with an important clue by introducing the notion of a 'teleological suspension of the ethical'. Whereas Abraham, I surmise, is representative of a culture where religion and morality is more or less indistinguishable, speaking of a 'suspension' once again reveals Kierkegaard as firmly anchored in the mentality of modernity. For this demonstrates his awareness not only that religion and morality are distinct spheres of validity and meaning, but also that morality has, in large measure, become the 'judge' or arbiter of religion. The sphere of public morality may be suspended for some time, but it cannot be abolished. And even today there may be situations (although Abraham's is certainly not one of them) where a person's conscience will lead her to suspend the ethical for a 'higher' purpose. This is commonly called 'civil disobedience', and no democracy can in the long run thrive without it. We should not overlook a crucial difference, however: Whereas Abraham suspended the ethical for the purely *private* reason of complying with a capricious and radically monotheistic God, civil disobedience, by definition, should always have a worthier *telos*, i.e. one covered by basic human rights.

With faith and its relation to morality being the theme of Part One, *Part Two* has addressed a similar problematic under its modern and contemporary form of religion's relationship to democracy. Chapter Four, however, was intended to establish a bridge between the two parts, between antiquity and modernity, by making the claim that it is by virtue of a cultural *evolution* that religion and morality have become differentiated. As an important trend in this process, secularization has paved the way for the *pluralism* of comprehensive doctrines which, as we have seen, is the overall challenge Rawls intended to confront with his version of political liberalism.

In outlining its basic ideas in Chapter Five, I have tried to make plausible a reading which sees *Political Liberalism* as joining forces with some of the best intentions of American pragmatism, and thus as marking a break with the Kantian and contractarian basis of *A Theory of Justice*. Besides, I believe that an interpretation along these lines is in accord with Rawls' own intentions. The other major figure of this chapter is Jürgen Habermas who also played an important role in the chapter on cultural evolution. As a political philosopher Habermas joins Rawls in advocating a 'deliberative' democracy, although his preferred version is that of a Kantian republicanism. In defending this, however, Habermas (and now in contrast to Rawls) relies on an elaborate philosophical argument. In addition, in his latest works Habermas has also dealt extensively with religion, and now (in contrast to his earlier views briefly outlined in Chapter Four) he displays a clear awareness of the rich semantic resources of religion and argues that democratic societies should be careful not to place asymmetrical burdens on the shoulders of religious citizens. Although having great sympathy for Habermas, in the end I prefer Rawls primarily for two reasons: One is his conscious *pragmatist* orientation which serves, I believe, to make his version of political liberalism more widely acceptable. The other reason is that Rawls stays (and wisely, I believe) on the level of comprehensive doctrines, whereas Habermas, by trying to accommodate to the sensibilities of individual believers, gets tangled up in unnecessary problems.

My treatment of some of the critical debates (Chapter Six) has demonstrated the extent to which political liberalism, despite its modest 'political' assumptions, has been the target of sharp criticism from theologians as well as philosophers. Although generally sympathetic towards Rawls' basic intentions, the critics have primarily focused their attention on political liberalism's allegedly negative and discriminatory consequences for religion and religious citizens. Political liberalism, it is complained, not only excludes religion from the public sphere but also violates the spirit of free expression. In trying to evaluate the validity of this criticism, I have found it important to dispel a grave misunderstanding which may, somewhat ironically, be at least partly to blame on Rawls himself, even though he explicitly rejects the usual distinction between 'public' and 'private'. The problem here, and what is likely to cause confusion, is that Rawls, as a consequence of his narrow view of 'public reason' uses the term 'non-public' for what in common parlance is called 'public'. By referring to it as 'non-public' however, some critics may have been misled into understanding it as 'private'. And in fact, by consciously limiting the *proviso* to the narrow area of the 'public political forum' Rawls' position is considerably less restrictive than is commonly supposed.

Finally, in Chapter Seven, I have turned to more theological considerations and argued for the need, at least when considered from a theological perspective, to strive for a certain degree of integration between political philosophy and philosophy of religion. At the same time, the purpose of the chapter was to take up the challenge presented by Rawls in advising religious citizens to say that 'such are the limits God sets to our liberty'. By revisiting Kierkegaard and *Fear and Trembling* and by introducing some ideas from the Christian personalism of Nicolas Berdyaev, I have tried to formulate a contemporary solution to the classic problem of balancing the demands of the realm of Caesar with the realm of God. Equally important, however, I found in Berdyaev a strong commitment to contribute to an ongoing process of 'purification' of religious consciousness. This commitment, in turn, led Berdyaev to effectively distancing Christianity from the 'abstract monotheism' of Judaism and Islam. Hence, he may be said to be an ally in my proposal for 'taking leave of Abraham'.

Looking back on the previous chapters, I have tried in this book to demonstrate that it is possible to engage and converse seriously with political philosophy without thereby surrendering the 'message' of Christianity or abandoning the task of theology. Turning, finally, to the message of the book itself, I have chosen from the outset to summarize it in the title. 'Taking leave of Abraham' is, I would say, a call to all democratically minded adherents of the three Abrahamic religions; a call to protect and pledge loyalty to the fundamental principles of democracy and human rights. However, in reality I may be speaking to but a small part of Western Christians. Those, and hopefully some others as well, I encourage to engage in critical religious reflection. To put it short: Contemporary Christianity should finally liberate itself from its Abrahamic captivity.

'Taking leave of Abraham' implies rejecting Abraham as the 'Father of faith' and as a paradigm to be emulated. Instead, we should muster the courage to say: 'This is not *my* faith. It may have been valid once, in primordial times, but it is not valid today, and besides it is not the faith that Jesus preaches in the Gospel.' Theologically, however, I am of course aware that 'taking leave of Abraham' entails even more far-reaching implications. Recalling Levenson's theology of the beloved son (briefly outlined in Chapter One), we should embrace the possibility of conceptualizing Christian soteriology *not* in sacrificial terms but by seeing God as someone who 'gives' his son freely as a spiritual gift to be enjoyed by all those who come to believe in the kingdom of God.

'Taking leave of Abaraham', finally, is not a call for excluding religion from the public square. And it is certainly not a proposal for 'privatizing' religion. Rather, it may be regarded as a plea for *more* religion in public life, provided that it is religion of a non-authoritarian kind. A form of religion, I might add, which is aware (and even proud) that we live in a secular age.

REFERENCES

Adams, N. (2006) *Habermas and Theology*. Cambridge: Cambridge University Press.

Andersen, S. (2005) Human Rights and Christianity. A Lutheran Perspective. In Lars Binderup & Tim Jensen (eds.), *Human Rights, Democracy & Religion In the Perspective of Cultural Studies, Philosophy, and the Study of Religions*, 98-104. Odense: University of Southern Denmark.

Arens, E. (ed.). (1989) *Habermas und die Theologie*. Düsseldorf: Patmos Verlag.

Assmann, J. (2003) *Die Mosaische Unterscheidung – oder der Preis des Monotheismus*. Munich: Carl Hanser Verlag.

Audi, R. (1997) The State, the Church, and the Citizen. In *Religion and Contemporary Liberalism*, edited by Paul J. Weithman, 38-75. Notre Dame: University of Notre Dame Press.

Audi, R. (2000) *Religious Commitment and Secular Reason*. Cambridge: Cambridge University Press.

Audi, R. and N. Wolterstorff (1997) *Religion in the Public Square. The Place of Religious Convictions in Political Debate*. Lanham: Rowman & Littlefield Publishers.

Balkin, J. M. (1998) *Cultural Software. A Theory of Ideology*. New Haven: Yale University Press.

Barclay, L. (2005) How Much Religious and Cultural Diversity Can Liberalism Tolerate? In *Human Rights, Democracy & Religion In the Perspective of Cultural Studies, Philosophy, and the Study of Religions*, edited by Lars Binderup and Tim Jensen, 62-74. Odense: University of Southern Denmark.

Berdyaev, N. (1944) *Slavery and Freedom*. New York: Charles Scribner's Sons.

Berdyaev, N. (1949) *The Divine and the Human*. London: Geoffrey Bles.

Berdyaev, N. (1950) *Dream and Reality. An Essay in Autobiography*. London: Geoffrey Bles.

Berdyaev, N. (1952) *The Realm of Spirit and the Realm of Caesar*. Translated by Donald A. Lowrie. London: Victor Gollancz Ltd.

Berger, P. L. (ed.). (1999) *The Desecularization of the World. Resurgent Religion and World Politics*. Grand Rapids: William B. Eerdmans Publishing Company.

Bruce, S. (2004) Did Protestantism Create Democracy? *Democratization* 11 (4): 3-20.

Brun, Lars K., et al. (2007) *Abrahams spor. Abrahamfiguren i religion, filosofi og kunst*. Copenhagen: Forlaget ALFA.

Brunkhorst, H. (2007) Globalizing Solidarity: The Destiny of Democratic Solidarity in the Times of Global Capitalism, Global Religion, and the Global Public. *Journal of Social Philosophy* 38 (1): 93-111.

Capps, D. (1995) *The Child's Song. The Religious Abuse of Children*. Louisville: Westminster John Knox Press.

Carter, S. L. (1993) *The Culture of Disbelief*. New York: Doubleday.

Clanton, J. Caleb (2008) *Religion and Democratic Citizenship*. Lanham: Lexington Books.

Cooke, M. (2006) Salvaging and secularizing the semantic contents of religion: the limitations of Habermas's postmetaphysical proposal. *International Journal for Philosophy of Religion* 60: 187-207.

Dalferth, I. U. (2006) Problems of Evil: Theodicy, Theology, and Hermeneutics (unpublished manuscript).

Damgaard, F. (2007) Skygger og allegori. Origenes' og Chrysostomos' homilier over Isaks ofring. *Patristik* 5, 1-26. http://www.patristik.dk/Patristik.htm.

Davie, G. (1999) Europe: The Exception That Proves the Rule? In: Peter L. Berger (ed.): *The Desecularization of the World*, 65-83. Grand Rapids, Michigan: William B. Eerdmans Publishing Company.

Dostert, T. (2006) *Beyond Political Liberalism. Toward a Post-Secular Ethics of Public Life*. Notre Dame: University of Notre Dame Press.

Doukhan, J. (1995) The *Akedah* at the "Crossroad": Its Significance in the Jewish-Christian-Muslim Dialogue. In F. Manns (ed.) *The Sacrifice of Isaac in the Three Monotheistic Religions*, 165-176. Jerusalem: Franciscan Printing Press.

Evans, C. S. (1981) Is the Concept of Absolute Duty to God Unintelligible? In *Kierkegaard's Fear and Trembling. Critical Appraisals*, edited by Robert L. Perkins. The University of Alabama Press.

Evans, C. S. (2004) *Kierkegaard's Ethic of Love. Divine Commands and Moral Obligation*. Oxford: Oxford University Press.

Evans, C. S. (2006) *Kierkegaard on Faith and the Self. Collected Essays*. Waco, Texas: Baylor University Press.

Gauchet, M. (1997) *The Disenchantment of the World: A Political History of Religion*. Princeton: Princeton University Press.

Gellman, J. I. (1994) *The Fear, the Trembling, and the Fire. Kierkegaard and Hasidic Masters on the Binding of Isaac*. Lanham: University Press of America.

Graf, F. W. (2006) *Moses Vermächtnis. Über göttliche und menschliche Gesetze*. Munich: C. H. Beck.

Green, R. M. (1986) Deciphering *Fear and Trembling*'s Secret Message. *Religious Studies* 22: 95-111.

Green, R. M. (1993) Enough is enough! *Fear and Trembling* is *Not* about ethics! *Journal of Religious Ethics* 21: 191-209.

Green, R. M. (1993a) A Reply to Gene Outka. *Journal of Religious Ethics* 21: 217-220.

Habermas, J. (1976) *Zur Rekonstruktion des Historischen Materialismus*. Frankfurt am Main: Suhrkamp.

Habermas, J. (1981) *Die Theorie des kommunikativen Handelns* (2 vols.). Frankfurt am Main: Suhrkamp.

Habermas, J. (1983) *Moralbewusstsein und kommunikatives Handeln*. Frankfurt am Main: Suhrkamp.

Habermas, J. (1996) *Die Einbeziehung des Anderen. Studien zur politischen Theorie*. Frankfurt am Main: Suhrkamp.

Habermas, J. (2001a) *Zeit der Übergänge*. Frankfurt am Main: Edition Suhrkamp.

Habermas, J. (2001b) *Glauben und Wissen*. Frankfurt am Main: Edition Suhrkamp (Sonderdruck).

Habermas, J. (2005) *Zwischen Naturalismus und Religion. Philosophische Aufsätze*. Frankfurt am Main: Suhrkamp.

Habermas, J. (2006) Religion in the Public Sphere. *European Journal of Philosophy*, 14:1, 1-25.

Habermas, J. (2007) Ein Bewusstsein von dem, was fehlt. Über Glauben und Wissen und den Defaitismus der modernen Vernunft. *Neue Zürcher Zeitung*, Feb. 10, 2007. www.nzz.ch.).

Hendriks, C. M. (2006) Integrated Deliberation: Reconciling Civil Society's Dual Role in Deliberative Democracy. *Political Studies* 54: 486-508.

Henriksen, Jan-Olav (2007) Religionens overraskende 'tilbagekomst': trekk av religionsforståelsen hos den senere Habermas. In *Habermas: kritiske læsninger*, edited by O. Lysaker and Gunnar C. Aakvaag. Oslo: Pax forlag, pp. 34-52.

Keane, J. (2000) Secularism? In *Religion and Democracy*, edited by D. Marquand and R. L. Nettler. Oxford: Blackwell Publishers.

Kierkegaard, S. (1983) *Fear and Trembling. Repetition*. Edited and Translated by Howard V. Hong and Edna H. Hong. Princeton: Princeton University Press.

Koch, K. (1999) Monotheismus als Sündenbock? *Theologische Literaturzeitung* 124 (9): 874-884.

Kukathas, C. (ed.) (2003) *John Rawls: Critical assessments of leading political philosophers* (Vol. IV: *Political Liberalism* and *The Law of Peoples*). London and New York: Routledge.

Lee, J. H. (2000) Abraham in a Different Voice: Rereading *Fear and Trembling* with Care. *Religious Studies* 36: 377-400.

Levenson, J. D. (1993) *The Death and Resurrection of the Beloved Son*. New Haven: Yale University Press.

Lippitt, J. (2003) *Kierkegaard and 'Fear and Trembling'*. London: Routledge.

Macedo, S. (2003) Liberal Civic Education and Religious Fundamentalism: The case of God v. John Rawls? In Chandran Kukathas (ed.), *John Rawls: Critical assessments of leading political philosophers*, edited by Chandran Kukathas (Vol. IV: *Political Liberalism* and *The Law of Peoples*), 145-171. London and New York: Routledge.

Manns, F. (ed.) (1995) *The Sacrifice of Isaac in the Three Monotheistic Religions.* Jerusalem: Franciscan Printing Press.

McBride, C. (2005) Deliberative Democracy and the Politics of Recognition. *Political Studies* 53: 497-515.

Milbank, J. (1995) Stories of Sacrifice: From Wellhausen to Girard. *Theory Culture Society* 12 (15): 15-46.

Mooney, E. F. (1981) Understanding Abraham: Care, Faith, and the Absurd. In *Kierkegaard's Fear and Trembling. Critical Appraisals,* edited by Robert L. Perkins. The University of Alabama Press.

Mooney, E. F. (1986) Abraham and Dilemma: Kierkegaard's Teleological Suspension Revisited. *International Journal for Philosophy of Religion* 19: 23-41.

Mooney, E. F. (1991) *Knights of Faith and Resignation: Reading Kierkegaard's* Fear and Trembling. Albany: State University of New York Press.

Nanda, S. and R. L. Warms (2007) *Cultural Anthropology.* 9th edition. Thomson / Wadsworth.

Nørager, T. (2003) *Hjertets længsel. Kærlighed og Gud religionsfilosofisk belyst* ['The Longing in our Hearts: Love and God in the Perspective of Philosophy of Religion']. Copenhagen: Forlaget Anis.

Nørager, T. (2008a) Love, Sacrifice, and Gender: Is There A Solution to Abraham's Dilemma? Paper presented at the European Society for Philosophy of Religion conference on 'Sacrifice', Oslo, August 28-31, 2008.

Outka, G. (1993) God as the Subject of Unique Veneration. A Response to Ronald M. Green. *Journal of Religious Ethics* 21: 211-215.

Owen, J. J. (2001) *Religion and the Demise of Liberal Rationalism. The Foundational Crisis of the Separation of Church and State.* Chicago: The University of Chicago Press.

Pailin, D. A. (1981) Abraham and Isaac: A Hermeneutical Problem Before Kierkegaard. In *Kierkegaard's Fear and Trembling. Critical Appraisals,* edited by Robert L. Perkins. The University of Alabama Press.

Paczkowski, M. C. (1995) The Sacrifice of Isaac i Early Patristic Exegesis. In F. Manns (ed) *The Sacrifice of Isaac in the Three Monotheistic Religions,* 101-121. Jerusalem: Franciscan Printing Press.

Perkins, R. L. (1981) For Sanity's Sake: Kant, Kierkegaard and Father Abraham. In *Kierkegaard's Fear and Trembling. Critical Appraisals,* edited by Robert L. Perkins. The University of Alabama Press.

Perry, M. J. (2003) *Under God? Religious Faith and Liberal Democracy.* Cambridge: Cambridge University Press.

Quinn, P. L. (1997) Political Liberalisms and Their Exclusions of the Religious. In *Religion and Contemporary Liberalism*, edited by Paul J. Weithman, 138-161. Notre Dame: University of Notre Dame Press.

Quong, J. (2004) The Scope of Public Reason. *Political Studies* 52: 233-250.

Rambo, A. T. (1991) The Study of Cultural Evolution. In *Profiles in Cultural Evolution*, edited by T. A. Rambo and K. Gillogly, 23-109. Ann Arbor, Michigan: University of Michigan Press.

Rawls, J. (1997) The Idea of Public Reason Revisited. In: John Rawls: *Political Liberalism* (Expanded Edition), 440-490. New York: Columbia University Press, 2005.

Rawls, J. (2005) *Political Liberalism* (Expanded Edition). New York: Columbia University Press.

Schmidt, T. M. (2001) Glaubensüberzeugungen und säkulare Gründe. Zur Legitimität religiöser Argumente in einer pluralistischen Gesellschaft. *Zeitschrift für Evangelische Ethik* 45: 248-261.

Shah, T: S. (2000) Making the Christian World Safe for Liberalism: From Grotius to Rawls. In *Religion and Democracy*, edited by D. Marquand and R.L. Nettler. Oxford: Blackwell Publishers.

Stepan, A. (2000) Religion, Democracy, and the "Twin Tolerations". *Journal of Democracy* 11 (4): 37-57.

Stiltner, B. (1993) Who Can Understand Abraham? The Relation of God and Morality in Kierkegaard and Aquinas. *Journal of Religious Ethics* 21: 221-245.

Stout, J. (2004) *Democracy and Tradition*. Princeton: Princeton University Press.

Stout, J. (2007) The Spirit of Democracy and the Rhetoric of Excess. *Journal of Religious Ethics* 35: 3-21.

Søltoft, P. (2000) *Svimmelhedens etik*. Copenhagen: Gads Forlag

Taylor, C. (2002) Democracy, Inclusive and Exclusive. In: Richard Madsen et al. (eds.), *Meaning and Modernity. Religion, Polity, and Self*. Berkeley: University of California Press, pp. 181-194.

Taylor, C. (2007) *A Secular Age*. Cambridge MA: The Belknap Press of Harvard University Press.

Taylor, M. C. (1977) Journeys to Moriah: Hegel vs. Kierkegaard. *Harvard Theological Review* 70 (3-4): 305-326.

Thiemann, R. F. (1996) *Religion in Public Life: A Dilemma for Democracy*. Washington D.C.: Georgetown University Press.

Trigg, R. (2007) *Religion in Public Life: Must Religion Be Privatized?* Oxford: Oxford University Press.

Wainwright, W. J. (2005) *Religion and Morality*. Aldershot: Ashgate.

Wamberg, J. (2006) *Landskabet som verdensbillede*. Århus: Aarhus University Press.

Weithman, P. J. (ed.) (1997) *Religion and Contemporary Liberalism*. Notre Dame: University of Notre Dame Press.

Westphal, M. (1987) *Kierkegaard's Critique of Reason and Society*. University Park, PA: The Pennsylvania State University Press.

Wolterstorff, N. (1997) Why We Should Reject What Liberalism Tells Us about Speaking and Acting in Public for Religious Reasons. In *Religion and Contemporary Liberalism*, edited by Paul J. Weithman, 162-181. Notre Dame: University of Notre Dame Press.

Young, I. M. (2003) Rawls' *Political Liberalism*. In *John Rawls: Critical assessments of leading political philosophers* (Vol. IV: *Political Liberalism* and *The Law of Peoples*), edited by Chandran Kukathas, 20-30. London and New York: Routledge.

Yunis, A. (1995) The Sacrifice of Abraham in Islam. In *The Sacrifice of Isaac in the Three Monotheistic Religions*, 147-157, edited by Frédéric Manns. Jerusalem: Franciscan Printing Press.

C

call to selfhood 93
Capps, D. 72, 79ff, 238
Caravaggio 10, 49
Cardinal Ratzinger 152, 156
Carter, S.L. 121, 212
Cartoon Controversy 171
Casanova, J. 103
categorical imperative 40
child sacrifice 18, 31, 34, 39, 63, 76
Christian consciousness 99
Christian reading 94, 95
Christ's death and resurrection 68
Chrysostomos, J. 35
Church Fathers 34
church-state relations 170, 179, 208
civic virtues 100, 132, 157, 185, 187, 188, 219
civil disobedience 79, 223, 238
civil religion 177, 206, 221
civil society 144, 145, 151
Clanton, J.C. 197, 224
Clement of Alexandria 36
cognitive dissonance 155
Cohen, L. 16, 18, 77, 238
communicative rationality 152, 159, 160
comprehensive doctrine 129, 136, 142, 146,
    147, 152, 174, 180, 191, 196, 198, 200,
    210, 211, 213, 214, 223, 239
conditions of belief 106
consensus 139, 152, 163
conservative Christians 164, 165
consocial position 184, 212
constitutional democracy 127, 141, 221, 235
constraints 145, 166, 180, 181, 183, 191, 210,
    218
contingency 86

Cooke, M. 161
cooperative translation 167, 213
counter-secularization 102
courage of faith 60, 67, 82, 92
criterion of reciprocity 133, 135, 141, 143
critical self-reflection 224, 238
critique of religion 107
crucifixion of Jesus 35
cultural anthropology 112
cultural evolution 12, 13, 99, 119, 121, 122,
    212, 217, 224, 239
cultural software 119

D

Dalferth, I.U. 86ff
Damgaard, F. 35, 36
Davie, G. 103ff
Dawkins, R. 107, 119
deliberative democracy 13, 127, 142, 144,
    151, 165, 168, 239
democracy 12, 48, 228, 238
democratic citizenship 142
Dennett, D. 107
depth psychology 79
developmental logic 124
Dewey, J. 192
discourse ethics 152
disenchantment 109, 118, 123
divine command 41, 87
divine command ethics 57, 71, 72, 73, 77, 90
divine grace 94, 95
divisiveness of religion 208
doctrine of the Trinity 231
Dostert, T. 194, 199ff, 203
Dostoyevsky, F. 227